THE PRACTICE OF ISLAM IN AMERICA

The Practice of Islam in America

An Introduction

Edited by
Edward E. Curtis IV

NEW YORK UNIVERSITY PRESS
New York

NEW YORK UNIVERSITY PRESS
New York
www.nyupress.org

© 2017 by New York University
All rights reserved

References to Internet websites (URLs) were accurate at the time of writing. Neither the author nor New York University Press is responsible for URLs that may have expired or changed since the manuscript was prepared.

Library of Congress Cataloging-in-Publication Data
Names: Curtis, Edward E., 1970– editor.
Title: The practice of Islam in America : an introduction / edited by Edward E. Curtis IV.
Description: New York : New York University Press, [2017] | Includes bibliographical references and index.
Identifiers: LCCN 2017008038| ISBN 9781479882670 (cl : alk. paper) | ISBN 9781479804887 (pb : alk. paper)
Subjects: LCSH: Muslims—United States. | Islam—Customs and practices. | Religious life—Islam.
Classification: LCC BP67.U6 P73 2017 | DDC 297.0973—dc23
LC record available at https://lccn.loc.gov/2017008038

New York University Press books are printed on acid-free paper, and their binding materials are chosen for strength and durability. We strive to use environmentally responsible suppliers and materials to the greatest extent possible in publishing our books.

Manufactured in the United States of America

10 9 8 7 6 5 4 3 2

Also available as an ebook

To Vernon Schubel and Ahmet Karamustafa

CONTENTS

ACKNOWLEDGMENTS

It is my pleasure, first, to acknowledge the volume's twelve contributors. They put up with my devotion to deadlines and, more importantly, rendered a rich and vibrant portrait of Islamic religious life in the United States.

In July 2016, many of us came together on the campus of Indiana University-Purdue University Indianapolis (IUPUI) to critique one another's drafts and offer constructive suggestions for improvement. This meeting improved the quality of the volume and gave us a rare opportunity to share ideas in a collegial, supportive setting.

As part of our meetings, we held a dinner in which Muslim community members from every part of the greater Indianapolis metropolitan area came together to hear about our progress and provide feedback. My community partners were essential to pulling this off. Gratitude goes to Rima Khan Shahid of the Muslim Alliance of Indiana, Imam Michael Saahir of Nur Allah Islamic Center, Imam Ismail Abdul-Aleem of Masjid al-Mu'mineen, Vice President Muhammad Safder of the Muslim Community Center, Sr. Habibe Ali of the Islamic Society of North America, and Dr. Sohel Anwar of al-Huda Foundation. We were also honored by the presence of retired Judge David Shaheed and City Controller Fady Qaddoura.

Lauren Schmidt of IUPUI's Center for the Study of Religion and American Culture coordinated both the authors' meeting and the community dinner, and it couldn't have been better organized or implemented. Nate Wynne also offered essential assistance. My thanks go to both of them.

Financial support for these events was provided by Indiana University's New Frontiers in the Arts and Humanities Program and by a collaborative research grant from the American Academy of Religion. I thank Dr. Faith Kirkham Hawkins, IU's associate vice president for research, for helping me navigate the grant application and its implementation. None of these parties is responsible for the content of this book.

My academic home, the IU School of Liberal Arts, provided a supportive environment for planning the volume, recruiting the contributors, editing the first drafts, and then finishing the manuscript.

For years, NYU Press senior editor Jennifer Hammer and I have been looking to collaborate on a project, and I am grateful that I had the chance to work with such a consummate professional. Also at the press, Amy Klopfenstein and Dorothea Stillman Halliday were very helpful indeed. Usha Sanyal copyedited the manuscript, and Jeremy Rehwaldt, Ph.D., proofread the galleys.

I conceptualized this volume as a book that could be used by college teachers to introduce their students to Islamic religious practice. And so, it is appropriate that I have dedicated the volume to two of my own Islamic studies teachers: Vernon Schubel, professor at Kenyon College, and Ahmet Karamustafa, now professor at the University of Maryland. Vernon and Ahmet are everything that anyone could want in a teacher— inspiring, brilliant, helpful, and encouraging. I remain so deeply grateful to them.

Introduction

EDWARD E. CURTIS IV

Muslims were practicing Islam on American soil long before the United States declared its independence in 1776. Perhaps the most famous Muslim to set foot in the British North American colonies was Ayuba Suleiman Diallo (1701–1773), better known in U.S. history as Job ben Solomon. "Very constant in his devotions," according to his biographer Thomas Bluett, Diallo was a highly educated religious leader who was a member of the ruling family of Futa Toro in Senegambia, West Africa. Enslaved in 1730 and brought to Annapolis, Maryland, he was sold to a settler who lived on Kent Island in Chesapeake Bay, where he lived until 1733. At first made to work as a hand in the tobacco fields, Ayuba, or Job, eventually became a cattle herder. "Job would often leave the cattle," according to Bluett, "and withdraw into the woods to pray." As a trained imam, or prayer leader, Ayuba would likely try his best to point his body toward Mecca, Arabia, just as other Muslims do when they prostrate their bodies in the direction of Islam's most important shrine. "But a white boy frequently watched him," recounted Bluett, "and whilst he was at his devotion would mock him, and throw dirt in his face."[1]

Bluett said this harassment "very much disturbed Job," but it did not prevent him from continuing his religious practice. Bluett first discovered that Ayuba was a Muslim when Ayuba "pronounced the words Allah and Mahommed; by which, and his refusing a glass of wine we offered him, we perceived he was a Mahometan [Muslim]." Even though he could not speak English, Ayuba believed, correctly, that invoking the names of Allah, the Arabic word for God, and the Prophet Muhammad, whom Muslims revere as the Messenger of God, would successfully communicate his identity as a Muslim. Bluett was impressed by the sincere reverence that seemed to accompany Ayuba's every mention of God's name: "he showed upon all occasions a singular veneration for the

1

name of God, and never pronounced the word Allah without a peculiar accent and a remarkable pause." In addition, Ayuba's refusal to accept the hospitable offer of a glass of wine was a sign of Ayuba's ethical commitment to abstinence from alcoholic beverages. During a 1733 sea voyage to England, Bluett wrote, "we often permitted him to kill our fresh stock that he might eat of it himself; for he eats no flesh, unless he has killed the animal with his own hands, or knows that it has been killed by some Mussulman [Muslim]. He has no scruple about fish; but won't touch a bit of pork, it being expressly forbidden by their Law." Bluett was observing Ayuba's ethical commitments to eating *halal*, or permissible, meat. Based on Bluett's description, it seems that Ayuba insisted on following the dietary guidelines of Shari'a, which Bluett called Islamic "law" but could also be translated as an Islamic "way of life" or "path to salvation." Once Ayuba had learned English, he and Bluett discussed the Christian belief in the Trinity, the idea that the one God is also three persons: the Father, Son, and Holy Spirit. After he "perused it with a great deal of care," Ayuba declared that his Arabic New Testament contained no mention of three gods.[2] For him, God was One, not Three in One.

Ayuba Suleiman Diallo was one of tens of thousands of Muslim Americans who were performing Islamic rituals and following ethical norms outlined in the Shari'a before the United States became an independent nation in 1776. Today approximately 1 to 2 percent of the U.S. population is Muslim, meaning that there are perhaps 3 to 6 million Muslims in the United States.[3] Their religious traditions have been part of the American experience since the moment that Europeans and Africans arrived in the Western hemisphere, but Muslims have always been religious minorities, and the general public's knowledge about basic Islamic beliefs and practices remains limited.[4] Islam is sometimes seen mainly as a political rather than a religious concern, and it is often associated with controversy rather than curiosity.[5]

This book is driven by the desire to provide clear answers to essential, but basic, questions about how observant Muslim Americans practice Islam: How do they pray? What religious holidays do they celebrate? How do Muslim Americans welcome a child into the world, get married, and bury their dead? What dietary rules do they follow? What kinds of charitable activities do they do? What is it like for American Muslims to go on *hajj*, the annual religious pilgrimage to Mecca? What role does the Qur'an play in Muslim Americans' daily lives? Is there anything like religious music or sacred dance in Muslim America?

The book's contributors, all experts on some aspect of Islam in the United States, take us to homes, religious congregations, schools, workplaces, cemeteries, restaurants, the Internet, and all the way to Mecca to see how Muslim American individuals discuss, debate, and implement answers to such questions in their daily lives. Their engaging narratives illuminate what Islam looks like as a lived religion in the United States. Muslim Americans have fashioned a set of religious institutions, ethics, and rituals that would be both familiar and strange to Ayuba Suleiman Diallo. This volume brings that vibrant world of religious practice to life. Points of commonality among Muslim Americans often include a shared love of the Prophet Muhammad and the Qur'an, the seventh-century scripture that he recited. And for many, but certainly not all Muslim Americans, the Shari'a provides specific guidelines on how to pray, what to eat and wear, how to bury the dead, when to fast, and how to perform the hajj. But even as the majority of Muslim Americans identify with a shared history, sacred texts, and authoritative religious interpretations, Muslim Americans themselves often point out that diversity is built into the religious DNA of Islam. As readers will learn, this diversity applies to questions as basic as "where should Muslims place their hands as they perform their daily prayers?"

The diversity of Islamic religious practice in the United States also reflects the fact that Muslim Americans are the most racially diverse religious community in the United States. According to the Gallup organization, "Muslims are the only religious group to lack a majority race or ethnicity, with 36% self-identifying as non-Hispanic black, 27% as non-Hispanic white, 21% as Asian and 8% as Hispanic."[6] While some Muslim Americans marry, worship, and socialize together across these racial divides, Muslims are divided by race just like other U.S. religious communities. This pattern of "racialization," as it is sometimes called, can affect nearly every aspect of U.S. culture from where people live and what religious congregation they attend to the quality of their educational opportunities and their intimate relationships, and the same is often true in Muslim American communities.[7] As this volume reveals, while Muslim Americans of many racial backgrounds share many of the same practices of prayer, pilgrimage, fasting, and charity, the meaning and significance of these religious practices are also shaped by the particular circumstances in which they are practiced, and race is one of those important circumstances.[8]

The very success of Islam's spread in the United States depended on its racial diversity. As we have seen, the first major population of Muslims in the United States were enslaved West Africans.[9] While they continued to practice Islamic religion in the United States as individuals throughout the 1800s, there is (as yet) no evidence that they established self-sustaining, multigenerational Muslim American communities. The first Muslim religious congregations and other institutions were instead established from the late 1800s through the first half of the 1900s by American-born whites, African Americans, and immigrants from the Middle East, Southeastern Europe, and South Asia. By the 1920s, Muslim Americans had established dozens of Muslim religious congregations and groups that not only offered very different interpretations of the Islamic religious heritage but also appealed to people across the American racial spectrum.[10]

The diversity of Islamic religious practices can also be traced to the community's enormous ethnic diversity. While the largest ethnic groups of Muslims are African Africans, Arab Americans, and South Asian Americans, perhaps every single ethnic group in the United States finds some sort of representation in the Muslim American community. During the late 1800s, most Muslim immigrants arrived from various parts of the Ottoman Empire, including the contemporary countries of Lebanon, Syria, and Bosnia, but important early Muslim figures and communities also came from Egypt and Sudan, and Bengal and Punjab in British India. After President Lyndon Johnson signed a bill that reformed immigration policy in 1965, Muslims began coming in much larger numbers, and from all over the world. Hundreds of thousands, perhaps more than a million, Muslims immigrated not only from the Middle East, North Africa, Southeastern Europe, and South Asia, but also from West Africa, East Africa, Central Asia, Southeast Asia, Canada, Mexico, and other parts of the Americas. Over the next several decades, these immigrants joined American-born whites, African Americans, and Latino/a Muslims to create thousands of new Muslim religious congregations, philanthropic organizations, Muslim media outlets, Muslim businesses, Islamic schools, and other communal institutions vital to Muslim American life.[11]

In addition to their ethnic and racial diversity, Muslim Americans are diverse by sect or religious group. The majority may be classified as Sunni, meaning, at least in historical terms, that they are *ahl al-sunna wa jamaʿa*, or people who follow the Sunna, or Tradition, of the Prophet Muhammad and the consensus-driven religious opinions of traditional scholars. The Sunna is contained in sacred scriptures called the *hadith*, which are reports about what the Prophet Muhammad and his Companions did and said. Because it applies to the vast majority of the world's 1.8 or so billion Muslims, the label "Sunni" may mean little in terms of how individuals implement the teachings of Islam in their daily lives. The second largest sectarian group of Muslim Americans are Shiʿa Muslims, meaning that they follow the tradition of Islam that arose out of historical struggles over who should lead the community of Muslims in the absence of the Prophet Muhammad. Traditionally, Shiʿa Muslims believe that the family of the Prophet through the line of his daughter, Fatima, and his son-in-law and cousin, Ali, are the rightful heirs to the mantle of the Prophet. In the United States, the majority of Shiʿa Muslims are part of a subgroup called the Twelvers, the tradition of Shiʿism most popular in Iran, Iraq, and Lebanon, among other places. A vibrant but influential minority of Shiʿa Muslims are Ismaʿili (pronounced Iss-ma-ee-lee), and some of them are followers of the religious leader called the Aga Khan. In addition to exploring how these Muslim American sectarian groups practice Islamic religion, this book includes the stories of people who insist that they are "just Muslim," neither Sunni nor Shiʿa, and also of people who follow alternative visions, such as members of the Nation of Islam.[12]

Muslim American religious culture and practice are also deeply shaped by gender. As with other religiously observant Americans, whether Christian, Jewish, Hindu, Buddhist, Wiccan, Sikh, or some other religious identity, one's identity as a man or a woman has an important impact on the roles that one plays in religious congregations, religious rituals, family life, and other Muslim American spaces.[13] Gender can be seen in everything from the clothes that one wears to one's personal interpretations of Islamic religion. Similarly, an understanding of the role of sexual orientation is essential to any comprehensive study of both public and private practices of Islam in the United States.[14] Economic status is another factor evident in the development of Islamic institutions such as mosques, charitable organizations, and schools.[15] By paying attention to the way that Islamic religion is practiced in the lives of specific people living in specific times and places, contributors to this volume capture the subtle interplay of all these factors in the ways that Islam is lived in the United States.

In Part 1, readers learn about Muslim American rituals of prayer and pilgrimage. This section begins with a description and explanation of what is the most frequently performed religious ritual in Islam and often the most frequently featured image of Muslims presented in the media—namely, the prostration of the body in the direction of Mecca. Rose Aslan's chapter on *salah*, also called *namaz*, takes us to Irving, Texas, where Nicole Fauster, a native of the greater Atlanta area, readies herself to pray *maghrib*, or the sunset prayer. Aslan also depicts the prayers of Nsenga Knight in New York City, and Hajj Ahmad in Durham, North Carolina, as she explains step-by-step the meaning and function of the ablutions, bodily movements, words, and feelings that are part of daily prayer. We learn about differences and similarities between Sunni and Shi'a traditions of salah, and about the existence of other forms of prayer in Islam, including *du'a*, or supplicatory prayers, and *dhikr*, meditative and sometimes joyous religious litanies.

While Aslan's chapter mainly focuses on salah, Rosemary R. Corbett's chapter explores different forms of dhikr. Corbett paints a rich picture of various Sufi Muslim groups in New York who perform dhikr often by incorporating chanting, music, and/or dancing into their religious ceremonies. Sufism, known as the mystical branch of Islam, is a catch-all term used to describe several different phenomena: popular Islamic religious devotions, formal organizations in which one studies with a spiritual master, and philosophical and spiritual literature. Sufism is not a sect of Islam, but rather a method or path in which the individual believer pursues a closer, more intimate, and loving relationship with God. Historically speaking, both Sunni and Shi'a Muslims have embraced various aspects of Sufism, though today some reform-minded Muslims criticize some Sufi traditions as un-Islamic. Introducing us to Sufism in New York, Corbett takes us to three locations: the financial district of Manhattan; the Upper West Side of Manhattan; and Spring Valley, which is located upstate. Even though each of the groups she discusses is associated with the same Sufi organization, the Halveti Jerrahi Sufi order, Corbett's thick descriptions of the rituals performed at each site reveal the fantastic variety of Muslims who ecstatically sing praises to God and the Prophet Muhammad and whirl their bodies around and around, or, contrariwise, quietly and sedately chant litanies to aid the mind and body in achieving a peaceful, more meditative state of mind.

Hussein Rashid then takes us on a different kind of spiritual journey, to Mecca, site of the hajj, or annual pilgrimage. Rashid depicts this often once-in-a-lifetime experience for several Muslim Americans who represent a wide variety of ethnic, racial, and sectarian backgrounds. We learn about the pilgrimages of Khizer, a health care professional from Washington, D.C.; Zahra, an attorney from California; Debra, a college professor from Wisconsin; Suehaila, a professional recruiter from Dearborn, Michigan; and other Muslim Americans as they walk counterclockwise around the Ka'ba, pray outside Mecca at Mina and Mt. Arafat, reenact Hagar's desperate search for water, and symbolically stone the devil, among other rites. In addition to providing essential background on each of these practices, Rashid asks these pilgrims what all these rituals mean to them and what they hope to gain by coming on hajj. As a result, we come to know not only about the logistical problems and gripes of pilgrims, but also about the failed relationships that led a couple of the pilgrims to seek solace or healing in Mecca in the first place.

Part II of the book begins with a celebration, or more precisely, the two most celebrated Islamic holidays in the United States. Before the celebration, though, comes the fasting. Jackleen Salem captures what it is like to fast from dawn to sunset during the Islamic month of Ramadan—a practice that most Muslims associate with the very heart of their faith. Salem takes us to "Little Palestine" in the southwest suburbs of Chicago, Illinois, where we follow Aminah Salah and other Muslims as they set aside more time to read the Qur'an, go to the mosque for extra prayers, share huge family meals during the evenings, and buy lots of presents for the kids in preparation for the big party, or eid, that ends the month of fasting. We accompany Aminah Salah's family and fifteen thousand other people to Toyota Park to attend communal prayers on the day of Eid al-Fitr, which literally means the festival of the breaking of the fast, and then afterward to the family's now traditional consumption of nachos and cheese at the Bridgeview Mosque Foundation's community party. Salem then explores what is technically, from the standpoint of authoritative Islamic religious traditions, the larger of the two main eids. Eid al-Adha, the festival of the sacrifice, commemorates the occasion on which God tested Abraham's faith by asking him to sacrifice his son, Ishmael, but at the last minute replaced Ishmael with a ram. Instead of focusing only on the celebration of Eid al-Adha in Chicago, Salem explores this holiday around the country with Muslims from a variety of ethnic backgrounds.

Michael Muhammad Knight then introduces readers to Ashura, a holiday of central importance to Shi'a Muslims. Ashura occurs on the tenth day of the Islamic month of Muharram, and commemorates the tragic death of Husayn, the Prophet Muhammad's grandson, at the hands of the ruling Umayyad Muslim dynasty in 680 C.E. in Iraq. Knight allows us to see how for many Shi'a Muslim Americans, this is "the central event in God's destiny for humankind, a moment in which oppression and salvation intertwine." This chapter brings to life the ritual mourning that occurs in different commemorations around the United States—one led by a female religious leader called a *zakira*, who recounts in dramatic fashion the noble sacrifice of Husayn, and another in which men first beat their chests in mourning and solidarity with Husayn and then further honor him by donating their blood at a Red Cross mobile donation center. Knight also reveals how Husayn's memory is evoked in the Ansaaru Allah Community (AAC), an African American Muslim group established in the 1960s.

The final Islamic holiday covered in this book is *mawlid* or *milad an-nabi*, the birthday of the Prophet Muhammad. Though far less popular in the United States than in countries across the Afro-Eurasian landmass, milad is an expression for some Muslim Americans of their love of and devotion to the Prophet. Marcia Hermansen's chapter on the Prophet's birthday shows us how some South Asian Muslim Americans recite Urdu devotional poetry and prayers specifically tailored for this occasion in San Diego, California. Changing locations, Hermansen welcomes us into a posh suburban Chicago home where the most popular poem ever written about the Prophet Muhammad, a thirteenth-century piece called the *Burda*, or Cloak, becomes a focus of rituals of devotion performed by both males and females. Her chapter includes a visit to the University of Chicago's Rockefeller Chapel, where Muslim chaplain Tahir Umar Abdullah convenes an annual birthday celebration for the Prophet.

Part III of the book introduces readers to the life cycle rituals of Muslims in the United States. Maria F. Curtis examines religious practices that accompany the birth of a child in the greater Houston area. Muslim mothers such as Aliya, who traces her Isma'ili roots to Kenya and India, let us know about the Islamic traditions used to prepare mothers in their families for labor and birth. Erin, a Creole convert to Islam from Louisiana, similarly describes the Islamic teachings that she studies in order to prepare herself to be a mother. Readers are taken to hospital rooms where the words "Allah" and "Muhammad" are whispered into a newborn's ears. New clothes are purchased, families may make special charitable donations, and a huge feast might be held. Curtis managed to talk with a remarkably diverse group of mothers about how they combine various U.S. cultural traditions with ethnic traditions from abroad, from holding baby showers, to naming their children, to caring for them in particular ways during their first forty days of life.

Juliane Hammer then presents detailed portraits of three Muslim American weddings as a way to discuss not only the nature of the "big day" itself, but also the implications of a traditional Islamic marriage contract in the context of the United States and the ways that Muslim American marriages are shaped by ethnic and national background, religious affiliation, economic status, education, and locality. Hammer introduces readers to three different couples. We attend a simple mosque-based marriage ceremony of an African American woman who was raised Muslim to a recent white male convert and the modest reception that follows. Then, it's on to an elaborate hotel wedding in which two Pakistani Americans are wed; this wedding features a lengthy ceremony and an exquisite South Asian buffet dinner. Finally, Hammer visits an Arab American home where the uncle of the bride oversees the signing of the marriage contract and then hosts a dinner for the family. The formal wedding in this case is different from the wedding reception, which is held later and includes some four hundred guests, a band, a Palestinian dance troupe, and a Levantine buffet dinner.

The discussion of Muslim American life cycle events then turns to the rituals that accompany the end of life. Amir Hussain presents research on how Muslim Americans at the King Fahad Mosque in Culver City, California, prepare Muslim bodies for burial, pray for the dead, and conduct burials in a Muslim cemetery. Hussain also includes coverage of what became the most watched funeral in history of a Muslim American. The funeral prayers and interfaith memorial service for Muhammad Ali in

Louisville, Kentucky, not only memorialized the man who was likely the most well-known Muslim American in history, but also introduced millions of viewers to some of the basic rites of Sunni Muslim funeral prayers.

Part IV concludes the volume with discussions of Islamic ethical practices and religious culture. Danielle Widmann Abraham surveys Muslim American philanthropy and social giving, including *zakat*, or the alms tax, which is the most popular form of Islamic philanthropy in the world. Widmann Abraham shows how Muslim American philanthropy is a "way of making connections and establishing a sense of belonging" in U.S. society. Donating money to various nonprofit organizations is only one form of social giving, she points out. Widmann Abraham describes the Imam-e Zamana Mission, an India-based Shi'a Muslim organization that seeks charitable contributions to aid educational and development projects around the globe as well as provides space for the celebration of Shi'a Islamic practices and holidays such as Ashura. Depicting a very different philanthropic organization, she then visits the ILM Foundation in Los Angeles, a grassroots African American Sunni Muslim group known for its organization of "Humanitarian Day," which focuses on the problems of homeless people. The chapter ends with an examination of Islamic Relief USA, one of the largest nonprofits in Muslim America. Agency staff emphasize the importance of implementing best practices in nonprofit management as a way to meet their religious obligations and to maximize the benefits of their fundraising and program development.

The next chapter is about food. Though previous chapters in the book describe the diversity of Muslim American foods consumed during holidays and life cycle events, Magfirah Dahlan focuses on the ethical rules governing the production and consumption of food. Rather than giving us a dry explanation of legal codes on this topic, she asks a wide variety of Muslim Americans what they actually eat and their reasons for doing so. She explains how Muslim Americans decide which foods are halal, or permissible, to eat. And she also delves into the growing popularity of *zabiha* meat, that is, meat slaughtered in accordance with ethical rules outlined in the Shari'a, and simultaneously, she reveals how some Muslims are led by their own sense of Islamic ethics to become vegetarians or vegans.

In the last chapter of the book, written by Muna Ali, readers learn about the Arizona-based Qur'an Academy, the Institute of Islamic Education in Chicago, the Texas-based Bayyinah Dream, and many other sites to learn about the Qur'an in Muslim American life. Ali helps us to hear the melodic recitation of this sacred scripture, and she reveals how religious congregations and Sunday school classes teach about and interpret the Qur'an. In the last half of the chapter, Ali shows how the Qur'an's place in U.S. society is a barometer of interfaith relationships as well as intra-Muslim divisions along lines of gender, race, and sectarian affiliation. Ali's conclusions about the Qur'an apply more generally to the meaning and function of Islamic religious traditions in the United States, and thus are especially appropriate for the end of the volume. In preserving, adapting, interpreting, and applying Islamic religious traditions in their daily lives, Muslim Americans "at once engage in an act of worship, a creative individual self-expression, and a form of cultural activism and civic engagement to challenge stereotypes and marginalization."

Overall, this book reveals a world of religious practice that is worth knowing about both because it is an inherently engaging, rich, and vibrant aspect of human culture and because it is vitally important to the present and the future of religious cooperation and public life in the United States. The volume provides practical information to all those simply curious about Islamic religious practices, but, more importantly, it tells the stories of individuals for whom these practices, matter. Understanding Islamic religious practices as lived by actual people, some of whom are our neighbors, is a powerful means to challenge false stereotypes about Muslims. It is essential to encouraging dialogue and mutual respect across some of the most stubborn divides of our historical moment.

NOTES

1 Thomas Bluett, ed., *Some Memoirs of the Life of Job, the Son of Solomon, the High Priest of Boonda in Africa* (London: Richard Ford, 1734), docsouth.unc.edu.

2 Ibid., 20–26, 51–52.

3 No one knows exactly how many self-identifying Muslims there are in the United States, but the Pew Research Center estimates that as of 2015, the number was 3.3 million. See Besheer Mohamed, "A New Estimate of the U.S. Muslim Population," Pew Research Center, January 6, 2016, www.pewresearch.org.

4 Peter Moore, "Poll Results: Islam," YouGov and *Huffington Post*, March 9, 2015, today.yougov.com.

5 The formal academic study of Islam in the United States reflects this bias, as well. Though this vibrant and growing field of study is changing, its main focus has been on issues such as security concerns, the assimilation and integration of

Muslim immigrants, Islam and gender, the ethnic and racial diversity of Muslim Americans, the development of Islamic institutions, and high-profile figures such as Malcolm X and Elijah Muhammad. See Edward E. Curtis IV, "The Study of Muslim Americans: A History," in *The Cambridge Companion to American Islam*, Juliane Hammer and Omid Safi, eds. (New York: Cambridge University Press, 2013), 15–27.

6 Mohamed Younis, "Perceptions of Muslims in the United States: A Review," Gallup, December 11, 2015, www.gallup.com.

7 See Eduardo Bonilla-Silva, *Racism without Racists: Color-Blind Racism and the Persistence of Racial Inequality in America*, 3d ed. (Lanham, Md.: Rowman & Littlefield, 2006).

8 For various angles on race in Muslim America, see Su'ad Abdul Khabeer, *Muslim Cool: Race, Religion and Hip Hop in the United States* (New York: NYU Press, 2016); Zareena A. Grewal, "Marriage in Colour: Race, Religious, and Spouse Selection in Four American Mosques," *Ethnic and Racial Studies* 32, 2 (2009): 323–345; Jamillah Karim, *American Muslim Women: Negotiating Race, Class, and Gender within the Ummah* (New York: NYU Press, 2009); and Sherman A. Jackson, *Islam and the Blackamerican: Looking toward the Third Resurrection* (New York: Oxford University Press, 2005).

9 Sylviane Diouf, *Servants of Allah: African Muslims Enslaved in the Americas*, 15th anniversary ed. (New York: NYU Press, 2013); and Michael A. Gomez, *Black Crescent: The Experience and Legacy of African Muslims in the Americas* (New York: Cambridge University Press, 2005).

10 See Kambiz GhaneaBassiri, *A History of Islam in America* (New York: Cambridge University Press, 2010), 95–227; and Edward E. Curtis IV, *Muslims in America: A Short History* (New York: Oxford University Press, 2009), 25–71.

11 GhaneaBassiri, *History of Islam in America*, 228–377; Curtis, *Muslims in America*, 72–96; and Yvonne Y. Haddad and Jane I. Smith, eds., *The Oxford Handbook of American Islam* (New York: Oxford University Press, 2014), 159–321.

12 Coverage of all these groups can be found in Edward E. Curtis IV, ed., *The Encyclopedia of Muslim-American History*, 2 vols. (New York: Facts on File, 2010).

13 Coverage of Muslim American women is particularly robust. For example, see Juliane Hammer, *American Muslim Women, Religious Authority, and Activism: More than a Prayer* (Austin: University of Texas Press, 2011); Leila Ahmed, *A Quiet Revolution: The Veil's Resurgence from the Middle East to America* (New Haven: Yale University Press, 2011); and Carolyn Moxley Rouse, *Engaged Surrender: African American Women and Islam* (Berkeley: University of California Press, 2004).

14 Though not focused on the United States, one place to begin this discussion is Scott Siraj al-Haqq Kugle, *Living Islam Out Loud: Voices of Gay, Lesbian, and Transgender Muslims* (New York: NYU Press, 2014).

15 See, for example, Pew Research Center, "Muslim Americans: Mostly Middle Class and Mainstream," May 22, 2007, www.pewresearch.org.

PART I

Prayer and Pilgrimage

1

Salah

Daily Prayers in Muslim America

ROSE ASLAN

A 2009 short film entitled *Forbidden Love* opens with a scene of a female college student casually hanging out with her friends on a Southern California campus.[1] The protagonist is a punk. She has lots of piercings and other punk paraphernalia. Given the film's title, viewers probably think that they are about to watch a romance, perhaps a story of unrequited love. Instead, we eventually discover that the protagonist is not only a punk but also a Muslim. A female punk Muslim. Her forbidden love is not a person, but a religious practice. She loves to pray, or more specifically, she loves *salah*, the prescribed prayers performed five times a day by Muslims all over the world.

As the film gets going, the protagonist runs into a headscarf-wearing friend, a Muslim. Her friend warmly greets her, "as-salam alaykum," peace be upon you, and the characters hug. The friend invites the punk to pray with other Muslims on the university quad. The punk Muslim wants to. But she sees some non-Muslim friends in the distance and she is too ashamed to pray in front of them. She wants a safe and private place to perform her salah. First, she stops in a stairwell, puts on a headscarf, and gets ready to pray. Still worried about being seen in public with a headscarf, she covers her hair with her hoodie. She is ready to begin. But she hears footsteps. Someone is coming. A male student gives her a suspicious look. She scurries away. She then attempts to pray in a classroom and even a bathroom—which is considered unsuitable for prayer because of its state of uncleanliness—but is interrupted both times. She looks at her watch and shrugs her shoulders.

Finally, she boldly walks to the same spot on the lawn where her Muslim friends just prayed. Still nervous, she cautiously pulls her headscarf out of her backpack. She looks around apprehensively. Having overcome her timidity, she dons her headscarf and begins her prayers. Soon, a tall, blonde woman who was watching her walks over, puts on a headscarf, and then joins her. Then, an African American woman wearing a head wrap joins the growing congregation. The female punk Muslim is now actually leading the prayers. The film ends with the three women prostrating in unison.

The short film raises a number of concerns addressed in this chapter. First, it begins to suggest how important daily prayer is to Muslim Americans. It also shows the racial and ethnic diversity—not to mention the diverse fashion styles—of Muslim Americans. Finally, it depicts the concerns and even feelings of vulnerability that some U.S. Muslims have when trying to maintain their religious practices as religious minorities.

This chapter examines what it looks like, sounds like, and feels like to perform salah as a Muslim living in the United States. Salah is one of the most basic and important rituals of Muslims, scholars and lay people, men and women, poor and rich, young and old. It is easily performed by anyone who can memorize a few lines of the Qur'an and *du'as*, or supplications, in Arabic. For the vast majority of Muslims, whether Sunni or Shi'a, there are five prayer times in a day: *fajr*, the predawn prayer; *dhuhr*, the noon prayer; *'asr*, the mid-afternoon prayer; *maghrib*, the sunset prayer, and *'isha*, the evening prayer. These prayers can be performed alone or in unison with a congregation behind a prayer leader. According to a Pew Research Center survey, Muslims perform salah more frequently than any other Islamic ritual.[2] And yet there are virtually no studies of salah in the United States.[3] As Marion Holmes Katz has noted, prayer has often received less attention in the study of Islam than other topics such as gender, law, and politics, in part because it has been overlooked as a simple ritual.[4] This chapter shows that prayer is more than a simple ritual. It is a richly meaningful practice to Muslims in the United States.

Prerequisites for Salah

In his home in Durham, North Carolina, Hajj Ahmad is preparing for the sunset prayer, *salat al-maghrib*. Raised as a Conservative Jew in Tuscon, Arizona, Hajj Ahmad Abdul Hakeem is a convert to Islam in his late sixties. As a young man, he dropped out of university and spent a few years as a hippie. He used a lot of illicit substances, and then ended up working as a counselor in a drug abuse clinic while also studying for a B.A. in psychology. He has been Muslim for nearly forty years, having first become interested in Islam by studying Sufism. Hajj Ahmad converted to Sunni Islam at the age of thirty in 1978. Five years later, he embraced a Shi'a interpretation of Islam. He eventually earned an MBA and moved to South Africa, where he pursued business projects and continued to follow a spiritual path.

Every day, Hajj Ahmad gathers himself, silencing the extra noises in his head. He carefully performs *wudu,* or ritual washing, concentrating on the meaning of this ritual meant to wash away the impurities of daily life. He rinses his mouth and then his nose three times each. He washes his face with water that he has collected in his cupped right hand, starting from the hairline and proceeding to just below the chin. He is sure to include the sides of the face too. It is sufficient to do this once, but if the believer desires it can also be done twice. Hajj Ahmad then collects water in his cupped left hand and washes his right arm from the elbow to the tips of the fingers on both the front and back of the arm. He then washes the left arm in a similar manner. He uses the remaining water in his right hand to wipe the top of his head downward from the middle of the head to the hairline. This is done only once. Finally, whatever moisture is left is used to wipe the top of each foot, beginning with the right foot from the ankle to the end of the toes. Once a Muslim is ritually pure and mentally and spiritually prepared, he or she is ready to engage in one of the most important practices in Islam: salah.

According to most Islamic traditions, Muslims must fulfill several prerequisites before beginning their salah. First, they must wear clean clothes and must find a clean place to pray. Next they must do their wudu. Sunni and Shi'a Muslims have slight variations in practicing wudu. The most significant difference is that Sunnis wash their arms from their wrists to their elbows and Shi'as wash their arms from their elbows to their wrists. In addition, Sunnis must thoroughly rinse their feet three times, while Shi'as need only wipe their feet (or socks) with whatever water remains on their hands (after wiping their hair on their head). In order to be in a ritual state of purity for prayer, Muslims must perform ablutions after they use the toilet, pass gas, sleep, or have sex, among other activities.[5]

Preparing for salah can be a challenge for U.S. Muslims when they are outside their homes or mosques. First, the requirements of wudu are difficult to carry out in a regular sink, especially when it comes to the feet. It can be even more awkward to do so in a public restroom.[6] Many short humorous Internet video clips depict young Muslim Americans finding themselves in awkward situations while performing wudu in public restrooms. Muslim Americans have come up with innovative solutions for these problems. A newly established company called Wudu Gear sells waterproof socks that allow Muslims to avoid washing their feet in the sink.[7] The website even includes a copy of a fatwa, or a nonbinding legal opinion, from an Islamic institute in South Africa to prove that their products are religiously permissible. Previously, very strict Muslims could only wear leather "socks" if they wanted to avoid washing their feet in public restrooms.

Hajj Ahmad does not pray in public. His town is located right next to Chapel Hill, North Carolina, where three young Muslim college students were murdered in February 2015. Those murders have struck fear in the hearts of many Muslims in the area. Since he is an older, white male, few people guess that Hajj Ahmad is a Muslim, and he chooses not to bring additional attention to himself by praying in public. He also avoids wearing any clothing that might signify his Muslim identity. If he is out of the house during prayer times and cannot find a private space for prayer, he will make up his salah once he returns home.[8]

Embodying and Performing Salah

In a living room somewhere in Irving, Texas, a young woman checks the time on her phone and puts down her Arabic textbook. Nicole notices that the sun has gone down and that it is time to pray the sunset salah. She walks down the hallway of her shared apartment to the bathroom where she performs wudu slowly and mindfully. She washes away physical impurities as well as the stress and worries of the day so that "my soul can be affected," she says. She then goes to her room, where she pulls out her favorite prayer clothes from a drawer. The brown paisley outfit is trimmed with white lace. It consists of a long cotton skirt and a long veil that completely covers her hair and her body down to her hips. Her sartorial choices partly express religious requirements and partly her personal sense of style. The main requirement for clothing worn during prayer is that it be clean and modest. According to the Shari'a, which is sometimes known as Islamic law and ethics but could also be understood as the Islamic way of life, men must wear modest clothing that covers their body between the navel and thighs. Women must cover their bodies, leaving visible only their hands, face, and sometimes feet. Nicole's garment is simple but replete with meaning for her. She purchased it from a store outside Jerusalem's Haram al-Sharif, or the Temple Mount, considered the third most sacred site in Islam. Whenever she dons the outfit, she is taken back to the sacred sites in Jerusalem, where she wandered the ancient alleyways of the city and met Palestinians from all walks of life. Once she is physically prepared for salah, Nicole attempts to clear her mind and focus on her Creator. She steps onto her prayer rug, which she always leaves open in her room, and begins her salah. She goes through the cycles of salah, bending down and prostrating her head to the ground while reciting verses from the Qur'an and also du'as.

Nicole Fauster is a young U.S. Muslim woman of Ugandan descent in her early twenties. Raised by a single mother in the suburbs of Atlanta, Georgia, Nicole attended an Islamic middle school but otherwise was a student in public schools. When she enrolled at the University of North Carolina at Chapel Hill for her bachelor's degree, she became active in the Muslim Student Association. Nicole learned about the significance of salah from her mother, who kindled a real love for prayer in her daughter. Nicole describes herself as a burgeoning civil and human rights activist. She aims to fight anti-Muslim discrimination and wants to increase the access of the U.S. Muslim community to legal aid.[9]

Apart from reading the Qur'an, she identifies salah as central to her practice of Islam, as something that "is necessary for me to do as a Muslim." As she put it, "this is something Allah has required of his servants to perform five times a day for my own benefit." Nicole works hard to realize the spiritual dimensions of prayer and the serenity that it can produce. "I try to feel something in salah," she said. In the past, she continued, "I used to go through the motions . . . but now salah has become a place where I try to tap into a certain place, where the soul is, the heart, the chest, the abdomen. . . . It's like a muscle I am trying to get working. . . . It takes a lot of effort to make salah a point of connection to where I can physically feel something in my heart or chest." She also prays to make sure everything in her life stays on track. When she prioritizes other activities ahead of salah, she feels a sense of dread that she is "putting the *dunya*, or material world, ahead of the responsibility [she] has to God."

Salah is an Arabic word generally translated in English as prayer, but it means something more specific. (U.S. Muslims from South Asian, Persian, or Turkic backgrounds also refer to the practice as *namaz*, the Persian word for salah.) In Arabic, salah specifically refers to the formal prayers that Muslims perform daily according to their particular *madhhab*, or Islamic legal and ethical tradition. Muslims pray because the Qur'an requires it: "Truly I am God, there is no god but I. So worship Me, and perform the prayer for the remembrance of Me."[10] The Qur'an also makes clear that the desire to pray is natural since it is deeply embedded in human nature. According to the Qur'an, God "created . . . humans to worship God" (51:56).

Nicole describes salah as bringing her to a place of deep spirituality. During salah, her feeling of spirituality in her chest fluctuates. Sometimes it grows increasingly strong and overpowers her. Other times she has to focus more to evoke any sort of feeling during her salah. She likens salah to a lawnmower whose starter cord must be pulled a few times before it gets going. For Nicole, the lawnmower starts humming once she recites, "You alone we worship and from You alone we seek help" (Qur'an 1:5). She feels connected, at peace. As she recites the Qur'an, she embodies the meaning of the verses in her physical movements. Sometimes she is physically shaking as she recites the last verse of the opening chapter of the Qur'an, in which the supplicant asks to be among those whom God has blessed and "not of those who incur wrath" (Qur'an 1:6). Letting her body feel the verses helps her connect physically to the meaning of the Qur'an. Oftentimes she cannot help but rock back and forth as she contemplates its meaning.

When she was younger, Nicole would sometimes miss prayer times because she was involved in sports or other extracurricular activities. She would make up all the prayers when she went home. For some Muslim Americans, observing the prayers throughout the day is not always easy. Religious accommodations vary in American schools and workplaces. It isn't always feasible to leave in the middle of a class, a basketball game, or a business meeting to make one's prayers. The sects of Islam differ on how to deal with such challenges. Generally speaking, Muslims who follow the largest Shi'a group, the Twelvers, are permitted to combine the prayers that one is supposed to make throughout the day. Sunni Muslims are also allowed to combine prayers in case of travel or extreme hardship, and women who are menstruating or who have just had a baby are excused from making prayers altogether. Overall, however, many modern Sunni teachers emphasize the importance of praying at the designated times.

Since leaving home to attend college, Nicole has made sure to pray all five daily prayers right on time. As Nicole started learning more about Islam with her peers at the Muslim Student Association, she also became more committed to the ritual requirements of Islamic religion. Because she is often out during the specified salah times, Nicole finds creative ways to make her prayer. Her favorite strategy is to find a big store like Walmart or, if she is in the mall, to step into a clothing store. Because she wishes to avoid arousing any suspicion from praying in public, she takes clothing to "try on" in a dressing room. There she prays in relative privacy, far away from prying eyes. Praying in public for Nicole is nerve-wracking, and when she finds herself in other kinds of places such as libraries, bookstores, or cafés, she will try to find a nook where she hopes "that no one will ask me what's going on." As she said to me, "I don't know if it's a good thing or bad thing, but when I am praying in public, I feel so conscious of what is happening around me that even if someone happens to pass by, I break salah and pretend I am looking somewhere else. I wait for them to pass by and then start over." While Nicole feels awkward praying in public, she has no problem talking about salah or asking non-Muslim friends if she could pray when she is visiting their homes.

On a Saturday evening, at a cozy home in Durham, North Carolina, Hajj Ahmad and Hajjah Fatimah, his wife of thirty-six years, sit down with their family of six grown children and their spouses along with eight grandchildren.[11] Hajj Ahmad and his wife have prepared a tasty meal of lamb, couscous, baked vegetables, and a mixed salad. It is an unusual event: a full family affair that gathers all the children, who live as far away as Arizona and the Arabian Gulf. Everyone at the table is savoring the delicious food and heartfelt conversation. The baby boomer parents are enjoying having all their children and grandchildren at their home for the gathering.

After the family meal at his house, Hajj Ahmad's adult children clean up and wash the dishes while the grandchildren play together. The sunlight is waning so Hajj Ahmad peers out a window to see how dark it is and senses that the sunset is fast approaching. Dessert and tea will have to wait until after prayer. As a Shi'a Muslim, Hajj Ahmad must wait to pray until fifteen to twenty minutes after the sun has set, while Sunnis, in contrast, pray as soon as the sun sets just below the horizon. This is one example of how Shi'a and Sunni Muslims share the same ritual practices but differ slightly in their interpretation of how to carry them out. Hajj Ahmad checks the website of his local mosque for the exact time to pray. Ten minutes before salah, he shouts to his family, "Maghrib, you guys. Make your wudu!" No one can hear him above the noise, so he has to shout it out several times until he is sure he has been heard. The Shi'a often pray maghrib, the sunset prayer, and 'isha, the night prayer, one after the other. They can choose to break them up by an hour and a half or so, just like the Sunnis, but they usually follow the ruling that allows the prayers to be joined.

"Let's go," exhorts Hajj Ahmad, trying to hurry his family members along to prayer. He adjusts the knitted white *kufi*, or skullcap, on his head. The worshipers all gather in a room designated for prayer in Hajj Ahmad's house. Hajj Ahmad then declares his intention to pray and focuses on his experience of *khushu'*, which is an Arabic term that he describes as "having a sense of awesome presence of God" and that also can be defined as spiritual humility. He then recites the *iqama*, or a formulaic announcement in Arabic that prayer will begin.

For Hajj Ahmad, salah is an "anchor" that "offers a direct connection to the inner meaning of the Qur'an and to the prophetic consciousness— which is the purest reflection of the Absolute Divinity." Salah among Sunni and Shi'a Muslims is mostly the same, with some slight variations in the placement of hands and, for Shi'as, additional du'as recited out loud during salah. When it is time for prayer, in most mosques the imam or sometimes a male congregant will recite the *adhan*, or the call to prayer, which includes the exhortation to come to prayer. Some Muslims might have an app on their cell phones that calls the adhan right on time. Others might recite it quietly to themselves. The adhan and iqama contain nearly the same formulaic prayer in Arabic. The Sunni and Shi'i adhan and iqama, the second call to prayer that occurs immediately before the prayer, are virtually the same. Shi'as add one extra phrase: "Ali is the Protector or Friend of God," a statement indicating their belief that Ali, the son-in-law and cousin of the Prophet Muhammad and first Imam, or spiritual leader of the Shi'a, is the representative of God.[12]

Salah begins when Hajj Ahmad raises both hands to his ears and calls out, "Allahu akbar," meaning there is nothing greater than God. His family members line up behind him in rows, the male members in the first row and the female members in the second row. They place their arms by their sides. When Muslims pray, the position of their hands generally indicates the madhhab, or school of Islamic law and ethics, that they follow. It is important to remember that some Muslims are not aware of these different schools of practice and some reject the whole idea of different schools, saying they are just Muslims. But many others follow the particular ritual requirements of the madhhab based on whatever their family of origin or community teaches them. For adult converts, it depends on who teaches them about Islam or what sources they use when reading about it. Since no one Islamic madhhab is dominant among Muslim Americans, adult Muslims can always adopt a different madhhab based on their own research about Islamic religion.

Twelver Shi'a Muslims follow the Ja'fari madhhab, so they place their hands at their sides when praying. Among Sunni Muslims, followers of the Shafi'i school usually place their hands between the chest and navel. Followers of the Hanafi school place their hands on their navel. Followers of the Hanbali school place their hands just below the navel. Malikis usually hang their hands by their side similar to Shi'a Muslims, but some place their hands above the navel. Each salah session lasts between three and ten minutes, depending on the time of day and the length of Qur'anic recitation of the *imam*, the person leading the prayer. Muslims pray different numbers of *rak'ahs*, or cycles of prayer, depending on the time of day: two cycles for the predawn prayer, four cycles for the noon prayers, four cycles for the mid-afternoon prayer, three cycles for the sunset prayer, and four cycles for the evening prayer.

While performing salah, Hajj Ahmad uses a smooth, pure-black stone that he found in the Adirondack Mountains in 2004. His wife uses a large *turba*, or clay tablet, which a friend brought back from Karbala,

Iraq, where Imam Husayn, Muhammad's grandson, was killed by fellow Muslims. While Sunni Muslims may pray on any surface, Shi'a Muslims are required to pray on a natural surface. That is, if they pray on surfaces other than wood or dirt, they must place natural material at the spot where their foreheads touch the ground. Usually, Shi'a Muslims use a ritual item called a turba in Arabic or *mohr* in Persian, a clay tablet often made from the soil of Karbala or another holy Shi'a city such as Najaf, Iraq. These tablets can include an image of one of the shrines of the Imams, a short prayer phrase, or the name of an important Muslim such as Ali. In the absence of a tablet, Shi'a Muslims can use an item that comes from the earth—natural stones, paper, or anything else made of organic material, such as tissues, which are made of cotton.[13]

After his salah, Hajj Ahmad also recites du'as, or supplicatory prayers. Du'as can include well-known Arabic formulae as well as less formal prayers uttered in any language. Whereas salah is a set ritual that leaves little room for innovation, du'a allows Muslims to use their own words to speak directly to God. Du'a thus offers Muslims a chance to ask for everything from world peace to help with personal problems. Because there are different kinds of prayers in Islamic religion and U.S. Muslims wish to distinguish among them, they often use the Arabic terms *salah* and *du'a* in everyday speech. For example, Muslim Americans frequently ask friends and family to "make du'a" for them. Before performing an action such as waking up, eating, or entering the bathroom, Muslims might utter a du'a. U.S. Muslims can purchase pocket-size books of du'as that include the prayers written in Arabic in addition to their transliteration and translation into English. But in recent years, more and more Muslims access du'as through hundreds of phone apps. One can find the right du'a for nearly any occasion.[14]

For members of the Isma'ili group of Shi'a Muslims, du'a means something slightly different. Shi'a Isma'ili Muslims, who likely number in the tens of thousands in the United States, generally follow the Islamic teachings of the Aga Khan, their forty-ninth living Imam. Many Isma'ilis pray three or five times a day like their Sunni and Shi'i counterparts, but they also perform devotional worship at sunrise and at sunset that they call du'a.[15]

In addition to praying the five regular prayers, Muslims, no matter what their sect, can choose to perform recommended but not required prayers before or after the *fard*, or mandatory prayers. Performing extra prayers is purported to give believers spiritual rewards and earthly success. Sometimes, Muslims pray these extra prayers because they find them to be the most spiritually satisfying. For example, Nsenga Knight's favorite time to pray is in the middle of the night when her son is asleep. This is when she makes *tahajjud*, or nighttime prayer. Nsenga finds tahajjud "nourishing." It is a chance to "experience peace and quiet."

In her mid-thirties, Nsenga is the daughter of Caribbean migrants to Brooklyn. Her father is from Trinidad and her mother is from Guyana. Her parents converted to Islam in their early twenties, and she grew up in a large family in the Caribbean-majority neighborhood of Flatbush. As a child Nsenga attended a predominantly Black mosque, and she identifies as both Black and Caribbean American. Nsenga holds an MFA from the University of Pennsylvania and is an emerging visual artist who draws inspiration from Islamic rituals and African American and Black Muslim experiences. She seeks to tell the story of her communities through her art.

Nsenga seeks to pray the five prayers on time, no matter whether she is at home or away. She views a missed salah as a burden. Once, while shopping on a weekend afternoon at a food co-op in Durham, North Carolina, she realized that she had not yet prayed the mid-afternoon prayer and that the sunset prayer would be arriving soon. Her solution was to leave the co-op and walk to an ethnic grocery store owned by Muslims, who gave her a space to pray. This is her go-to solution for finding a hospitable place for prayer when she is outside her home. Nsenga has developed an uncanny ability to locate Muslim-owned businesses. It's different when she finds herself in an airport or a shopping mall during prayer times. She generally finds a quiet corner, sometimes near a stairway in the mall or even in a dressing room, and prays on the bare floor or on a sheet of paper. She once prayed in the yoga room at the San Francisco airport. Nsenga attributes her penchant for praying in public to her background as a New Yorker. Residents of New York City are a diverse lot, used to seeing people do strange things in public. There is also a large population of Muslims in New York, where approximately one in ten public school children is Muslim, and males often make their prayers right on the sidewalk.

But it is in the safe confines of her home that she often finds the most nurturing space for her spiritual life. As she creates her art in her home studio, she finds that salah helps her break up her day into manageable chunks. She schedules her day based on the salah times, and she has come to sense, quite automatically, when it is time to pray. For Nsenga, salah is both an obligation and a pleasure: "After praying, I feel like I just had a meeting, like I just had an appointment. . . . I feel like I go to salah as a way to fulfill an obligation, not as a form of drudgery." This obligation "helps me reorient myself throughout the day so it's not just an action that I am doing. I am constantly developing. Over the past couple of years I try to investigate it myself and figure out what it means to have khushu' [spiritual humility]. I ask myself how can I remain conscious and aware of my salah with every movement and prayer?"

After finishing up a charcoal sketch, Nsenga dusts off her hands and senses that it is time to pray the sunset prayer. She looks out the window and notices the sun is just dipping below the horizon. She reaches for her phone and navigates to Islamicfinder.com to verify the exact time for maghrib. Many Muslims now use social media and information technologies (IT) to help them keep track of and communicate with others about salah. In addition to using their cell phones and computer applications to keep track of prayer times, Muslims can also use applications on their cell phones to point themselves toward Mecca, find mosques in their locale, look up various du'as, listen to recitations of the Qur'an, and more.[16]

One popular website is Productive Muslim, which tries to show the benefits of praying, even while at work. A short video called "Just Go Do It and Recharge Your Iman with Salah!" depicts a non-Muslim and Muslim employee.[17] The video is short and simple but conveys a clear message to Muslims: salah on time leads to success in life and career; missing salah makes it hard to get through the day. Productive Muslim uses a popular American coaching model to teach Muslims to be more efficient in their lives so they can learn how to find more time for worship.[18] Productive Muslim also has a counterpart called Productive Muslimah (a female Muslim), presumably aimed at stay-at-home Muslim mothers. In one video entitled "Forget the Madness of Life with the Calmness of Salah," we see a woman wearing an *abaya*, or long dress, and headscarf grappling with a crying baby, a boiling teapot, and a ringing phone all at the same time.[19] She stops to perform salah, and suddenly an aura of peace surrounds her despite the chaos around her. The video conveys the message that if a Muslim prays on time, salah can bring a person back to a place of equanimity.

Nsenga is just such a Muslim mother. When it is time to pray, her toddler son accompanies her as she walks over to her closet to take out her special prayer clothes: a purple zip-up *jilbab*, or long dress, and headscarf that she reserves especially for salah. She puts on the jilbab over her colorful outfit, spreads out her blue and green prayer carpet on the ground in the direction of Mecca. She places her prayer beads on the floor next to her carpet and mentally prepares herself to pray. Nsenga raises her hands beside her ears and then quietly whispers, "Allahu akbar," before she lowers her hands to her chest and begins reciting the first chapter of the Qur'an.

Children, who are not required to keep the prayers until after they reach puberty, often start imitating their parents at a young age. For example, while Nsenga recites from the Qur'an and goes through the cycles of salah, her toddler follows alongside her on his own little prayer rug. He imitates his mother and loudly recites the adhan before the prayer in his childish Arabic. He bends down in bowing and in prostration. In between being serious, he lets out a few giggles and looks askance at his mother. He grins at her but she remains absorbed in her prayer. He then walks in front of her demanding to be picked up, and without hesitation, Nsenga reaches down in the middle of her prayers and brings her son to her chest. She holds him in her embrace until she finishes her prayers and turns her head to her right and left to give a symbolic greeting to the angels. Her son gives her a big hug and kiss and jumps out of her arms toward his play area and works on building a tower out of his blocks. As her son plays next to her, Nsenga reaches for her prayer beads and does *dhikr* for a few minutes before reaching out her hands in du'a. Apart from learning through observation at home, children also learn how to perform salah if they attend a full-time Islamic school and/or weekend school at their local Islamic centers. Muslim parents also purchase picture books and DVDs that teach children about salah.[20]

After making salah, Nsenga enjoys reciting dhikr, literally meaning remembrance. Dhikr is yet another form of Islamic prayer discussed in depth by Rosemary R. Corbett in the next chapter of this book. Throughout the Qur'an, God commands people to remember their Creator, declaring that "surely in the remembrance of God [dhikr] do hearts find peace" (13:28). Dhikr can simply refer to Muslims engaging in constant awareness and remembrance of God. But there are also specific formulaic dhikrs that Muslims are recommended to recite upon completing salah.[21] One of them is reciting the following phrases thirty-three times in Arabic: *subhanallah*, all glory be to God; *alhamdullilah*, all praise is to God; and *Allahu akbar*, or God is the greatest.

Praying at the Mosque

For many Muslims, the most important prayer of the week is *jumu'a*, or Friday congregational prayers. The Qur'an invokes the importance of Friday as a day of rest, at least for part of the day, akin to the Jewish Sabbath, stating, "O you who believe! When you are called to congregational prayer, hasten to the remembrance of God and leave off trade. That is better for you, if you but knew."[22] In countries that include Friday as part of the weekend (such as Egypt, Iran, and Pakistan), Muslims have the day off to spend with family, attend the prayer, and relax. In the United States, Muslims who work have to receive special accommodation from their workplace to take off enough time to visit a nearby mosque. In some workplaces such as universities, hospitals, or corporate offices, employees organize their own Friday prayer on site.[23] In addition to the prayer itself, Friday services include a sermon, sometimes given by a professional Muslim clergy member but more often than not, offered by a volunteer male preacher. Hajj Ahmad of Durham, North Carolina, is one of them. He sometimes delivers the *khutba*, or Friday sermon, at the local Shi'a mosque where he is the president of the mosque's board.[24]

Generally speaking, the mosque is a gendered space. Following rules articulated in the Shari'a, men and women do not sit or pray together in the mosque. Men sometimes pray in separate rooms than women. At other times, they pray in front of or beside women. The 2005 documentary *Me and the Mosque* follows filmmaker Zarqa Nawaz on a journey throughout Canadian and U.S. mosques to discover not only the different arrangements that Muslim men and women use but also how they feel about the separation of men and women in the mosque. Nawaz says that when she was a child, she prayed behind the men in the same prayer hall; for her, this felt inclusive. It was only when she grew up that her mosque—and other North American mosques—began to prevent women from praying in the main prayer hall. Nawaz interviews feminist activists such as Asra Nomani, who spent years fighting the board of her local mosque in West Virginia to be included in the main prayer hall. Nawaz also interviews male leaders of mosques who argue that barriers are necessary to keep men from becoming distracted by women in mosques. Unconvinced by such arguments, Nawaz dramatically depicts the female experience at mosques where women are placed in different rooms or behind large barriers: they feel ignored, censored, and generally marginalized within the community. Nawaz reminds her viewers that this strict separation of men and women does not follow the model of the Prophet Muhammad's mosque in Medina, where women were in far closer proximity to men.

One media-savvy U.S. Muslim activist and public intellectual, Hind Makki, has asked people from around the world to send their photos of women's spaces in mosques.[25] She curates the images, many of which were taken at American mosques. They reveal women's prayer rooms that are also used as storage rooms or have leaking roofs or broken AC systems in the height of the summer. Many mosques erect a variety of barriers between men and women, designed in theory to protect the modesty of female congregants. Makki's blog also features mosques that are more inclusive of women by offering one prayer room for both men and women or a female prayer room that is as spacious and clean as the male prayer room.

Having grown up in predominantly African American mosques informed by the teachings of religious leader W. D. Mohammed, Nsenga has little patience with mosques that offer poor accommodations for women. In this group's mosques, men and women generally pray in the same room or prayer hall with women sitting behind the men without any sort of barrier. When Nsenga has visited other mosques, she has sometimes been guided by men to a separate prayer room that she has deemed unsafe, moldy, dirty, dark, and too small. In such cases, Nsenga disregards the rules and prays in the back of the main prayer hall. Doing this is not an act of rebellion for Nsenga; rather, she says that "for me praying in the space is not about them. I tell them, 'This is not your mosque, this is the house of Allah.' . . . I usually try to navigate the situation in a way when I can form an ally with a man there and explain why I need to pray in the back of the room and not in the desolate women's area. I tell them that I will be in the back, that I will be very discreet, and that they should not notice me during salah." Occasionally, men have made comments about her praying in the main prayer hall, but she is usually able to dissuade them from taking further actions because her explanations as to why she is not praying in the women's section are so confident.[26]

Disputes over where men and women should pray in the mosque have led to rifts in some communities. Some choose to leave the mosque. Nawaz's documentary makes the point that many younger Muslims are "unmosqued" because they refuse to participate in congregations that treat women without respect and dignity.[27] For these Muslims, what is regarded as gender discrimination inside the mosque is often connected to other forms of marginalization along lines of sexuality, ethnic background, language, dress, belief, and practice.[28] Another controversial issue for some Muslims is the practice of male-only leadership of mixed-gender congregational prayers. Like some Jewish and Christian groups, including the Roman Catholic Church, only men are able to perform certain rituals in some traditions of Islamic practice. A few feminist Muslims—both men and women—reject that interpretation. Since the early 2000s small groups of feminists have not only formulated new interpretations of Islam to support female leadership of prayers in the mosque but have also held mixed-gender prayers led by a female imam.[29] Such practices remain rare, and Nicole Fauster expresses the point of view of most Muslim American men and women when she says that she does not mind praying in mosques where women are separated in some way from men. She would prefer to pray in the same prayer hall as she believes this is more true to the practice of the Prophet Muhammad, but she says some Muslim communities are slowly becoming more inclusive.

Not all Muslim American places of prayer are organized along gendered lines. Instead of praying in what other Muslims call a masjid, or mosque, Shi'a Isma'ilis pray in a *jamatkhana*, or place of assembly.[30] Like other Muslims, they ritually purify themselves with water and remove their shoes before entering the prayer hall. The congregational prayers are led by lay leaders appointed by the living Imam, the Aga Khan. Men and women have equal access to the front of the prayer hall, and they sit on either side of the hall on the carpeted floors. Women do not usually cover their hair.

In addition to conducting religious activities, some Muslim Americans have begun to develop what they refer to as "third spaces." Third spaces are not mosques. But they aren't secular spaces either. They can be a bit of both. One of the first third spaces in the country, Taleef Collective, in Fremont, California, was founded in 2005 by converts to Islam. The Taleef complex includes a prayer room, a multipurpose room, a café, a film screening area, and an outdoor area for barbeques and other meals.[31] Women and men sit on opposite sides of the prayer hall separated by small bookshelves, but otherwise they mingle with one another in the complex's other spaces. The popularity of Taleef has been phenomenal, with hundreds of Muslims attending its events. In 2014, Taleef opened a branch in Chicago in addition to establishing a website and media channel that offers viewers original content and live-streaming of all their events. Taleef has inspired many nonobservant Muslims to begin praying again—often right in the middle of social events.

Integrating Islamic Prayer into America

Although it is a religious practice, salah has social and political ramifications in the United States. The sight of Muslim men prostrating toward Mecca is frequently used as a prop in political cartoons and other media representations to symbolize Muslim political activism and violent extremism.[32] Muslims who choose to pray in public have been the victims of discrimination. For example, in a 2006 case known as the "Flying Imams Incident," six imams were arrested, handcuffed, and led off a US Airways flight after having been seen praying together in the airport.[33] To cite a very different incident that may speak as much to a lack of knowledge about Islamic prayers as any sort of intentional act of discrimination, football player Husain Abdullah, a safety for the Kansas City Chiefs, was penalized in 2014 for briefly praying after scoring a touchdown for "unsportsmanlike conduct, going to the ground," and excessive celebration.[34] It is quite typical for Christian players to pray after scoring a touchdown, and many fans made the point that Muslims should be allowed to do the same thing. After reviewing the incident, the National Football League acknowledged that the penalty was an error.[35]

As these incidents show, the performance of salah in public has prompted both Muslim and non-Muslim Americans to address themes that are quintessential to U.S. history and life: How does the religious liberty guaranteed by the First Amendment of the U.S. Constitution apply to those who perform Islamic prayer? Is there space—both physical and symbolic—for the incorporation of Islamic prayer into the country's national culture? What might Muslims and non-Muslims do to make non-Muslims feel safe when they decide to pray in public?

One of the ultimate signs that Islamic prayer has become part of American culture is the fact that Muslim Americans have identified the topic as a source of comedy. *Forbidden Love*, the short film that I discussed at the beginning of this chapter, addresses a serious topic, but does so in a humorous way. Another short film, entitled *Bassem Is Trying*, follows a young man through a series of vignettes in which he tries to hide various aspects of his Muslim identity and Islamic religious practices from the eyes of non-Muslim coworkers and members of the public.[36] At the beginning of the film, he uses a pair of scissors to shorten his *shalwar kameez,* the long South Asian tunic worn by both men and women. Bassem tucks what is left of his shirt into his pants and goes to work. In another scene, a coworker walks in on him as he is praying at the office. She is surprised. In the very next cut of the film, we see that Bassem is not praying. He is doing push-ups. Then, Bassem is in a Mercedes Benz. The window is open and he is listening to a recitation of the Qur'an. A small red sports car driven by a white male pulls up beside him. Bassem quickly puts on hip hop music and busts a move. In the final scene, Bassem holds the elevator for a coworker who is moving slowly toward the door. Bassem grins widely, and even looks pleased with himself for doing a good deed. The coworker gazes not at Bassem's face, but at the brown paper bag that Bassem is holding. The films ends with the coworker silently asking himself, "What's he got in that bag?"[37]

Though the short film ends on a negative note by depicting the prejudice that Muslim Americans face in their daily lives, filmmaker Lena Khan's ability to make fun of that prejudice taps into a deep well of American ethnic and religious humor. By making light of the futility of Bassem's attempts to fit in, such laughter ultimately makes Bassem and the signs of his religious and ethnic identity less foreign. One of those signs is salah, which for many Muslim Americans is the most meaningful religious obligation that they perform.

NOTES

1 M. Hasna Maznavi, *Forbidden Love*, www.youtube.com. Maznavi is a U.S. Muslim woman living in Los Angeles who founded the Women's Mosque of America.

2 For a comprehensive survey of salah practices among Muslims around the word, see www.pewforum.org.

3 For an exception, see Daniel Winchester, "Embodying the Faith: Religious Practice and the Making of a Muslim Moral Habitus," *Social Forces* 86, 4 (2008): 1753–1780.

4 Marion Holmes Katz, *Prayer in Islamic Thought and Practice* (New York: Cambridge University Press, 2013).

5 Asad Tarsin, *Being Muslim: A Practical Guide* (Berkeley: Sandala Publications, 2015), 51–52.

6 For a poetic take on this issue, see the short poem by Syrian American poet and novelist Mohja Kahf, "My Grandmother Washes Her Feet in the Sink of the Bathroom at Sears," www.poetryfoundation.org.

7 www.wudugear.com. Some legal opinions permit a Muslim to wear leather socks after having performed ablutions. Once on, they need only wipe their wet hands over the socks instead of having to wash their entire feet. This makes the process of performing ablutions in public much simpler.

8 J. E. Mikell, phone and email interview by author, March 24, 2016.

9 Nicole Fauster, Skype interview by author, January 13, 2016.

10 Qur'an 20:14; all English translations of the Qur'an have been taken from Seyyed Hossein Nasr, *The Study Quran: A New Translation with Notes and Commentary* (New York: HarperOne, 2015).

11 While I refer to my other subjects by their first names, Hajj Ahmad requested that I refer to him using the honorific title "Hajj," indicating that he has gone on Hajj. In his Muslim circles he is known as "Hajj Ahmad" and explains that everyone in his Shi'i community in Durham is addressed by various titles to indicate their social rank in the community or level of religious learning.

12 *Imam* with an uppercase "I" refers to the Imams in the Shi'i tradition who are seen as both political and spiritual leaders of the Muslim community, whereas *imam* with a lowercase "i" refers to any person who leads a community of Muslims in prayers and/or is employed as the religious leader of a mosque/community center. For more background on the development of Shi'i thought and ritual practices, see Arzina R. Lalani, *Early Shī'ī Thought: The Teachings of Imam Muḥammad Al-Bāqir* (London: I. B. Tauris, 2000).

13 For more on the clay tablets used by Shi'i Muslims, see Robert Gleave, "Prayer and Prostration: Imami Shi'i Discussions of al-sujud ala al-turba al-husayniyya," in *The Art and Material Culture of Iranian Shi'ism: Iconography and Religious Devotion in Shi'i Islam*, ed. Pedram Khosronejad (London: I. B. Tauris, 2012).

14 Based on observations and experiences by author among U.S. Muslims.

15 For a description of how a subset of Ismaʻilis practice Islamic rituals, see Tazim R. Kassam, "Jamatkhana," and "Ismaili Muslim Americans," in *The Encyclopedia of Muslim American History*, 2 vols., edited by Edward E. Curtis IV (New York: Facts on File, 2010); and "The Daily Prayer (*Duʻa*) of Shiʻa Ismaʻili Muslims," in *Religions of the United States in Practice*, vol. 2, edited by Colleen McDannell (Princeton: Princeton University Press, 2001).

16 For a thorough overview of Islam on the internet, see Gary R. Bunt, *iMuslims Rewiring the House of Islam* (Chapel Hill: University of North Carolina Press, 2009).

17 "Just Go Do It and Recharge Your Iman with Salah!" www.youtube.com.

18 "The Daily Life of a Productive Muslim—It Revolves around Salah," www.youtube.com; and "Pray Fajr on Time!" www.youtube.com.

19 "Fight the Madness of Life with the Calmness of Salah!" www.youtube.com.

20 For a popular Islamic children's website, see one4kids.net; and for a video that teaches kids how to pray, see "Learn How to Make Salah and Wudu," www.youtube.com.

21 For more on dhikr, refer to Rosemary R. Corbett's chapter in this volume.

22 Qur'an 62:9.

23 For an overview of the significance of Friday prayers as well as further details about the ritual practices of *salah*, see Shelomo Dov Goitein and Norman A. Stillman, *Studies in Islamic History and Institutions* (Leiden: Brill, 2010), 111–125; and Marion Holmes Katz, *Prayer in Islamic Thought and Practice* (Cambridge: Cambridge University Press, 2013), 130–138; for a humorous Muslim-style riff of Rebecca Black's infamous "It's Friday" 2011 music video that went viral, see Raef Haggag's music video "It's Jumuah," www.youtube.com.

24 While most Sunnis and Shiʻa would not mind praying together, there are some people from both communities who would refuse to pray behind an imam from the other community due to differences in ideology and/or the difference in the format of salah.

25 See Hind Makki's blog sideentrance.tumblr.com.

26 Nsenga Knight, Google Hangout interview by author, January 26, 2016.

27 See 2014 film entitled *Unmosqued* for an overview of this issue, www.unmosquedfilm.com.

28 For a thorough treatment of American Muslim women and their roles in mosques, see Juliane Hammer, *American Muslim Women, Religious Authority, and Activism: More than a Prayer* (Austin: University of Texas Press, 2012).

29 For more on the debate between scholars on this issue, see Jonathan Brown, *Misquoting Muhammad: The Challenge and Choices of Interpreting the Prophet's Legacy* (London: Oneworld, 2014), 189–199; for an overview of the first prayers led by Amina Wadud in New York City in 2005 and related controversies, see Hammer, *American Muslim Women*. To answer the question of whether women are allowed to lead female-only groups of worshipers: in the Hanafi madhhab, it is not recommended that women lead other women in prayer and they are forbid-

den from doing so in the Maliki madhhab. No significant restrictions occur in the Shafi'i and Hanbali madhhabs on women leading other women in prayer.

30 For a full explanation of mainstream Isma'ili beliefs and practices, see Farhad Daftary, *The Ismāīlīs: Their History and Doctrines* (Cambridge, U.K.: Cambridge University Press, 1990); Andrew Rippin and Jan Knappert, eds., *Textual Sources for the Study of Islam* (Chicago: University of Chicago Press, 1990); Ali Asani, "Devotional Practices," in Farhad Daftary, Amyn B. Sajoo, and Shainool Jiwa, eds., *The Shi'i World: Pathways in Tradition and Modernity* (London: I. B. Tauris, 2015).
31 taleefcollective.org.
32 Peter Gottschalk and Gabriel Greenberg, *Islamophobia: Making Muslims the Enemy* (Lanham, Md.: Rowman and Littlefield, 2008), 95, 123.
33 Heena Musabji and Christina Abraham, "Threat to Civil Liberties and Its Effect on Muslims in America," *DePaul J. Soc. Just.* 1 (2007): 83.
34 www.sbnation.com.
35 www.nytimes.com.
36 www.youtube.com.
37 For a detailed overview of Muslims in film, sometimes portrayed in prayer scenes, see Hussein Rashid, "Muslims in Film and Muslim Filmmaking," in Yvonne Yazbeck Haddad and Jane I. Smith, eds., *The Oxford Handbook of American Islam* (New York: Oxford, 2014).

2

Dhikr

Remembering the Divine

ROSEMARY R. CORBETT

The flickering light of oil lamps, reflecting off the blue Turkish tiles and glass *mihrab*, a niche in the wall that indicates the direction of Mecca, casts moving shadows around the ten-sided room and up the high walls to the peaked ceiling, even before any human movement begins. A group of men kneel in the center of the space on sheepskin rugs while a female contingent occupies an overlooking platform off to one side. Separated but together, following the communal dinner that precedes their prayers, they start the ceremony. As the men rise and begin a choreographed dance, their rhythmic shouts echoing up to the wood rafters, the women lean left and then right—coordinating their motions and softer utterances with those happening on the floor below. The only unscripted movement comes from children who skirt the walls and occasionally dart across the room, as absorbed in their own activities as the whirling parents who brought them here. It is a typical Saturday night at the Chestnut Ridge *dargah*, home to the Halveti Jerrahi Sufi order of Spring Valley, New York. Yet, as far as Sufi *dhikr* ceremonies in the United States go, it is not typical at all.

The movements of some aspects of Islamic practice, such as the daily prayers (*salah*, see chapter 1 of this volume) are largely standard, with minor differences between Sunni and Shiʻa observances and additional differences between those and Ismaʻili *duʻa* prayers. In contrast, Sufi dhikr, or "remembrance," rituals vary tremendously. Before describing such rituals here, it is important to note that dhikr is not just a collective weekly ceremony undertaken by Sufis. Such rituals are certainly more elaborate among members of Sufi orders, or *tariqas*, whose practices of "remembering" the divine have been handed down over centuries.

Nevertheless, because such remembrance, or dhikr, is enjoined multiple times in the Qur'an, it is also an activity periodically undertaken by non-Sufis. Some Muslims occasionally pray special prayers of thanksgiving after their daily prayers, for example, while others argue that even saying "*alhamdullilah*" ("thanks be to God") before or after a meal counts as remembering God at that moment. For Sufis, however, dhikr has a more definite purpose. The point is not simply to give thanks for a particular blessing or even to remind oneself periodically of God's power and presence. Ultimately it is—through such practice—to take steps to become a more Godly human being, and to eventually enter the state of constant dhikr, continually mindful of God's closeness.[1]

Muslims in North America—particularly West Africans brought to the continent through the transatlantic slave trade—have engaged in Sufi dhikr since before the United States was a nation. Yet over time and across space, Muslims have undertaken such practices in very different ways. Many aspects of dhikr rituals are specific to particular Sufi orders. Among these is the *wird*, the litany of programmatic prayers, chants, and readings from the Qur'an handed down over the centuries from each order's founder. Not only do different orders make reference to different portions of the Qur'an or chant different selections of the ninety-nine attributes of God (such as "*Ya, Latif,*" meaning "Oh, Subtle One") when praising Allah during their ceremonies, the physical components of their traditions can also vary tremendously. Some use music while others do not, for example, and some incorporate a kind of ritual dance while others refrain. And while many Sufi orders are interracial or intersectarian in composition, others—such as the Mouride from Senegal—tend to be ethnically homogeneous. Even different branches of the same order may conduct their ceremonies somewhat distinctly, as I discuss below. As a result, no one dhikr ceremony fully represents the larger genre of practice, and no one description can sufficiently capture the sensory experience of participating in this ritual form. Like the stars of the night sky, the ceremonies of the different orders may—at a distance—seem like similarly bright lights scattered across space. On closer inspection, however, each proves to have its own characteristic elements. Although orienting the observer in the same direction, each one is irreducibly unique.

In this chapter, I describe three different versions of collective dhikr—practiced by Sufis related to the same order—so as to illuminate variations within this ritual form. I also put these collectivities in historical context to shed light on how their ceremonies changed over time. Although based on long-held traditions, Sufi practices are subject to alteration—sometimes because of the sheer impossibility of always engaging in the exact same actions in the exact same way, but also because of the variety of factors unique to Sufism in the United States. These include, but are not limited to, the multinational character of many orders, as practitioners migrate and attempt to enact time-worn traditions with new people in new places, as well as practitioners' responses to the sensitivity many Sufis feel about characterizations of their practices as un-Islamic. As I have discussed elsewhere, some African American Muslim communities practice collective dhikr but prefer not to call themselves Sufis because they already face scrutiny over orthodoxy from Arab and South Asian Muslims.[2] Then there are others who are less concerned about their Sufi identity.

Approximately forty miles south of Spring Valley, on a noisy street near Manhattan's financial district, dozens of worshipers pack a tiny storefront mosque that stands in stark contrast to the stately suburban dargah. The aesthetic here is minimalist, with white brick walls and white tin ceiling. The only ornaments in the hundred-foot-long prayer hall are the dangling glass chandelier; the handsome dark wood *minbar*, or podium, for delivering *khutbahs*—the sermons following Friday prayers; and six circular wall hangings on which "Allah," "Muhammad," and the names of the Prophet's Companions are inscribed in gold Arabic calligraphy on fields of forest green. Red and green Persian carpets cover the floor. This is also the home of a Jerrahi group—the Nur Ashki Jerrahis, whose leaders followed the same Turkish shaykh, Muzaffer Özak, as those in Spring Valley until the shaykh's death in 1985. Here, though, the privileged voice is female, belonging to Shaykha Fariha, the American woman who heads this community.

As in Spring Valley, Fariha's dervishes perform their prayers separated, with men standing in lines in front of the women's ranks. The dhikr ceremony is less segregated, however, and less scripted. The ritual begins each time with the same *wird*, the order of which is kept in white booklets and passed around so that dervishes can follow as it progresses. Like their primarily Turkish cousins in Spring Valley, these dervishes shift from chanting to dancing as time passes, and as the wird gives way to sung *ilahis*, or "hymns," and *sema'*, "a physically active meditation" in which dervishes "aim to reach the source of all perfection" by using music and movements to distract from one's self and to focus on God.[3] Unlike the northern group, however, the Nur Ashki Jerrahis' movements can be as eclectic as the nationalities and religious orientations of those gathered among them. And yet, for all their noticeable differences, the Spring Valley and Nur Ashki Jerrahis are remarkably similar when compared to the third group I describe: a newer Sufi community whose shaykh also holds—at least in part—a claim to Jerrahi lineage, but whose dhikrs are quiet, contained, and stationary, involving no music or dance at all. As I discuss, these last Sufis are the least physically demonstrative in their ceremonies and thus the least likely to run afoul of reformist Muslim leaders. Nevertheless, they may well be the ones to test the limits of the flexibility of Sufi traditions in a new country.

Jerrahis Coming to America

Approximately six miles north of the Nur Ashki Jerrahis' Manhattan dargah, and twenty-six miles south of the Halveti Jerrahis' Spring Valley meeting place, is a one-bedroom apartment on Manhattan's Upper West Side. For nearly ten years, until 2007, this residence served as the gathering place for the Sufi group led by Feisal Abdul Rauf, an Egyptian American shaykh who once also "took hand" (or *bay'a*, a ritual of initiation to join a Sufi order, among other things) with Muzaffer Özak and performed dhikr with the Nur Ashki Jerrahis.

Despite the fact that this house of worship is more of an actual house than most, the apartment's devotional purpose was evident in its arrangement. Outside the front door sat shoe racks awaiting the footwear of arriving dervishes. In the tiny kitchen were stacks of plastic cups, plates, and utensils to be used in the communal meal preceding the ceremony and for the sweets and tea served afterward. Aside from couches lining two walls of the living area, the main room of the apartment was sparsely furnished. A desk in one corner often held books, tapes, and CDs about Islam and Sufism available for purchase. Like at the downtown dargah, the walls featured gold-leaf calligraphy that traced qur'anic passages and some of the ninety-nine names of Allah chanted during dhikr. Here, though, the orientation for prayer was marked by a floor lamp festooned with an orange shade.

While the surroundings for these Sufis were more cramped than those for their Jerrahi cousins, the dervishes themselves were no less earnest or intent in their devotions. Before turning to the similarities and differences between this group's practices and those of other Jerrahis, a bit of history is in order. Although he joined the Jerrahis under Shaykh Muzaffer in 1983, Rauf—this order's leader—also took hand with a Moroccan Qadiri shaykh in 1996. That is not the only important distinction between Rauf and the leaders of the other Jerrahi groups, though. While the Spring Valley Halveti Jerrahis and the Tribeca Nur Ashki Jerrahis generally appealed to first-generation audiences (first-generation Turkish immigrants, in the first case, and first-generation Muslim converts, in the second), Rauf oriented his Sufi practice to appeal to second-generation Muslim Americans—the children of immigrants or of converts who had grown up as Muslims in the United States.

The first American leader to meet Muzaffer was Tosun Bayrak, a Turkish expatriate, artist, and professor. Bayrak was not a pious Muslim before joining the Jerrahis. He experienced a crisis after his mother's death in Turkey in 1974, however, and began to seek out Sufis while there to mourn her. This search led him to Muzaffer.[4] Three years later, at Muzaffer's urging, Bayrak turned half his house in Spring Valley into a dargah for the newly established Jerrahi order of America. "Find a place," Muzaffer had told him, "invite people you know; offer them food. Treat women, children, and minorities especially kindly."[5] An ornate and stately dargah would follow later.

Many of the Muslims Bayrak knew in the United States at that time were Turkish, and the Spring Valley community took on a Turkish flavor immediately. Accustomed, also, to a historically Turkish chain of transmission (Shaykh Muzaffer was nineteenth in the line of succession to the original founder in Istanbul), Bayrak did not foresee that he would one day compete for his shaykh's legacy with an American convert, much less a woman.[6] In just a short time, however, the Halveti Jerrahi tariqa would be reinterpreted for a religiously eclectic American audience.

Shaykha Fariha, born Philippa de Menil to the oil heiress and art patron Dominique de Menil and her husband, John, first met Muzaffer a few years after Bayrak did and was largely responsible for bringing Muzaffer to New York during the decade that followed. Under Muzaffer's leadership, the Jerrahis began to perform their ceremonies—described as both traditional Turkish folk rituals and devotional ones—at cultural festivals around Europe.[7] It was through the popularization of such "whirling dervish" dances that the de Menils first learned of the Sufis. After their first visit to the United States in 1978, and with Philippa's help, Muzaffer and his Jerrahis retured twice annually for several weeks at a time until his death in 1985. Not only did Philippa financially sponsor these journeys, but she and her husband, Heiner Friedrich, bought and renovated an old firehouse on Mercer Street in Manhattan. The new dargah contained a mosque and living quarters for Muzaffer and was bedecked with the work of groundbreaking contemporary artists Philippa and Heiner supported through their Dia Art Foundation. Muzaffer named it Masjid al-Farah: the mosque of divine ease.[8]

In 1979, Philippa took hand with Muzaffer, joining his order. During the ceremony, Muzaffer granted her a new name: Fariha. Not long after, Muzaffer transformed Fariha and another New Yorker from dervishes into *khalifas* (deputies). The other person was Lex Hixon, later known as "Shaykh Nur," after whom the Nur Ashki Jerrahis get their name. Hixon, who had written several works on the essential unity of the world's religions, hosted the popular radio talk show "In the Spirit" on New York's WBAI from 1972 to 1989. He first met Muzaffer in the late 1970s when he interviewed him for the program, with Bayrak serving as a translator, and became a dervish shortly thereafter.[9] As Hixon later recounted the khalifa transmission ceremony:

> In the Islamic year 1400, which was 1980 of the Common Era, I became one of the formal successors of Muzaffer Effendi. I knelt before him, side by side with my spiritual sister Fariha al-Jerrahi, at the Mosque of Divine Ease, the Masjid al-Farah, in New York City. After placing his magnificent green and gold turban upon my head, the Grand Shaykh opened his palms and offered supplication: "May whatever has come into me from Allah and from the Prophet of Allah now enter into him." After this brief prayer, Shaykh Muzaffer removed his turban from my head and placed it on the western woman beside me.[10]

After that, during Muzaffer's extended absences from New York, Shaykh Nur led the Manhattan community. Sufi and other so-called "Eastern" traditions had become quite popular in the United States during the 1970s—what many called the "New Age" of esotericism that developed out of the 1960s counterculture[11]—and Muzaffer's new followers in Manhattan quickly grew to rival the original, traditionally Turkish, contingent that met in Spring Valley.

Three years after the khalifa ceremony, Feisal Abdul Rauf first visited Masjid al-Farah. Shortly thereafter, he also joined the Nur Ashki Jerrahis and accepted Muzaffer's charge to deliver khutbahs there, effectively serving as imam.[12] When Rauf became imam at the downtown dargah in 1983, he did so on the condition that he not be drawn into the rivalries between the New York City Nur Ashki Jerrahis and the Spring Valley Halveti Jerrahis.[13] In contrast to Fariha and Nur (who was also an Orthodox priest and trained to become a Zen master, and whose group adheres to Nur's belief in the mystical reality underlying all religions), Bayrak's order describes itself as a "traditional" Islamic one.[14] Rauf would eventually outline a middle path: praising the ethical and mystical parts of the divine reality he believes other religions share, while faithfully practicing the tradition into which he was born.

Two years later, the Nur Ashki Jerrahis endured several changes. The transitions started with a takeover at the Dia Art Foundation that involved Fariha's removal as head of the board. After a drop in oil prices slashed the organization's assets (and with the foundation already on the verge of insolvency—despite tens of millions of dollars from Fariha), Dia was forced to sell property in Manhattan, among other things. Although the Mercer Street mosque and dargah were closed, Heiner and Fariha reestablished them in a much smaller three-story building sandwiched between two bars in Tribeca. Shaykh Nur called their new home the "jewel box" after the great spiritual treasures held within the tiny space.[15]

The Dia coup and closure of the Mercer Street dargah coincided with another loss for the Jerrahis—the death of Muzaffer. Taking this as a divine sign, Fariha turned all her attention to her Sufi community, of which she and Nur assumed direction while Bayrak continued to direct the Halveti Jerrahis in Spring Valley.[16] The two groups met together occasionally, but tensions over practice often surfaced between the leader of the traditionally Muslim segment of the order and the leaders of the more eclectic and religiously inclusive community.

When Nur passed away in 1995, leadership of the Nur Ashki Jerrahis, which by then had outposts across the United States, passed directly to

Fariha. Unsettled by the new situation, Rauf traveled to Morocco and soon joined the order of a Qadiri shaykh there. Before long, that shaykh tasked him with bringing knowledge of their Qadiri traditions to America "in ways it can understand."[17] Still delivering khutbahs at the mosque under the charge given him by Muzaffer, Rauf went on to start his own Sufi organization, the American Sufi Muslim Association, or ASMA, in 1997, and to hold separate Friday night dhikrs at his home in New Jersey or in the Manhattan apartment of his wife and ASMA cofounder, Daisy Khan.

Unlike the Halveti Jerrahis, whose primarily Turkish contingent was comprised mostly of immigrant families, or the Nur Ashki Jerrahis, whose ethnically and religiously diverse members were mainly American converts, Rauf sought to reach American-born Muslims—often the children of immigrants who wanted an Islamic practice that resembled neither what they saw as the overly cultural traditions of their parents nor the overly eclectic American traditions of New Age converts. Blending the influences of the shaykhs who had inspired him, Rauf offered a sober Sufism shorn of dancing and singing—a kind of ritual based in a deep, Qur'an-focused practice that seemed accessible to Muslims of all backgrounds, not just those of certain ethnicities or nationalities. This practice—focused on orthodoxy but open to the insights of other religions—allowed Muslims in Rauf's group to feel fervent about Islam without feeling fanatical (an image Muslims were often tarred with by the media), and to enjoy a form of devotion that did not run afoul of Muslim authorities who regard many Sufi traditions (particularly those involving music and dancing) as inauthentic. Within a decade, however, even this community would feel the strain of adapting to a changing American environment.

Turkish Immigrants and Their Dhikr

In Spring Valley, on a frigid February evening in 2015 male dervishes donning the white cap of Jerrahi initiates exchange greetings and chat, the lights of the dargah burning brightly as they intermingle and eventually take their places, standing in formation in two rows on either side of the room. Young boys, also festooned with little white hats one might otherwise see on a baker or sous chef, dart here and there around the ranks, settling finally into a row behind the older adherents on the right.

It is not a special occasion this evening and there are no dignitaries visiting from Turkey, so the dervishes are clad in jeans and khakis rather than in the long white skirts over white pants and the short white jackets that flare out so dramatically during official or particularly ceremonial dhikr performances. (Few other orders have such elaborate ceremonial garb.) In contrast to those special performances, when the dargah's gleaming wood floor is cleared to make way for the white sheepskin carpets on which each dervish kneels, the floor this evening is covered in a crimson Turkish carpet that stretches from the potted palms on the right side of the room to the raised women's section on the left side, set apart by a small wooden railing. The only sheepskin carpet out this evening is placed perpendicular to the dargah's ornately tiled mihrab on the easternmost side of the room.

"*Bismillah*" ("In the name of God") rings out above the din and the chatter quiets as an elderly man with a cane walks to the mihrab and bows in its direction. Moving carefully and slowly as a result of his age, he coughs and leans back on a stool placed on top of the sheepskin there. Like many others, he is wearing a white cap and what appears to be a kind of sweater vest. The colors of vests in the room range from white to tan to charcoal, but all are cut in the same fashion. The elderly shaykh begins prayers in Arabic, and the assembled dervishes, male and female, immediately join in with a collective "*Huuuuuuu*" ("He," in Arabic, referring to Allah) that vibrates through the room. They repeat their chant as the shaykh continues. The older man's voice is muffled and he is not using a microphone, so his words are hardly decipherable above the hum from the dervishes. Nevertheless, they follow along with him intently, not even needing the aid of a printed program to guide them for the hour-long ceremony.

Shortly after, the room falls silent. The shaykh continues his prayers with no underlying chanting, and dervishes switch to occasional "ameen"s as their leader invokes the memory and spirit of various past Sufi leaders. They then pray together silently, still standing, each dervish passing palms over face upon finishing. Following this, they break out in song, voices lilting and lulling as they draw out the words:

> Allahumma salli wa sallim wa baarik
> 'ala Sayyidina Muhammad wa 'ala aalihi . . .

[Oh, Allah, exalt and greet and bless
our Master, Muhammad, and his family . . .]

While only a few of the participants are fluent Arabic speakers, all have memorized the many stanzas of the *ilahi*. Upon completing it, they collectively recite from memory a portion of their order's wird and the many praises of God it entails, bowing slightly when uttering the name of the Prophet. A moment of silence follows, the clearing of throats, and then the older man's muffled voice rings out again, cuing people to join him in another paean to Allah. This time a younger man's song climbs above the rest, overlaying their common refrain of "Allah, Allah," with a voice like that of a classically trained singer of traditional Arabic *maqams* (scaled melodies). The men in their rows sway gently, left and right, in time and bow to each side repeatedly at the beginning of the dance that will be this evening's dhikr. The women move similarly on their platform to the side, though they will not be nearly as mobile as the cohort on the main floor during the proceedings.

The dervishes transition to a new sung chant of "*la 'ilaha 'illa-llah*" (the beginning of the Muslim profession of faith: "There is no god but God"), bowing deeper each time they sway to one side or the other. The chant slows at points, then quickens again, the men's movements increasing in intensity, palm fronds fluttering slightly as bodies brush the potted plants. The voice of the soloist fades out and a segment of the gathered contingent takes up a new song, layering it above the running chant of the others. Then, by some unseen cue, they all fall silent and still. The quiet lasts only a moment, however, before their leader calls out the beginnings of a new ilahi and the rest join in just syllables later. For this next part, they do not sway. Nevertheless, some cannot help but nod rhythmically or rock back and forth on their heels. Again, the singing ends, and the group utters another prayer from the wird in a call-and-response refrain.

Moments after the group has begun a new chant, one of the older men in a row on the right side of the room steps out of his place and moves slightly closer to the center, turning toward the shaykh as he begins a new solo. Someone else claps loudly and shouts out, "Hu!" Several men follow, interjecting the divine pronoun into the smallest space between song cycles, while the rest maintain their deep rhythmic chanting of "Allah, Allah." The swaying begins again and a new collective song fills the room with at least three different parts sung by those gathered. Moments later, three dervishes bearing large circular drums walk down the aisle between the rows of facing chanters. Each presents his instrument to the shaykh and receives it back after a brief blessing. They move to their posts on the left side of the room and a female musician moves out of the women's section to join them. Soon, the musicians are swaying along with the rest, and before long the deep thump of a drum strike tolls out, the tinkling of the mini cymbals attached to the drum chiming along with it.

As the drums become rhythmic, five more men step out of their places in line and move to the front of the room, gathering in a semicircle behind the shaykh. They too begin to sway and a new soloist's voice punctuates the otherwise rhythmic chanting and pounding. The men in the facing rows begin to step forward in time with their swaying, moving the rows closer to each other with each drumbeat, until opposing dervishes are very nearly brushing their cheeks together as they bow from side to side. They retreat and return, with young boys ranging in ages from four to twelve bobbling along behind them unevenly. It almost appears as if one flank of dervishes advances against the other, pushing them to one side of the room, before the other flank rallies and pushes back. In other kinds of dhikr, known as Devran and often performed prior to the ceremony described here, the drummers move to the center of the room and the dervishes form one large circle around the male musicians. Additional female musicians, clad—like the other female worshipers—in long dark garments topped by black *hijabs*, or head coverings, remain outside the circle, and the sound of an instrument resembling a pan flute joins the chorus of voices rising to the ceiling.[18] But tonight's dhikr is just a short one

The swinging, swaying, and thumping intensify. The men return to their original ranks and well-timed shouts pepper the otherwise steady cadence. Finally, the elderly shaykh rises from his stool and, swaying in time, moves to join hands with a dervish on his right. The others follow, bringing the opposing ranks into unified circles, one inside the other, that turn together clockwise in the center of the room. The circles then slow and come to a stop, dervishes moving closer together into a pulsating huddle. The five men who stood behind the shaykh approach the throbbing mass and, placing their hands to their right ears, begin to sing out strands of prayers above the chanting crowd. "*Ya, Hayy*" ("Oh, Everlasting One"), "Ya, Hayy! Ya, Hayy!" the encircled dervishes exclaim, throwing their heads back on the second syllable, passing several minutes this way. A joint drumbeat of "Hayy! Hayy! Hayy!" takes over and the female drummer behind the group bounces along with the rest. The dervishes finally begin to slow their movements as the drums cease, and draw out their utterances until the group sounds like one giant heaving individual, breathing a noisy, labored breath. "Hayyyyyyy," it finally exhales. The huddle breaks apart, men slowly shuffling back to their ranks as their shaykh calls out a new refrain and resumes his place of honor.

Back in their rows, the dervishes proceed once more to sway and sing, their melody eventually giving way to a chant of "Hu, Hayy! Hu, Hayy!" The chanting, swinging, and swaying continue, various choruses carrying up into the dargah's rafters, and one dervish calls out the first English utterance of the ceremony. "Bless Allaaah," he sings melodically, before switching back into Arabic. The dervishes fold their arms over their chests, standing silently, as their shaykh takes the lead. They are quiet again as his aged voice, quavering, issues a prayer in thickly accented English:

Oh, the Creator Allah, Honorable . . . Oh, the most compassionate one.

Oh, the forgiver of all sins; Oh, the loving one; Oh, the beautiful one. Oh, Lord, you say that if we do not love each other as human beings, our faith is incomplete. Your beloved, who you have sent as our Prophet, said that his *umma* [community] is like one single body. If the finger aches, the whole body aches. He said Muslims [are] like one brotherhood, that we are all brothers and sisters. He also said, "he who loves each other for your sake in this world, will be together in this world and in the hereafter."

"Ameen," echo the dervishes, periodically concurring with the prayer.

Increase the love which we feel in our hearts for each other. Ya, Allah, be beautiful our hearts with your love and the beloved of yours, Mohammed Mustapha, *salla llahu 'alayhi wa-alihi wa-sallam* [the prayer of God and peace be upon him and his family]. You have brought us in this humble mosque this day; on the day of last judgment bring us all together also in the safe place under the divine hum and close to the one who you have sent, and the intercessor of the sinners such as ourselves. You have sent him as your mercy upon all mankind . . . bless us with the *adab Moham-medin* [character and ethics of Mohammed]. Give us the character and morals of the one you have given the most beautiful character. So that by chance we may have a chance to hope for his intercession. Bless my *ikh-wan* [brothers and sisters] with the intercession of the intercessor.

The shakyh calls out the beginning of further prayers in Arabic and the dervishes join him, ending in extended "Alllllllaaaaaaah," "Alllahhhh-hhhhh," as another dervish calls out more prayers. The underlying hum sounds vaguely like the drone of bees, until the dervishes collectively bow with a "Ya, Allah, Huuuuu." The elderly shaykh rises, the head of his cane grasped firmly in his palm, the foot of it digging into the floor as he lifts himself with great effort. The group issues one last collective prayer, and then the shaykh takes his leave, walking on three legs down the center aisle between devotees. The dervishes turn to each other and exchange hugs or the very Turkish kiss on either cheek.

The fellowship among dervishes that follows the dhikr, like the time over the meal that preceded it, is less formal but no less important. It is yet another instantiation of the directives and example of their deceased shaykh. Muzaffer was particularly known for emphasizing love. In fact, his full title was Muzaffer Özak 'Isqiyyu'l-Jerrahiyyu'l-Khalwati. The Jerrahi and Halveti (or, in Arabic, *Khalwati*) portions of his name, one of his dervishes explains, indicate the specific branch of the Sufi order to which Muzaffer belonged. But the adjective *'Isqi*—from the Arabic *'ishq*, or intense love—"specifies his style and emphasis within the spiritual path."[19] For these dervishes, like their Manhattan cousins, the time communing together outside the formal dhikr ceremony is as meaningful in different ways as the time spent in ritual prayers of remembrance.

An American Convert Community

Dhikr at the Manhattan dargah of the Nur Ashki Jerrahis is not altogether distinct from that which occurs forty miles north. The singing begins with English-language "mystic hymns" set to the same tune (though they are not literal translations) as some of the ilahis sung in Arabic in Spring Valley. Fariha's voice rises above that of the mixed-gender choir, white caps upon the dervishes' heads, just as they are donned forty miles north, as one male dervish's strong baritone moves symmetrically beneath the rest. Other singers come in after a few words.

> Allah, most high, shower your blessings sublime, Allah, upon our
> master, Mohammed, the exalted, and upon his noble
> Companions.
> Mystic presence shines through his heart, most merciful.
> O, Thou, boundless mercy.
> Allah, most high, shower your blessings upon our master,
> Mohammed, the dawning sun, and upon his noble Companions . . .

The Nur Ashki Jerrahis continue this hymn for several more refrains before turning to a collective enunciation of the divine pronoun that echoes the utterances made by their cousins: "Huuuu, Huuuuu, Huuuu." As they proceed with their dhikr, sung prayers are interspersed with the hymns, with the underlying baritone sounding almost like the monotone drone of a Tibetan chant, and additional percussion occasionally added by the rifling of pages, as dervishes flip through the wird to find their places.

Before long, Fariha calls out, and the collective singing ceases as female dervishes take up a new tune:

> Most Precious Allah, please shower the supreme blessing of mystic
> union upon our spiritual master and guide, Mohammed,
> as long as this vast creation lasts.
> Allah Most Merciful, please convey to his exalted soul and to the
> sublime souls of his spiritual lineage your divine peace and
> blessings
> and abundance, and abundance, and abundance.

After a few more verses, all join in singing again, but it is not long before Fariha's voice climbs above the rest once more, as she chants prayers alone in English with the baritone "Hu" still resonating in the background. Like in Spring Valley, Fariha invokes the memory and spirit of sages past. In a more ecumenical style than the Halveti Jerrahis—one that reflects both her history and her community—she does so by beginning with the people that Jews, Christians, and Muslims believe to be the first humans created by God and, continuing on, she includes figures regarded differently among the different religions. The other dervishes sit silently, listening.

> Most precious Allah, please manifest at the center of this mystic circle of love the light of all 124,000 noble human beings sent into the world to call the human heart back into its source.
>
> Oh, Allah, please manifest the blessed souls of Adam and Eve, mother and father of humanity.

When Fariha comes to Abraham, the patriarch recognized by all three religions, and his first two sons, about whom there is disagreement (Muslims believe the firstborn, Ishmael, was the sacrifice Abraham intended to make as a sign of covenant with God, while Jews and Christians believe it was Isaac, the second-born), she makes no distinctions: "please manifest . . . Sarah and Hagar, the mothers of the faithful in Ismael and Isaac, the holy sacrifices."

Fariha proceeds, invoking Moses and Jesus and including in her prayer numerous women, as well as men, thus making the petition as egalitarian in gender as it is in religion. She then invokes the Prophet Muhammad. Although Muslims consider Muhammad to be the "seal of the Prophets," meaning the final prophet sent to reveal the same message earlier prophets brought to other communities at other times, Fariha is far from finished with her prayer. She invokes the Prophet's family, including his wives, his Companions who led the early Muslim community, and his grandsons "Hassan and Husayn, the mystic roots of Islam, and all the twelve Imams bearing the nectar of prophecy." The last reference in this litany is to leaders accepted as authoritative by Shi'a Muslims, who are in the world's minority, but not often by Sunnis. Fariha has thus made the prayer as inclusive in intrareligious matters as it is in interreligious ones.

"Oh Allah," she continues, moving into the heart of the prayer, "please manifest the early Sufis." She begins to call these early Sufis out by name, male and female, and then proceeds to the founders of other branches of Sufism: Qadiri, Chishti, Naqshbandi, among others. "Oh Allah, please manifest all the sages, both women and men, both known and unknown," Fariha exhales, making the prayer as radically inclusive as possible. Then getting specific, she turns to the "living *silsila*," or chain of transmission, that is, the Jerrahis, and includes in her invocations the order's original founder, several of the shaykhs who led the order in the three hundred years before Muzaffer's headship, and finally, "Muzaffer . . . this Pir," or Sufi teacher, "of the West," and "his noble son of light, Shaykh Nur . . . Pir of the new humanity, gatherer of the tariqas, gatherer of the sacred traditions." While all the previous sages and prophets mentioned had revealed parts of the universal message, Fariha believes, Shaykh Nur had gathered them together and shown them to be one.

Still not finished, Fariha then turns to the other living leaders of the Jerrahis, asking God to bless the various shaykhs in Istanbul, the ones in the United States who have led the Spring Valley community since Muzaffer's death, and the Nur Ashki Jerrahi shaykhs who follow Nur's teachings and have since spread across the continent. Finally, she concludes, "bless humanity and all the teachers and all their communities." The epic prayer seems to stretch into eternity but has actually taken only six minutes to recite. It is one of the many points at which time seems elastic during these ceremonies.

The dervishes follow Fariha's prayer with a collective recitation of the *Fatiha*—the first chapter, or "opening," of the Qur'an, which is prayed during daily prayers. They then join in song briefly. Fariha quickly directs a few words at her dervishes, moving them out of the quietly meditative state of the early dhikr and into what will be the more energetic portion of the evening. The atmosphere in the room is relaxed, the dervishes holding soft postures and smiling gently. Fariha then calls out the first few words of another mystic hymn, and the energy in the room shifts—as if this were the moment for which everyone has been waiting. The volume of collective singing increases dramatically and harmonies begin to break out. The joint refrain here too is "la ilaha illa-llah" ("there is no god but God").

At one point, Fariha calls out to a dervish, "Ali," and a male voice takes over, singing rhythmically in Arabic, his words ringing out with the cadence and timbre often emanating only from muezzins trained in the Middle East. When he pauses, the collective song rises slightly in speed and pitch, and Ali begins his mesmerizing tune again. The energy in the room intensifies, and after a short time, the chanting increases to an even more fervent pace. Some dervishes sway with eyes closed; someone claps a few beats, then claps again moments later as the chanting again quickens. The air in the dargah begins to feel rarified, as if there is not quite enough to breathe fully. A dervish coughs between chants, the others raise the pitch again, and 'Ali begins to draw out the syllables of his sung prayers in a longer, lower, and more resonant register that hovers just above the evening's constant baritone. The droning chant returns once more, subtly, beneath the rest of the voices.

The dervishes continue this way for a few more minutes, with Fariha modulating the pace and pitch of the chanting, until she draws out the first syllable of the refrain in a long "laaaaa" that causes all the others to catch their breath and follow. The chanting slows and a woman's voice periodically climbs above the rest, replacing 'Ali's. Soon after, singing turns to chanting. The pace quickens dramatically within the next minute, and over the minute following quiets almost to a whisper until Fariha draws out the last "Alllaaaaaah." Only half an hour has passed since the beginning of dhikr, and several dervishes, breathing heavily, seem already exerted. Within a few minutes, they have found their places and joined again in communal song, reciting "Allah, Allah," over and over in ascending and descending scales, deep quick breaths preceding each refrain until Fariha again calls out, "Allaaaahhh" and the rest follow, transitioning to a rapid, almost hyperventilating, repetition of the sacred appellation.

The dervishes continue to follow Fariha's direction, switching cadence, pitch, speed, and volume in matters of mere seconds as she leads them through wandering cycles of invocation and then back from "Allah" to the ever-resonant "Huuuuuuuuuuuu." The cycles slow briefly, the dervishes breathe deeply, then the chanting accelerates once more. At this point in the ceremony, one hardly has time to fill the lungs completely for more than two or three breaths between rapid exhalations of divine names. "La 'ilaha 'illa-llah," Fariha finally breathes out, almost forty minutes in, and the rest fall silent and regroup.

After another prayer from Fariha finished by a collective "Huuuu," the community begins singing in English again, with harmonies resounding as someone begins to thump a tambourine. Fariha calls out affirmations and prayers above the rest of the voices, and then the group together recites a brief honorific before one of the male singers begins an Arabic call and response song with the other dervishes. Before long, all join again in reciting the Fatiha, after which Fariha leads them once more in chanting "Huuuuuu, Huuuuu, Huuuuuu."

The cycles of singing, chanting, and prayer continue for another hour and fifteen minutes, with soloists' voices sometimes rising above the rest and rhythmic chanting by a select few grounding the group chorus at other times. There seems to be no direct orchestration of parts, each person apparently assuming the role into which he or she feels moved. If one forgets the words or tune of a particular hymn, one can almost always take up the background chanting. Before long, with the first of what will soon be many ecstatic shouts, instruments accompany the voices: most specifically, *tablas*, or Indian drums. The dervishes are no longer stationary, with sitting and swaying giving way to rising and twirling. Except for the traditional turning posture, with one hand raised to the heavens and one pointed toward the ground, the movements are as loosely choreographed as the voices, some legs moving faster than others, some arms raised higher, as Fariha occasionally gives direction. The chanting continues in Arabic, the singing in English, the sound of thumping drums permeates the hall, and dervishes are turning in various spots throughout the small space. Even on cold nights, the poorly insulated building begins to radiate, with the sound of euphoric utterances and the warmth of turning bodies reflecting off the white brick walls as if off a mirror, feeding back into the increasingly euphoric assembly.

The movement and song rise again to an ecstatic pitch. Then, after nearly two hours, the singing, chanting, and turning wind down into a communal refrain of "Huuuuu." After the formal ritual has concluded, dervishes linger in the hall for some time, many gathered in a circle around Fariha, sharing with her dreams that she interprets for them, and in other ways communing and seeking guidance on the path toward spiritual perfection.

The Next Generation: Cyber Sufis

Feisal Abdul Rauf's dhikrs on Manhattan's Upper West Side have a very different flavor from those of the Halveti Jerrahi and Nur Ashki groups. As mentioned, there is no music or dance. Nor is there the invocation prayer that blesses and recalls past and present prophets, sages, and Sufis. Instead, following the evening communal prayer, dervishes take their seats in gender-segregated areas of the small space and open the Qur'ans from which they chant their litanies. There are no white caps signaling the Jerrahi lineage, as Rauf is not recognized by other Jerrahis, and no choreographed movements. The only supplementary items are the *tasbihs*, or prayer beads, that dervishes pull through their fingers to keep count of the number of times each praise of Allah is uttered. During most of the dhikr, the dervishes follow their leader in reciting honorifics: first they say "la 'ilaha 'illa-llah" one hundred times, followed by "Ya, Latif" ("Oh, Subtle One") fifty times, for example, and so on through the glorifying utterances that constitute this form of dhikr, also called *tasbih*, which involves short repetitive praises to Allah. The tones and volume are much more subdued than those of the other Jerrahis in the years after 9/11. They had not always been quite so hushed.

Just a few years after Rauf began leading dhikr ceremonies, a journalist spent a summer documenting the religious habits of some members of the community. At that time (the year 2000), Rauf and Khan focused most of the ASMA Society's work on the Sufism after which their organization was named. On some evenings, forty or fifty people would gather for dhikr in Khan's apartment. After an hour of "repetitive mantras," the journalist chronicled, Rauf and the dervishes would move into a "singsong" session of chanting only the name "Allah." This part of the ceremony, with tempo and volume alternating between crescendo and decrescendo, was often the most intense, despite its apparent simplicity.

> At times the entire group would sound like cars honking in some celestial traffic jam, at other times, like flocks of geese following the leader. . . . There would be evenings of turbulence, others in which you heard just the bare struggling of unmatched voices weakly trying to keep up, and a few where the sound did seem amplified by Dolby stereo. Those were the evenings in which the angels were apparently singing backup, at least according to the spiritual connoisseurs in the group, who would recap the event. "How was your *dhikr*?" they would ask probingly afterward.[20]

Like Fariha and many shaykhs before them, Rauf would also linger with his dervishes long after dhikr ended, interpreting dreams and dispensing advice. As in Fariha's dhikr, one could often find Christians and Jews among the dervishes and sense an openness to others. Rauf, however, was uncompromising about observing established rituals and regulations. "Don't look at members of the opposite sex when you're doing your dhikr," he would tell the community, for example. "Stay focused within."[21] Further, Rauf kept his ceremonies sober for a reason. He did not want his dervishes to enter ecstatic emotional states—the kind of "drunken" practice, as some Sufis call it, that religious authorities often disapprove of and that even Sufis fear can lead to unorthodox beliefs or behaviors. Some, but certainly not all, Sufi sages believe that such a state is what gives rise to Sufi dance.[22]

The ecstatic, emotional experience is one of several spiritual and psychological *ahwal*, or "states," that many Sufis believe they transition through as they move from lower to higher *maqamat*, or "stations," on the Sufi path of attempting to acquire perfect character and God-like ethics.[23] This "intoxication," known in Arabic as *sukr*, of being overcome by the feeling of closeness to God, is desirable in some respects. Yet it is also regarded as a very vulnerable state to be in, during which a Sufi—filled with the vision of God's nearness to all of creation—might begin to see God in everything to the extent that she loses the ability to differentiate God from creation, good from bad, right from wrong, Islam from that which is not authentically Islam.[24] It is partly because of such vulnerability that the ministrations of a shaykh, who is learned in the teachings handed down by previous leaders, are seen as so necessary. And it is partly because Rauf could not always be with his dervishes during dhikr—particularly after 9/11—that he made sure their practice was sober and contained.

Following the 2001 terrorist attacks on the World Trade Center and Pentagon, Rauf and Khan began devoting ASMA's work as much to fostering a "culturally American Islam" as to Sufi practice. Within a few short years, they had established another organization, the Cordoba Initiative, designed to "heal" the rift between "Islam and the West."[25] Although Sufi practice remained important to Rauf and Khan, their emphasis on Sufism began to wane in the years that followed—to the extent that Khan changed the ASMA Society's name to the American Society for Muslim Advancement. Rauf and Khan also began to travel more often, with Rauf—by the end of the decade—spending months at a time working from an office in Malaysia and trying to guide his dervishes via email. One of Rauf's Sufi deputies, who had helped cofound ASMA in 1997, served as a surrogate shaykh for the dervish community until 2006, when he began to question the direction in which ASMA and Rauf were moving. After that, another, younger dervish generally led dhikr sessions. The longer Rauf was absent, the lower the attendance at dhikr became and the softer the volume of the ceremonies.

Rauf was certainly not the first shaykh to use the Internet as a means of staying in contact with his dervishes. A few other orders have tried this with varying degrees of success when they have had communities in multiple locations but only one shaykh to guide them. Challenged by the lack of in-person contact with their shaykh, many dervishes made the best of the situation, even creating a temporary website for members of their community to access Rauf's older sermons and *sohbets*, or messages delivered to the dervishes after dhikr. Some aspects of this long-distance relationship with their leader were not so easily overcome, however.

In 2006, with Rauf and Khan frequently traveling, Rauf's dervishes found themselves lacking a stable location for their meetings. After an evening of gathering for dhikr in a Times Square Starbucks because the apartment was unavailable at the last minute, the dervishes rented a carpeted storage area in a municipal office for their ceremonies. Although the space was less than ideal, their earnestness was as keen as ever as they carried out furniture usually stowed in the room and prepared it for their gatherings. Mariachi music from the Friday night festivities in the Mexican restaurant on the building's ground floor filtered through the dhikr services, and the location had none of the comforts of Khan's apartment. Nevertheless, a distinctly communal ethos emerged as members of the group cooperated in creating a reconstituted, and rather independent, community.

A few weeks later, Rauf returned briefly from his travels. Reestablishing his authority after a long absence, he reminded his dervishes of the path Muzaffer Özak had once set him on.[26] (He did not mention his Moroccan shaykh.) He then blessed their endeavors and urged them to recommit themselves to him as their shaykh and to serving their community—something that would require more of them than it had in the past, as he would be traveling even more often. Most dervishes rededicated themselves and, in so doing, embarked on yet another phase of tailoring Sufi practice to the changing American environment.

Conclusion: Everything New Is Old Again

As a Sufi who has attended all three ceremonies once remarked, Rauf's dhikr is akin to "chamber music," whereas Fariha's dhikr is more like a jazz concert, and the Halveti Jerrahi dhikr is "dinner and a show."[27] In other words, Rauf's ceremonies are the most quiet and composed, Fariha's can be the most improvisational without being any less impactful, and the Halveti Jerrahis of Spring Valley follow a scripted choreography from which they do not intentionally deviate. Not surprisingly, these three dhikrs appeal to different Muslim American audiences of different generations.

The Halveti Jerrahis perform a traditional Turkish ritual that has been handed down over centuries and was regarded as most authentic by recent immigrants to America, although the community now is comprised of more than just Turkish expatriates. In contrast, Fariha's Nur Ashki Jerrahi rituals—once so eclectic that they seemed only loosely affiliated with Islam, but increasingly oriented around Sunni tenets—have generally appealed to American converts who are initially more attracted to Sufi aesthetics and to New Age philosophy than to what they assume are the more rigid conventions of formal Islam. Finally, for some, Rauf's Sufism feels the most authentic although it is perhaps the least traditional in that it grows out of the influence of two different shaykhs and sometimes involves virtual communication rather than in-person communing. This practice appeals to young American-born Muslims who want neither what they see as the overly traditional cultural expressions of previous immigrant generations, nor the overly American practices of religiously eclectic converts. Rather, these Muslim Americans want a Qur'an-based practice that feels to them most in keeping with the Prophet Muhammad's likely tradition. And since these Muslims can be highly mobile and have yet to settle in one location, some also want a shaykh who can travel with them—virtually, if not physically. These are only three of the varieties of dhikr undertaken within the Muslim American community, but they give a sense of some of the changes and challenges Muslim Americans have faced while endeavoring to practice time-worn traditions in a continually changing environment.

NOTES

1   For an introduction to these practices and their history, see Carl Ernst, *The Shambhala Guide to Sufism* (Boston: Shambhala, 1997). Edward Curtis also briefly describes Sufism in the Introduction to this volume.

2   Rosemary R. Corbett, *Making Moderate Islam: Sufism, Service, and the "Ground Zero Mosque" Controversy* (Stanford: Stanford University Press, 2016).

3   Tosun Bayrak, *Memoirs of a Moth: The Life of Shaykh Tosun al Jerrahi* (Istanbul: Timas Publishing, 2016), 258. Sema' is derived from the Arabic *sama'*—to listen intently to Qur'anic recitation or music.

4   Ibid., 74–109.

5   Bayrak, 108–126 (quote from 126).

6   Brad Gooch, *Godtalk: Travels in Spiritual America* (New York: Alfred A. Knopf, 2002), 343.

7   Sheikh Muzaffer Özak, *The Unveiling of Love: Sufism and the Remembrance of God* (New York: Pir Press, 2001), 16–21.

8   See Bob Colacello, "Remains of the Dia," *Vanity Fair*, September 1996, accessed November 7, 2009, www.vanityfair.com.

9   According to Hixon's website, the interview occurred in 1979 (see "Radio," accessed January 10, 2008, www.lexhixon.org), but Muzaffer elsewhere describes it as occurring during his first visit to the United States in 1978 (Özak, *The Unveiling*, 21).

10 Lex Hixon Nur al-Jerrahi, *Atom from the Sun of Knowledge* (Westport, Conn.: Pir Press, 1993), v–vi.

11 See Catherine L. Albanese, *A Republic of Mind and Spirit: A Cultural History of American Metaphysical Religion* (New Haven: Yale University Press, 2008); and Leigh Eric Schmidt, *Restless Souls: The Making of American Spirituality from Emerson to Oprah* (San Francisco: HarperOne, 2005).

12 Feisal Abdul Rauf, *Islam: A Search for Meaning* (Costa Mesa, Calif.: Mazda Publishers, 1996), xi.

13 See Gooch, 352–353.

14 See Gooch, 348. According to the Nur Ashki Jerrahis' website, Nur's "vision of Universal Islam opens a new era of spiritual flowering." See "Lineage," accessed January 10, 2008, www.nurashkijerrahi.org. In contrast, Bayrak's Halveti Jerrahis define themselves as "A Traditional Muslim Sufi Order"—using the words "Traditional" and "Muslim" to distinguish their order from the Nur Ashki Jerrahis (accessed January 10, 2008, www.jerrahi.org). Thanks to Michael Wolfe for directing me to these websites.

15 Gooch, 346.

16 Quoted in Colacello.

17 Gooch, 356.

18 According to Shaykh Tosun Bayrak, the dhikr described here is known as Ushaki Kiyam (email communication, May 23, 2016).

19 Layla Amzi, "The Survival of Sufism in the Turkish Republic: Sheikh Muzaffer Özak and the Halveti-Cerrahi Order" (Master's Thesis, New York University, 2006), 7–8.

20 Gooch, 357.

21 Ibid., 356.

22 See William C. Chittick, *Sufism: A Short Introduction* (Oxford: Oneworld, 2000), 89–96.

23 Sufi scholars and leaders differ over the number of stations on the Sufi path. See Ernst, 100–107.

24 Chittick, 26.

25 For Rauf and Khan's organizations, see Corbett, *Making Moderate Islam*.

26 Personal observation, March 9, 2007.

27 As recorded in Michael Wolfe, "Invitation and Education: How Two American Branches of a Turkish Sufi Order Use the Internet to Educate Newcomers," unpublished paper for Islamic Education in the United States course, Columbia University, New York City, 2005, 3.

3

Hajj

The Pilgrimage

HUSSEIN RASHID

A city in the middle of the desert, distant from popular trade routes, seems like an unlikely place for people from all over the world to want to come to at least once in their lives. Yet Mecca is an international city that has served as a site for trade and pilgrimage for millennia. There is historical evidence that Mecca was a market city generations before London was settled.[1] The foods of Mecca reveal the types of people who pass through the city. One can find South Asian sweets, Central Asian rice dishes, and McDonald's.[2] Ultimately, the appeal of this city in a desert valley is tied to its religious role.

Muslims believe that the shrine at the heart of the city, the Ka'ba, was first built by Adam and Eve, called Adam and Hawwa in Arabic, when they were exiled from paradise after disobeying God. According to one tradition, the Black Stone, which is still affixed to the Ka'ba, fell to earth with Adam and Eve, showing them where to build the Ka'ba.[3] This Ka'ba was washed away in the flood during the time of Noah, known as Nuh in Arabic, who sought refuge on his ark. The Ka'ba was then rebuilt by Abraham and Ishmael, whose names are Ibrahim and Isma'il in Arabic. When Muslims go on Hajj, they remember the ethical examples of Abraham, Ishmael, and Hagar. As pilgrims circle the Ka'ba, they stop at the Maqam Ibrahim, the Station of Abraham, where they believe Abraham and Ishmael prayed. In performing what is called the *sa'y*, pilgrims run between Mount Safa and Mount Marwa, imitating Hagar's desperate search for water. When they drink the water of the Zamzam well, it reminds them of Ishmael. The animal sacrifice that occurs at the end of the pilgrimage during Eid al-Adha, the Feast of Sacrifice, then entangles them in the story of Abraham and Ishmael again.

Remembering Muhammad, the seal of prophets for Muslims, is also an essential part of the Hajj. It was Muhammad who, according to Islamic tradition, rededicated the space to the worship of Allah, the one God. Between the time of Abraham and that of Muhammad, the Ka'ba became a place where many gods were worshiped. From a Muslim perspective, Muhammad restored the true meaning of the site. Ancient rituals that were performed around the Ka'ba long before him were made Islamic, or "Islamized." For example, the Prophet helped to put the Black Stone, known as *al-hajar al-aswad* in Arabic, in its current location. Muslims approach the stone with reverence, as Muhammad did, to recommit themselves to being Muslim or to seek forgiveness for their sins.[4]

The Hajj is central to Islamic religious practice and identity. In order to explain what the Hajj means to American Muslims, I interviewed a dozen people either by phone or in-person, with an occasional email after the conversation for clarification. Their Hajj stories suggest the great variety of Muslim American Hajj experiences, but they also speak to some shared sentiments and concerns. These narratives resonate with one another as the Hajj experience becomes a shared lens through which pilgrims view Islamic religion.

The Story of the Hajj

Muslims wish to go on Hajj because it is considered a necessary act for those who are able. It is part of a Muslim's life cycle, and even when it cannot be completed, it is part of her understanding of what it means to be Muslim. There is no religious "penalty," however, if the Muslims are unable to go for financial or health reasons—or because they simply aren't lucky enough to get a visa to travel. Even for those who are unable to go on Hajj, it is often an important part of Muslim religious cultures. Indeed, Muslims all over the world participate in Eid al-Adha, the holiday celebrated at the end of the pilgrimage.

The rituals of Hajj are patterned on the Sunna, or Tradition, of the Prophet Muhammad. For Muslims, Muhammad is the model of a perfect Muslim and one seeks to emulate him while on Hajj just like in one's daily life. Khizer Husain from the Washington, D.C. area feels the Hajj is, at least in part, a ritual in which one walks "in the footsteps of great individuals like Prophet Muhammad." Similarly, Debra Majeed, a professor of religious studies in Wisconsin, believes that part of the Hajj's power is "to know that the Prophet Muhammad (May God grant him rest and peace) walked these grounds. I could close my eyes and imagine it. I was there with the dirt he shared." When Khizer and Debra say the Prophet's name, they utter *salawat*, sayings that praise the Prophet. This tradition is based on the Qur'an, which says that God and the angels call blessings on Muhammad, and Muslims should do the same (Qur'an 33:56). Muslims become closer to God by loving Muhammad, including during Hajj.

This is true no matter what interpretation of Islam the pilgrim follows. For example, Nargis Virani, a professor of Islamic studies in New York, leads groups of Shi'a Isma'ili Muslims to Mecca. Shi'a Muslims acknowledge that Muhammad named Ali ibn Abi Talib, his cousin and son-in-law, as his successor. Shi'a consider Hasan and Husayn, the children of Ali and Fatima, Muhammad's daughter, to be the rightful heirs of Muhammad's religious and political authority. Speaking about the centrality of the Prophet and his family to the experiences of Shi'a Isma'ili pilgrims, Nargis says that people join her group because they "want to be connected to the history of the Prophet and his family. They want to relive the experience of the Prophet."

The formal Hajj ritual spans five days in the lunar month of Dhu'l-Hijja, which literally means "possessor of the Hajj." It is the twelfth and last month in the Islamic calendar. This calendar is based on the cycles of the moon, which means that each month begins on a new moon. Lunar months are shorter than the solar months that constitute the Gregorian calendar. As a result, the Muslim calendar shifts back about eleven days every solar year. For example, if the Hajj began on October 23 one year, it would begin on October 12 the next year, and October 1 the year after.

In addition to the prophetic narratives, there is a tradition that Muhammad's cousin, Ali, was born in the Ka'ba. There is a crack in a wall of the shrine called Rukn al-Yamani, the Yemeni corner. According to Suehaila Amen, a Shi'a Ithna 'ashari from Dearborn, Michigan, it "is important because it serves as a reminder of the greatness of Imam Ali (*alayhi as-salam* [peace be upon him]), who we believe was born there. No matter how often they try to seal the crack, it returns, at the same place which once allowed the mother of Imam Ali (*alayhi as-salam*) to enter to give birth to him. At the end of the day, it will remind us that this is a home of the progeny of the Prophet."

The Logistics of the Hajj

The Hajj starts on the eighth day of Dhu'l-Hijja, and continues until the twelfth of the month. While it is possible to perform some of the rituals outside these five days, such a journey is not considered Hajj, but *umra*, or "minor pilgrimage." The specific dates are an integral part of completing the pilgrimage. Many people will go on umra to prepare themselves for the Hajj, but the events are not considered equivalent. Pilgrims will often combine the rituals of umra prior to starting Hajj rituals in a specific practice known as *umra at-tamattu'*, the *umra* of delight.

Muslims are nearly one out of every four people in the world, with a population of over 1.6 billion individuals. Though all these Muslims would never choose to perform the Hajj during the same year, the number of Muslims who wish to go exceeds the capabilities of the host country. As a result, Saudi Arabia, working with the Organization of Islamic Cooperation (OIC) sets a limit on how many pilgrims it can accept. Once that number is established, countries are issued Hajj visas, based on the percentage of the worldwide Muslim population the country represents. Under this system, countries like Indonesia, India, Pakistan, Bangladesh, and Nigeria receive large numbers of Hajj visas. In turn, each country has a system for allotting the visas to their populations.[5] For the last several years, the number of pilgrims during Hajj has been around 2 million, with approximately 1.3 million pilgrims coming from outside Saudi Arabia.[6] The large number of Hajjis, or pilgrims, coming from Saudi Arabia is misleading. While Saudis are disproportionately represented, there is also a large expatriate population living in Saudi Arabia. As a result, the 600,000 pilgrims that originated in Saudi Arabia may actually be coming from many different nations.[7]

In 2015, the United States received around 11,000 visas.[8] They were distributed through authorized agencies that worked with would-be pilgrims on their travel arrangements. While the estimates of the total American Muslim population vary from three to six million or even more, the number of visas (0.6% of the worldwide number of visas) far exceeds even a generous reading of the number of American Muslims (0.4% of the worldwide Muslim population). The discrepancy reveals that the process of issuing Hajj visas is not apolitical. The Saudi government utilizes access to the Hajj to reward its allies and punish its perceived enemies, and as a tool for foreign policy. In the case of the United States, the Saudis seem to recognize the important political relationship between the two countries.[9]

Making the Decision to Go

While Muslims who go on Hajj consider it a religious obligation, pilgrims are sometimes motivated to go for very personal reasons, including heartbreak. The idea that the end of a relationship or unrequited love might be tied to a religious obligation such as Hajj is quite typical in Islamic religious tradition. The story of Majnun and Layla, for example, is an old Arabic story of unrequited love. Similar to *Romeo and Juliet*—although predating it by centuries—it is about a man and a woman who cannot be together because of differences in social standing. The story is well-preserved in various Muslim cultures and is sometimes used as a religious metaphor: just as Majnun pines for Layla, so too does the human being desire a closer relationship with God. Omar Offendum, a Syrian American Muslim musician based in Los Angeles, makes an oblique reference to the Hajj in his 2011 song about the love story entitled "Majnoon Layla." Offendum voices the character of Majnun as he sings: "Your hand in mine, marriage as I was sad to find, wasn't written for us in the grand design. Set out for Mecca on Hajj." Offendum's version of the story has Majnun going on Hajj because of his heartbreak, and this rationale can be seen in the stories of other Americans who do likewise.[10]

Sarah, a media producer from the Washington, D.C., area, talks about how emotional distress precipitated her decision to go on Hajj. Sarah was in a relationship that ended badly, and decided during Ramadan that she would go on Hajj.[11] On the lunar calendar, Ramadan comes two months before Dhu'l-Hijjah, so her decision to go at the last minute was unusual. It often takes much more than two months to plan and arrange spots on tours, especially as visa requirements can slow down the process. She asked her brother to join her, and he agreed, so the logistics became doubly challenging. But she was able to secure visas fairly quickly and to book two open spots with a tour group led by a well-known and well-respected American Sunni religious leader. She found comfort in the fact that everything had worked out so quickly and so well. For her, it confirmed that going on Hajj was the right decision. She says she did not want her trip to be a "band-aid," but she did want it to transform her. Sarah was hoping it would enrich her spiritual life.

Similarly, Suehaila was planning a future with someone when she felt she was faced with a choice between the righteous path of God and a man who did not apply Islam in his daily life. His detachment from the faith made her feel she was no longer developing spiritually. She said that she wanted to have more spiritual growth. As a result, she broke off the relationship, focused on what her heart desired, and went on the Hajj to catalyze that change.

Sometimes the decision to go on Hajj is not a choice. When Maryam Sharrieff, now a university chaplain in the Boston area, went on Hajj for the first time in the 1980s, she was seventeen and a member of the Nation of Islam. She believed in God, but she rejected the teachings of the Nation of Islam and did not consider herself to be a Muslim. Her father forced her to go on Hajj, because for him it is a status symbol. During the Hajj, Sharrieff experienced something unfamiliar to her, a different way of being Muslim. And then something dramatic happened. During prayer time in Mecca, Sharrieff declined to join the crowds of Muslims from around the world in prostrating her body toward the Ka'ba. She was not a real believer, she said. But as she observed everyone else bending their bodies and standing as one, she also looked up and saw "birds doing *tawaf* around the Ka'ba." That is, birds were circling the Ka'ba in a counter-clockwise fashion, just as believers do. Sharrieff did not become a Muslim at that moment, but she did remember feeling genuine awe: "I acknowledged Allah as the Creator and a love for Allah. I *started* becoming Muslim."

Of course, many Muslims go on Hajj neither because of a breakup nor because of an insistent parent, but instead because they have dreamed of doing it since they were young. Khizer grew up knowing that he wanted to go on Hajj. "In our family, going on Hajj has always been something that has been given a lot of importance. My maternal grandmother went on Hajj as a teenager, and no one went that young in that period. I felt an urgency to do Hajj [as soon as I could]." He chose to go in 2001 during his graduate school years because he had the time, he could afford it, and his new wife was living in Mecca. It became a "Hajj honeymoon." His parents-in-law, who are South Asian but who also lived in Mecca at that time, were used to helping pilgrims and could assist their daughter and son-in-law.

Preparing for the Journey

Muslims tend to believe that both physical and spiritual preparation is needed before undertaking the Hajj. In premodern times, many pilgrims never returned from what could be a long and treacherous journey. They had to make sure that their affairs were in order before departing. Debts are settled and the Hajj is generally paid for prior to departing. Pilgrims are supposed to leave behind enough money to care for anyone in their charge. In modern times, air travel makes the journey to and from Saudi Arabia much quicker and more reliable, but Muslims still prepare for it as if they will not return. Any time millions of people gather in one place, accidents can lead to serious injury and death. For example, in 1997 there was a fire that caused the death of 2,000 people. In 2004, a stampede killed over 200 pilgrims. The year 2015 saw two tragedies: a crane collapse killed over 100 people and a stampede killed over 700 people.[12] And then some people die of natural causes. Khizer remembers that during his Hajj trip in 2001 an older gentleman got separated from his group. After searching for the man for twelve hours, they found him dead. He had apparently had a heart attack. For Khizer, that experience gave him "insight into Hajj being an intense experience in all forms and fashions."

There is also spiritual preparation. People seek forgiveness from others, and they make an official intention to perform the pilgrimage in a manner that will yield spiritual fruit. Maryam described it as an "invitation from Allah." Many Hajjis talk about being reborn through the experience of Hajj. Their old selves die away. In fact, the prominent twentieth-century Iranian intellectual Ali Shariati likened the *ihram*, the simple white garment worn by men and many women during the Hajj, to a burial shroud, and wrote that the pilgrim "witnesses his own dead body and visits his own grave." In so doing, the pilgrim is preparing for the transition to the eternal life. "The scene is like the day of judgment," Shariati declared.[13] Bawa Muhaiyaddeen, who was a Sufi Muslim American spiritual teacher, said that during the Hajj "the world within you dies and the good qualities come alive."[14] After practicing for the end of life, some pilgrims feel ready to begin a new life on earth. The pilgrimage becomes a purifying process, where the pilgrim becomes an agent for good actions in the world. For example, Sarah returned from Hajj committed to praying more regularly and doing so in a more focused way. She also wanted to experience more joy in her life.

For some Muslim Americans, the spiritual preparation for the Hajj includes studying the words of great Islamic teachers before they go. Khizer, for example, read Ali Shariati's book about the Hajj. Some Muslims read the works of a man who at one time was called America's best-selling poet—the thirteenth-century Persian legal scholar and mystic known simply as Rumi. Rumi cautions pilgrims that they should not go on Hajj until they have found God first. The Beloved, meaning God, is present inside each of us, according to Rumi, and Muslims need to understand that before going to God's house. If not, they will only be looking at a building with no one at home. In one of his poems about Hajj, Rumi concludes, "Why do you care for a bouquet of roses if you have seen the garden?"[15] The line indicates that people want to possess something, the bouquet, but miss the larger beauty available to them. In the same way, Rumi seems to worry about travelers who proudly claim to have been on Hajj but do not think to experience the Divine. Rumi is not the only Muslim teacher to encourage pilgrims to think deeply about the rituals of Hajj. Many Muslim teachers encourage pilgrims to meditate on what they are doing and why they are doing it.

Nargis explained the relationship between a mystical interpretation of the ritual and the ritual itself. Some people, she noted, went so far as to say that the physical ritual was unnecessary once the intention behind the rituals was understood. Nargis disagreed, at least for herself and her community. She emphasized that for her community, and for many other Muslim communities, spiritual practice cannot be a substitute for the physical practice. Both are equally important components of religious practice.

Arriving in Mecca for Hajj

Pilgrims arrive outside the city of Mecca. In the past, pilgrims would travel overland, on caravans, over long distances. As Muslims spread throughout the world, sea travel became common. Starting in the 1950s, air travel began to become the dominant mode of transportation. Many pilgrims fly into a special airport terminal in Jeddah, about sixty miles away from Mecca. Indonesia, which sends the largest number of pilgrims every year, leases airplanes to transport nearly a quarter-million passengers.

As prospective Hajjis approach Mecca and journey closer to the Ka'ba, they begin to make a spiritual transition from the demands of daily life to the demands of the Hajj. By the time they arrive at the Ka'ba many feel they are in a sanctified state. Jalal Al-e Ahmad, a twentieth-century Iranian intellectual, wrote a Hajj narrative titled *Khasi Dar Miqat*, often translated *Lost in the Crowd*, but actually meaning "dust in the presence of the holy." It conveys the sense of awe and wonder that Al-e Ahmad felt when he entered the sacred precincts.[16] During his 2001 Hajj, Khizer says that he felt a transformation happening on the pilgrimage. The change, he noted, was both "subtle and immediate." One night, his group had no hotel room in Mecca, so they left their bags in the hotel and slept in the sanctuary area around the Ka'ba. "This is God saying do this— which we wouldn't have if we had a hotel to sleep in," Khizer told me. That experience "nudged me in the direction of spirituality."

Many Muslims believe the Ka'ba to be a point where the distance between heaven and earth is shortest. The two planes of existence touch at that point. The area around the Ka'ba is liminal, belonging to two states of existence at the same time. The *miqat*, or stations, are boundary zones where one begins a transition from the familiar world to this new, transformational environment.

At the miqat, male pilgrims don special clothing called *ihram*. The root for ihram is H-R-M, which can mean forbidden or sanctified. When a pilgrim puts on the ihram, he is sanctifying himself by rejecting forbidden things. The term *ihram* refers both to the cloth and to the state of being sanctified. Women wear modest clothing from their respective cultures that reveals the hands and/or face.[17] Some women do choose to wear white, like the men. No matter what dress they choose to wear, all pilgrims are in a state of ihram, sanctified, and follow particular rules of behavior to remain in this state. The clothing of ihram for men is two pieces of white cloth, which remind the pilgrim of his own mortality. Muslims are traditionally buried in pieces of white cloth, and many pilgrims will keep their ihram for their own burials.[18]

Pilgrims have now entered sacred space where non-Muslims are not permitted to go. The space and the rituals of Hajj are not secret, but they are private. They are there for those who believe in what the Hajj means. There have been cases of non-Muslims sneaking into the Hajj, most famously the nineteenth-century British Orientalist Sir Richard Francis Burton, who wrote his own Hajj narrative, *A Personal Narrative of a Pilgrimage to Al-Madinah and Meccah*.[19] But such examples are rare.

Despite the spiritual transformation that occurs during a pilgrim's journey toward Mecca, Mecca is still an earthly, physical city that poses various challenges for pilgrims. Once they arrive, some of those problems become all too real. Sarah, for example, was concerned about the overcrowding.[20] At one point during her time in Mecca, she felt crushed by the crowd and was afraid that she would have an asthma attack. She thought to herself, "It would be so beautiful if all these people weren't here." But then she had a different thought. "All these people were me, doing what I wanted to do. I felt guilty and silly. We are human, we are flawed—even having that thought [that it would be better without the crowds] was normal." For Sarah, the overcrowding in Mecca created radical empathy with other people.

Crowds are not the only challenge in Mecca. Another challenge can be the government officials in charge of the place. Sarah felt that her gender posed a problem for some Saudi officials, and they attempted to discipline her. When she was in front of the Ka'ba, readying to offer evening prayers, a guard told her that women could not be present in that particular area. Their guide, a religious leader, sent the guard away. The guard returned and once more the group leader sent him away. Sarah started praying, and then someone started pushing her. Her prayer rug got ripped. It was the guard. He was physically forcing her to stop worshiping. The group leader tried to stop the harassment, and then another guard came and reprimanded the first guard. Sarah remembers feeling "humiliated and small at that moment." At the same time, she did not let the actions of human beings interfere with her spiritual quest. "The sweetest and most beautiful part was that I was able to pray looking at the Ka'ba," she said. She even used an Islamic teaching to put this harassment in perspective, finding comfort in remembering the Qur'anic verse that after every hardship there is ease (Qur'an 94:6). According to Sarah, "Allah had the last laugh."

Muslim American filmmaker and documentarian Anisa Mehdi was concerned about the increasing commercialization of the area, as international conglomerates establish chain stores in the area around the sanctuary (*haram*), and wealthy pilgrims book five-star hotel packages. People face the temptations of the material world regularly outside the Hajj experience, she said, and Hajj is an opportunity to "purge your bad habits." During the Hajj, she believes, "the body becomes less important than the soul." But the physical environment was diminishing the Hajj as a seat for the soul. "What we see in Mecca now is a pandering to the body. They might miss the chance to reject luxury and to see real people—fellow Muslims—struggling with hunger and poverty right in front of them [in the sanctuary.]"

Day 1—Talbiyah and Travel to Mina

On the eighth day of Dhu'l-Hijjah, the first day of the Hajj, as the hopeful Hajji leaves the miqat, she will utter a chant called the *talbiya*, an announcement of her presence, which begins *labbayk allahuma labbayk*: "Here I am, O Lord, here I am." The full chant makes it clear that the pilgrim is announcing herself as a servant of God, as she says "Here I am, O Lord, here I am. Here I am, You are peerless, here I am. Truly all praise and bounty are Yours, and You are the Lord. You have no peer, here I am." The pilgrim's declaration of presence is a humbling act that is a statement of awe as she approaches Mecca and the Ka'ba.

Suehaila recalled that when she saw the Ka'ba for the first time, she said the stupidest thing of her entire life: "It's so small." In the images she had known since her childhood, the Ka'ba was enormous. But that initial reaction did not detract from the powerful religious experience that she had in this sacred place. "I was standing near the Ka'ba, I was touching it, and was left alone for an hour to do *du'a* [prayers of supplication]. The police let me be. Later, we were able to walk through people doing *tawaf* [circumambulating the Ka'ba] and do it again for 1.5 hours." Suehaila was not the only pilgrim I interviewed whose preconceptions about the space were challenged by the actual building. Debra recalls:

I remember how different the experience in Mecca was than the images I had seen in television. I did not realize the Ka'ba was in its own mosque. I didn't realize how deeply I would be moved by seeing a cube with people walking around it, and realize I will make prayer and commune with God and not think about which way I faced. I arrived at night and as I entered the Grand Mosque and it looked like the Ka'ba was rising before me. [She says this with her eyes closed and near crying.] I can still see it. I was moving closer to the Ka'ba and the Ka'ba was getting closer to me. It didn't matter that there were thousands of people there, *I* was there.

After visiting the Ka'ba, pilgrims traverse five miles from Mecca to a town called Mina—throughout the Hajj people can either walk or travel by vehicle. During this procession, they will chant the talbiya. Mina is a "tent city," where pilgrims congregate in their various tour groups. Although the rituals of the Hajj are meant to emphasize equality among all the believers, material differences are noticeable, such as the tents in Mina. The tents of Americans who have paid for the privilege tend to be air-conditioned and placed closest to important sites and infrastructure.

Day 2—The Day of Arafat, to Muzdalifa

The next day, pilgrims will go nine miles further to the Plain of Arafat. There, they spend the entire day in prayer and reflection. Khizer described his experience of Arafat as feeling like he was at the center of the Muslim universe. He knew, deeply and truly, his place in time and space. He felt spiritually centered and aware of himself. Khizer, who is a Shi'a Bohra Muslim, utilized some of the prayers especially important to his Islamic community. During his time on Arafat, Khizer recited prayers from a book attributed to Zayn al-Abidin, Muhammad's great-grandson.[21] According to Zayn al-Abidin, Arafat is the place where a believer realizes that God is All-Knowing and Merciful. It is a play on the name of Arafat, which is related to knowledge, and the name of the hilltop on the plain, the Mount of Mercy.[22]

At the end of this day of prayer, the pilgrims move to Muzdalifa, about four miles away. Then, during the night of the ninth day of Dhu'l-Hijja, pilgrims collect forty-nine pebbles and sleep in the open air.

Day 3—Stoning, Sacrifice, and Sa'y

The next morning, the morning of the tenth, the pilgrims go to Mina, about two miles away. After a short stop at Mina, the pilgrims take a walk to Jamarat and cast seven of the pebbles they had collected at one of three pillars, which collectively represent Satan.

The pilgrims then sacrifice an animal. This act is a commemoration of Abraham's attempted sacrifice of his first-born son. In Muslim tradition, that son is Ishmael. It is a festival day for Muslims known as Eid al-Adha, or the Feast of the Sacrifice. Pilgrims will then cut their hair, sometimes symbolically, to signify the end of their sanctified state, and they will leave their ihram. They return to Mecca and circle the Ka'ba.

The pilgrim circles the Ka'ba seven times in the ritual called tawaf. On the face of the cube structure of the Ka'ba is the Black Stone. To start the tawaf, a pilgrim starts in line with the stone, and circles around the cube. After that, hopeful Hajjis will run between two hills, Safa and Marwa, in the sa'y ritual. They will run between them seven times, starting at Safa and ending at Marwa.

The running re-creates the acts of Hagar. In the biblical and qur'anic accounts of Abraham's life, Abraham had a son, Ishmael, with Hagar. Sara, Abraham's wife, initially encouraged Abraham to have a child with Hagar because Sara did not seem to be capable of having children. But after the birth of Ishmael, Sara did become pregnant, and gave birth to Isaac, or Ishaq in Arabic. She then became protective of her son and demanded that Abraham exile Hagar and Ishmael, which he did. While wandering in the desert, Ishmael began to cry from thirst, and Hagar ran between Safa and Marwa calling out for help. The Archangel Gabriel, known as Jibra'il in Arabic, appeared, and there are two prominent Muslim versions of what happened next. In one version, Gabriel struck his staff on the ground. In the other version, Ishmael struck his heel on the ground. The result of hitting the ground was that a spring of water appeared, called Zamzam. Pilgrims drink this water throughout the time they are in the mosque area, and particularly as they perform the sa'y.

For Debra, the experience of reenacting Hagar's search for water is a deeply moving one:

In Mecca, as a Black woman, as a womanist [a feminist of color, conscious of race and class], to know that there's a tradition that Hagar is buried beneath the Ka'ba is powerful. As people are pushing to get to the Black Stone, I didn't feel comfortable trying to get closer. I saw a woman who made it close to the wall, and I made a *du'a* [supplication] for her. I believe she represented all the people who want to get there. Instead I went to another corner where the remains of Hagar are believed to be. Such a difference to know the story of Hagar and Ishmael and to know the struggle and challenge she had to go through and the faith she had throughout it all. As a former Christian who was always told about the story of Hagar, to [know] the story of Hagar as a Muslim, complements an experience for me of what she went through as an African. She was a part of my legacy. It reminds me why social justice work is very necessary. It reminds me that Allah always takes care of those who put their trust in Allah.

Participating in the ritual clearly engaged Debra in what she considers to be the moral message of Hagar. This message resonates in the modern period and helps to inform Debra's view of the world.

The rituals of Hajj are full of breaks from expected patterns. For example, pilgrims will remove their ihram clothing on the third day of the pilgrimage, but they are still expected to behave in a sanctified state for the remaining two days of the Hajj. It represents a transition out of the experience, like the donning of the ihram at the miqat was a transition into the experience.

Days 4 and 5—The Stoning at Mina

The eleventh and twelfth days of the month are spent back at Mina. Each day, pilgrims will stone each of the three pillars seven times, using up the remaining forty-two pebbles they had collected on the night of the ninth of Dhu'l-Hijjah. On the twelfth, pilgrims will go around the Ka'ba for another cycle, and then get ready to depart Mecca. Once the last tawaf is done and a pilgrim leaves Mecca, the Hajj is officially over.

Pilgrimages beyond the Hajj

But some Muslims also visit Medina, about three hundred miles away, to make a stop at the burial place of the Prophet Muhammad. Nargis's recollection of her visit to Medina is representative of what many of my interviewees had to say about the experience. She says, "Visiting the site of the Prophet's Mosque in Medina is one of the most beautiful experiences for me because of the Prophet [having been] there. We went for a walk around the mosque after *fajr* [dawn] prayers."[23] Nargis noted that in recent times Saudi officials have been more understanding of people's desires to pray at the tomb. "In 2000," she said, "the police would beat you up if you stood for more than 30 seconds at the tomb of the Prophet. . . . Now, there are times after prayers where people are allowed in briefly to pray, but are reminded that they should not worship [Muhammad]. It's a stampede to offer the prayers, and now the security forces can't keep them back." Like many other Muslims, Nargis regrets what she regards as a lack of historical and spiritual awareness among Saudi officials, who have literally paved over large parts of early Muslim history. She feels that "it is heart wrenching to see that there is nothing of the family of the Prophet left there [in Mecca and Medina.]"

During his trip to Medina, Khizer set out to visit the tomb of the Prophet and many of his family members, who are buried in a cemetery called Jannat al-Baqi. Khizer remembered that when he went anywhere to honor Muhammad and his family, the Saudi police were looking for prayer books that pilgrims might use to pray for the family of the Prophet. Because praying for the family of the Prophet is taboo in Wahhabism, the interpretation of Islam that the government of Saudi Arabia supports, Khizer was worried that he would be prevented from fulfilling his obligations to pray for them. His solution was to memorize the prayers, and when his memory failed him in Medina, he uttered the best prayer he could muster "from the heart," as he said.

After the Hajj

After the Hajj pilgrims return to their homes and receive the title *hajji* or *hajja* to indicate that they have completed the pilgrimage. They return to much fanfare in their local communities. Pilgrims show off and also share the many gifts, especially souvenirs, that they procured during the Hajj. The ihram is the most obvious example for men. Other pilgrims get certificates commemorating their experiences. Some Hajjis will bring back pieces of the cloth that covers the Ka'ba, called the *kiswa*.[24]

Sarah talks about bringing back prayer beads, calligraphy on tapestries, and Zamzam water. Khizer offers a reflection on his Hajj souvenir, a prayer mat he bought for around $2.50. He says, "It's a part of me. It's bringing a piece of the Hajj with me. I carry it in a denim bag that was part of convention gear that was from an international AIDS conference. My worlds combine when I take it around."

It is also possible for non-Muslims to ask Muslims to pray for them on Hajj. Brie Loskota is the executive director of the Center for Religion and Civic Culture at the University of Southern California and co-founder of the American Muslim Civic Leadership Institute. While she is not Muslim herself, she knows many Muslims, and she shared this email from 2014:

> I wanted to share something good. My husband just got a nice and unexpected promotion at his work. It's lovely especially since he has had a really hard time in his job and basically wants to quit at least once a month. So here is the really lovely part. . . . [SJ] went on Hajj this year. She asked me if I had any prayers and I said, "Pray for [my husband] to get peace about his current job or insight into a future career path." When he got the news of his promotion last night, he actually seemed to be at home in his career and proud of his accomplishments—something that had really eluded him for the last five years.

Brie asked for these prayers and believes that they had an impact on her life. This type of interfaith exchange is becoming more typical in the United States. During her second trip on Hajj in 2015, Suehaila says, "For my friends, including my Christian friends, I bought prayer beads, took them to the *haram* [sanctuary], prayed on them, and then rubbed them on the Ka'ba. There is nothing more that I can give [them] than the prayers on these beads."

Like pilgrims before them, Muslim American Hajjis share stories of the Hajj with friends and families, and some commemorate the Hajj in their songs and in their artwork. The travel narratives of Hajjis are an important literary genre among Muslims. One of the most well-known American Muslim Hajj narratives is that of Malcolm X, a former leader of the Nation of Islam who became a Sunni Muslim toward the end of his life. In 1992, Spike Lee directed the film adaptation of *The Au-*

tobiography of Malcolm X, simply called *Malcolm X*.[25] As the film so beautifully portrays, Malcolm X's Hajj was an experience of spiritual transformation, a theme echoed by many other Hajjis. Michael Wolfe, who covered the Hajj for the ABC News program *Nightline*, edited an anthology of Hajj narratives called *One Thousand Roads to Mecca: Ten Centuries of Travelers Writing about the Muslim Pilgrimage*.[26] He includes Hajj narratives from medieval times until today. His own Hajj narrative is titled *The Hadj: An American's Pilgrimage to Mecca*. Both these books have become important sources for Muslim Americans, and several interviewees said that reading them had helped to prepare them for their own Hajj experiences.[27] Michael's role as editor, reporter, and now documentary producer demonstrates the changing media of Hajj narratives.

In addition to the written word, there are an increasing number of Hajj films. One of the most recent forays into this genre is *Journey to Mecca: In the Footsteps of Ibn Battuta*, produced in 2011.[28] Ibn Battuta was a fourteenth-century polymath and traveler, and this film explores what his first Hajj may have been like, with a discussion of the modern Hajj. It is narrated by British actor Ben Kingsley, who was born Krishna Bhanji and whose father comes from a Shi'a Isma'ili background. While his renown as an actor is most likely what the producers wanted to capitalize on, his religious heritage is fortuitous.

According to Anisa Mehdi, who who made a documentary on the Hajj for National Geographic called *Inside Mecca* and another film on the Hajj for PBS, creating a film narrative is not without difficulties.[29] She is the first person to cover the Hajj on location for American broadcast television. Her role as a Muslim and an observer and recorder raises issues for her about what it means to create Hajj narratives in film. She says she would not perform the pilgrimage while reporting it. Ultimately, for her, "no one makes Hajj without *niyyat* [intention], and that comes from within, as an invitation from God. My intention was to make the best film I could make and be the best narrator for these pilgrims. I would be cheating myself if I performed Hajj without the most clear of intentions." But because she's prayed sincerely at Arafat on the Day of Arafat—considered by some Muslims to be the essential day of Hajj—some people tell her she has indeed completed the pilgrimage. That is not how she herself views it.

Muslim Americans also sing about the Hajj. For instance, the devotional songs of Washington, D.C.–based hip hop group Native Deen include the song "Labbayk." This track, from their 2006 album *Not Afraid to Stand Alone*, is about the desire to go on Hajj. They chant the talbiya, specifically focusing on the first part, *labbayk allahuma labbayk*, "Here I am, oh Lord, here I am." This phrase becomes part of the chorus, which is: "*Labbayk allahuma labbayk* / It's the journey for Allah I want to take."

Conclusion

The Hajj is an evolving experience. As the Saudi authorities work to commercialize the area, they are also working to make the area more physically safe. As they continue to upgrade the logistics and infrastructure of the Hajj, more people are able to attend. With more people, there are sometimes more accidents and more deaths because of the overcrowding. The spread of infectious diseases, particularly airborne pathogens, remains a constant concern.[30]

For some pilgrims, the upgrades also detract from the spiritual nature of the journey. For example, if the path between Safa and Marwa is paved and mists of water spray pilgrims, then the runner may not fully experience the anxiety of Hagar as she runs to save her son's life and her own. There are other points where the ritual practices are sanitized, diminishing the struggle pilgrims experience. There is a tension between needing to keep pilgrims safe and removing the physical challenges that develop the spiritual experience.[31]

Yet there is a consistency that believers recognize in each others' stories of this fourteen-hundred-year-old ritual. The desire to remain true to the commands of the Qur'an and traditions of the Prophet Muhammad ensure that the key rituals of the Hajj are preserved. The Ka'ba itself also remains an important part of the imagination of Muslims. Children draw pictures of it; artists represent it; and academic books dealing with religion and science make reference to it.[32] "Hajj is my peace," said Suehaila. "That's why I'd rather go there than anywhere else. In Mecca, I felt I was home, where I belong. If I could go every year, I would." Debra had a similar feeling: "You're supposed to leave the Ka'ba area after finishing your last *tawaf*. I didn't want to do the last one because I knew it meant I had to leave it, and I did not want to let it go. As I left, I did not turn around, because I wanted that memory to hold forever. It was me and Allah for eternity." Sometimes the incredible feeling of solidarity with the rest of the Muslim world and closeness to God seems to fade. About six months after returning from her first trip in 2013, Suehaila called her Hajj leader and asked where that special feeling had gone. "It's like a honeymoon," he responded. "It's up to you to find that feeling in other ways in your life." Maryam calls the emotions associated with Hajj, including the desire to return, "Hajj fever."

For many Muslims, the fever is there even when they have not performed the Hajj. That fever is present from Detroit to Houston, from Los Angeles to Boston. All over Muslim America, there is an urge to cry out "Here I am!" at the House of God.

NOTES

1 For a discussion of trade and the Hajj, see Michael B. Miller, "Pilgrims' Progress: The Business of the Hajj," *Past & Present* 191 (2006): 189–228.

2 For more on food culture in Mecca, see Mai Yamani, "A Taste of Mecca," in *A Companion to Muslim Cultures*, edited by Amyn B. Sajoo (London: I. B. Tauris, 2011), 185–99.

3 Seán McLoughlin, "Pilgrimage, Performativity, and British Muslims: Scripted and Unscripted Accounts of the Hajj and Umra," in *Hajj: Global Interactions through Pilgrimage*, edited by Luitgard E. M. Mols and Marjo Buitelaar (Leiden: Sidestone Press, 2015), 50.

4 Robert Bianchi, *Islamic Globalization: Pilgrimage, Capitalism, Democracy, and Diplomacy* (Hackensack, N.J.: World Scientific Publishing, 2013), 25–26.

5 For more information on the international infrastructure of the Hajj, including how different governments help their citizens, see Robert Bianchi, *Guests of God: Pilgrimage and Politics in the Islamic World* (New York: Oxford University Press, 2004).

6 Royal Embassy of Saudi Arabia, "1,384,941 Foreign Pilgrims Participated in Hajj" (2015), accessed July 17, 2016, www.saudiembassy.net.

7 In 2015, an estimated 2 million pilgrims went on Hajj. See Don Melvin, "Millions of Muslims Mark Spiritual Climax of Hajj Pilgrimage" (2015), accessed July 7, 2016, edition.cnn.com. Subtracting the official number of nearly 1.4 million foreign pilgrims leaves us with approximately 600,000 domestic pilgrims. For the diversity of domestic pilgrims, see Bianchi, *Guests of God*, 11.

8 This number comes from the trend of visas issued over the last several years by the Royal Embassy of Saudi Arabia; "Saudi Embassy Releases 1435 (2014) Figures for Hajj Visas Issued in the US." (2014), accessed July 7, 2016, www.saudiembassy. net; and the visas expected to be issued in 2015 by the Ministry of Haj and Umra,

"Establishment of Motawifs of Pilgrims of Turkey Muslims of Europe America 1436h" (ND, accessed July 7, 2016, www.haj.gov.sa.

9   See, for example, Saud al-Sarhan, "The Saudis as Managers of the Hajj," in *The Hajj: Pilgrimage in Islam*, edited by Tagliacozzo Eric and M. Toorawa Shawkat (Cambridge, U.K.: Cambridge University Press, 2015), 196–212; Bianchi, *Guests of God*, 253–272; Robert Bianchi, "The Hajj by Air," in *The Hajj: Pilgrimage in Islam*, edited by Tagliacozzo Eric and M. Toorawa Shawkat (Cambridge, U.K.: Cambridge University Press, 2015), 131–52.

10 Cf. Neil Van Der Linden, "Hajj Music from Egypt, Syria and Lebanon: Some Reflections on Songs for the Pilgrimage," in *Hajj: Global Interactions through Pilgrimage*, edited by Luitgard E. M. Mols and Marjo Buitelaar (Leiden: Sidestone Press, 2015), 229–36.

11 For more on the month of Ramadan and its spiritual implications for Muslim Americans, see Jackleen Salem's chapter in this volume.

12 Rym Brahimi and Ayman Mohyeldin, "Hajj Stampede: 244 Pilgrims Dead" (2004), accessed July 7, 2016, www.cnn.com; Ben Hubbard, "Hajj Stampede Near Mecca Leaves Over 700 Dead" (2015), accessed July 7, 2016, www.nytimes.com; Unknown, "Report: Death Toll in Hajj Fire Actually Is 2,000" (1997), accessed July 7, 2016; www.cnn.com; Unknown, "Mecca Crane Collapse: 107 Dead at Saudi Arabia's Grand Mosque" (2015), accessed July 7, 2016, www.bbc.com.

13 ʿAlī Sharīatī, *Hajj*, translated by Ali A. Behzadnia (Houston: Free Islamic Literature, 1980), 9.

14 M. R. Bawa Muhaiyaddeen, *Hajj: The Inner Pilgrimage* (Philadelphia: Fellowship Press, 1998), 15.

15 W. M. Thackston, *A Millennium of Classical Persian Poetry* (Bethesda, Md.: Iranbooks, 1994), 42–43. Translation by author.

16 Jalal Al-e Ahmad, *Lost in the Crowd*, translated by Michael C. Hillmann (Lexington, Ky.: Mazda Publishers, 1985); Golnar Nikpour, "Revolutionary Journeys, Revolutionary Practice: The Hajj Writings of Jalal Al-e Ahmad and Malcolm X," *Comparative Studies of South Asia, Africa and the Middle East* 34, no. 1 (2014): 67–85.

17 Maria F. Curtis, "Hajj," in *Encyclopedia of Muslim-American History*, edited by Edward E. Curtis (New York: Facts on File, 2010), 223–26. For a broader discussion on gender, see William C. Young, "The Kaba, Gender, and the Rites of Pilgrimage," *International Journal of Middle East Studies* 25, no. 2 (1993): 285–300.

18 See Amir Hussain, "Funerals and Death Rites," in this volume, for more information on Muslim funerary practices.

19 Richard Francis Burton, *Personal Narrative of a Pilgrimage to Al-Madinah and Meccah* (London: Tylston & Edwards, 1893).

20 There is some research to suggest that crowd density on the Hajj may not be as dangerous as pilgrims perceive it to be: Hani Alnabulsi and John Drury, "Social Identification Moderates the Effect of Crowd Density on Safety at the Hajj," *Pro-

ceedings of the National Academy of Sciences of the United States of America 111, no. 25 (2014): 9091–96.

21 'Alī ibn al-Ḥusayn Zayn al-'Ābidīn, *The Psalms of Islam: Al-Ṣaḥīfat Al-Kāmilat Al-Sajjādiyya*, translated by William C. Chittick (London: Muhammadi Trust of Great Britain and Northern Ireland, 1988).

22 Mohammed Ali Ismail, "The Spiritual Aspects of Hajj: A Translation of Imam Zayn Al- 'Abidin's (a) Discourse on Hajj with Al-Shibli," *Journal of Shi'a Islamic Studies* 7, no. 3 (2014): 345–52.

23 See Rose Aslan, "Salah: Daily Prayers in Muslim America," in this volume, for more information on ritual prayer.

24 Venetia Porter, "Gifts, Souvenirs, and the Hajj," in *Hajj: Global Interactions through Pilgrimage*, edited by Luitgard E. M. Mols and Marjo Buitelaar (Leiden: Sidestone Press, 2015), 95–111.

25 Spike Lee, *Malcolm X* (1992).

26 Michael Wolfe, ed., *One Thousand Roads to Mecca: Ten Centuries of Travelers Writing about the Muslim Pilgrimage* (New York: Grove Press, 1997).

27 Michael Wolfe, *The Hadj: An American's Pilgrimage to Mecca* (New York: Atlantic Monthly Press, 1993).

28 Bruce Neibaur, *Journey to Mecca: In the Footsteps of Ibn Battuta* (Desert Door Productions, 2009).

29 Anisa Mehdi, *Inside Mecca* (National Geographic, 2003).

30 Valeska Huber, "The Pilgrimage to Mecca and International Health Regulations," in *The Hajj: Pilgrimage in Islam*, edited by Eric Tagliacozzo and M. Toorawa Shawkat (Cambridge, U.K.: Cambridge University Press, 2015), 175–95.

31 See Shahed Amanullah, "Hajj 2.0: Technology's Impact on the Muslim Pilgrimage," *Georgetown Journal of International Affairs* 10, no. 2 (2009): 75–82.

32 Nidhal Guessoum, *Islam's Quantum Question: Reconciling Muslim Tradition and Modern Science* (London: I. B.Tauris, 2011). The cover of the book has a magnet, like a Ka'ba, surrounded by ferromagnetic shavings that look like they are doing *tawaf* around the magnet.

PART II

Holidays

4

Ramadan, Eid al-Fitr, and Eid al-Adha

Fasting and Feasting

JACKLEEN SALEM

Aminah Salah's parents arrived in the United States from Colombia in 1965. Her father, a Palestinian from Sara, Palestine, a village captured during the 1948 Arab-Israeli War which no longer exists, and her mother, a Colombian from Bogota, met and married in Colombia.[1] Many years before she was born in Chicago, they resettled in the United States to provide their children with better life opportunities. Aminah grew up in the southwest suburbs of Chicago, in a place Google Maps categorizes as "Little Palestine." Her parents' home was in a little Muslim enclave in Bridgeview, Illinois, created by interstate highway 294 to the west and 95th street to the south. In the center of this enclave lies a beige brick structure with a brown dome that's slowly turning green. It's known as the Mosque Foundation of Bridgeview, Illinois.[2] It is surrounded by homes and two Muslim schools—Universal School and Aqsa School. Aminah's family built a pink brick house a block or two away from the mosque.

Wearing denim jeans, a white embroidered shirt, and a yellow jersey scarf, Aminah told me in an interview not only about her move to the Bridgeview area but also about her experiences during Ramadan, the Islamic holy month of dawn-to-sunset fasting. Though Ramadan traditions in the United States vary in accordance with family preferences and ethnic background, prayer, spiritual reflection, great food, and fun are common factors in many Muslim Americans' celebration of this sacred month. For Aminah and many other Muslim Americans, Ramadan is a time for increased religious worship and family gathering: "I am very blessed, I know. I am really lucky to have such great holidays with my family."[3] According to Aminah, "Ramadan consists of fasting from sunrise to sunset from all food and drink. It is a time of spiritual reflection when Muslims are encouraged to do good, like read more Qur'an, give charity, cook food for people. We are taught from when we are kids that every good deed you do in Ramadan is multiplied, so going to the mosque to pray is even better than praying at home or feeding the poor is even more blessed in Ramadan in deeds."[4] Observing the fast during the month of Ramadan is one of the five pillars of Islamic religious practice. For many Muslims around the world, it is a time of purification for the soul: "When you're not eating," said Aminah, "you should be reflecting. The hunger pains make you remember people who never get to break their fast because it's their life. Every mosque will have a dinner every night for anyone who needs to eat, and it can be anyone, not just Muslims."[5]

According to Islamic traditions outlined in the Shari'a, which is known as Islamic law but also might be called the Islamic way of life, during the days of Ramadan all healthy adults and postpubescent children are supposed to fast. They also aim to abstain from sexual relations, smoking, and other things that distract the person from remembering God. As with all rules discussed in Shari'a, however, there is considerable flexibility and endless debate about how the ideals of Islam should be put into practice on a case-by-case basis. If a mother is nursing or pregnant or a woman is menstruating, for example, she can abstain from fasting. If a person is ill or is traveling, he or she can likewise break the fast. Children are encouraged at a young age to try fasting and are supposed to begin observing daily fasting after reaching puberty. In addition, the timing of Ramadan, which is a month in the Islamic calendar, changes each year. Throughout the course of a person's lifetime, he or she might observe the month of fasting during the dead of winter and the height of summer. This too can have an important impact on whether one is physically able to observe the fast.

Since the Islamic calendar is based on the moon rather than the sun, the month of Ramadan begins with the sighting of a new moon. Aminah has always gone with the decision of her local mosque as to when the moon has been sighted, long an issue of contention among Muslim American communities. She gets a call and message from her mosque, and then she knows when to start.

In contrast, Tuscany Bernier, one of the other people whom I interviewed for this chapter, chooses to follow the decision of the Islamic

Society of North America (ISNA) since they are located in Indiana and that's where she resides.[6] Bernier converted to Islam at eighteen; she is of German ancestry on her father's side and Native American and Lumbee ancestry on her mother's. Dressed in her colorful *hijab* and *niqab*, which is a loose-fitting material covering her face, she talks of the confusion in her local mosque and felt it was a safer decision to go with ISNA. ISNA, one of the largest Muslim organizations in the United States, bases its calculations on the Fiqh Council of North America. According to this Muslim group, "the Fiqh Council of North America recognizes astronomical calculation as an acceptable Shari'a method for determining the beginning of lunar months including the months of Ramadan and Shawwal."[7]

Tahir Umar Abdullah, Assistant Director of Spiritual Life and Advisor of Muslim Affairs at the University of Chicago, takes yet another point of view. He is associated with two different crescent moon sighting organizations in North America—Crescent Watch and the Chicago Hilal Committee—both of which posit that the moon must be actually sighted by a human rather than using scientific calculations. According to Abdullah, "I give final authority to the Chicago Hilal Committee because it is comprised of scholars in my locale. I sometimes perform moon sightings by myself, or with others, and may even submit a report of my own to the aforementioned bodies."[8]

Shereen Yousef, a second-generation Twelver Shi'a Muslim from Hyderabad, India, who is working for her Ph.D. at the University of Wisconsin-Madison, says that there is also a lot of debate in the Shi'a community about this issue. She mentioned this in reference to the end of Ramadan: "The thing that is so ridiculous for me—this is my personal opinion—there has been a response . . . that has been quite adequate. So, for me, it tends to be surprising how often these debates come up. A lot of that derives from differences in interpretations, what constitutes the shared horizon which then indicates what date is the last date of Ramadan and what is the first day of the next month."[9] She believes that *marja'iyya* or the *marja'* system—in which scholarly experts are qualified to use independent reasoning in making legal decisions—means that there should be a clear way of determining when Ramadan begins and ends.[10] Most Shi'a Muslims follow one of these imams or clerics. But it is even more complicated in her own family since there are both

Sunni and Shi'a Muslims, and everyone ends up starting Ramadan on a different day.

In addition to praying, fasting, and spending more time with family members, some Muslim Americans celebrate Ramadan by decorating their homes. For Tuscany, decorating the two-bedroom apartment that she shares with her husband, Drew, and her three cats is part of creating a sacred space for practices associated with Ramadan: "I really strive to have a very family-oriented but also God-oriented atmosphere for the whole month. I make paper chains and I put them all around in the living room and sometimes in the kitchen. I put up a tree of Allah's [99 beautiful] names. I tend to try to listen to music a lot less. If I do, I listen to *nasheeds* [a cappella praise songs for the Prophet Muhammad and his family]. I listen to more Qur'an. I spend more time on *du'as* [supplicatory prayers] and try to focus on how hungry I'm not, or am. With every year it gets better. I'm not getting hungry as much."

Nikia Bilal, an African American lawyer who grew up in the Southside Chicago community of Imam W. D. Mohammed (the son of Elijah Muhammad who led hundreds of thousands to embrace Sunni Islam) makes sure her five children grow up feeling that Ramadan and Eid are important:

> For me growing up, Christmas was so depressing for me. . . . It just seemed like the best time that kids like, and I hated that we were missing out. And because most of my family is non-Muslim, I knew my family would be getting together and having this big dinner and my cousins are getting gifts and we would not go. My parents' stand was that we would not join the family for Christmas. I used to find it depressing. I felt like Eid [al-Fitr, the Muslim holiday marking the end of Ramadan] was not comparable, even as I got older. I understand why parents don't want to turn eid into Christmas. . . . But because of that, I did come into parenthood wanting to do things differently for my kids than I felt it was like for me. Once they were old enough to really notice and care, I borrowed ideas from Universal [the Islamic School in Bridgeview, Illinois]. Each classroom would have a door-decorating contest. I did stuff like that. . . . Every year I have started building up my holiday home decoration cache of stuff. First year I didn't have much. I just had streamers, which isn't much. It was pathetic to me. Each year it gets more blinged out here. . . . About a month before

eid, I start scouring the internet to see what new stuff is out there. We have those huge moons that light up. . . . I have star and crescent lights we put up and down the banisters. We have little figurines that are glittery and say "Ramadan Mubarak" that I put on the dining room table and other tables. We found these Moroccan lanterns. We put those up. Kinda get kids involved by plugging in the lights at *maghrib* [sundown] and get excited about it. . . . A couple of years ago I found this thing where people were putting prizes in balloons. Each day the kids would get to pop a balloon. First day of Ramadan we fill up thirty balloons with different candy and we would have to put a lot of it because there are a lot of kids. Each day at *maghrib* time one of the kids gets to pop a balloon and the kids go diving for candy. Which they love, even the big ones.

Decorating and creating activities for children has become a significant part of Ramadan for families with young children. As Nikia indicates, for many Muslims in the United States and abroad, Ramadan and Eid al-Fitr can sometimes be compared to Christmas and other holidays that involve decorations, gift giving, and food. Muslim American parents sometimes feel the necessity and even the pressure to make Ramadan just as festive and fun.

Suhur, the meal eaten right before *fajr*, or the morning prayer, is another tradition that Muslims in the United States and around the world practice during the month of Ramadan. Suhur is recommended by the Prophet Muhammad in his Sunna, or tradition, and many Muslims rise early before fajr to consume food and drink that help them prepare for the upcoming day. But there are some Muslims who work long days and find it challenging to wake up in the middle of the night to eat. Missing this meal can make the day harder since no other food or drink is allowed from the start of fajr prayer until sunset.

At first, Tuscany Bernier was one who skipped suhur. Tuscany's first Ramadan was tough and she got through only three days of fasting. As time passed, however, she learned the keys to maintaining the fast. She made sure to eat a lot of protein or milk during suhur to prepare herself for the day. According to Yvonne Maffei, a convert with Italian and Puerto Rican roots who converted to Islam in 2001 and is the author of *Summer Ramadan Cookbook* and *My Halal Kitchen*: "You need so much hydration, so I encourage people to eat watermelon and lots of fruits during the Ramadan meals. I try to avoid processed sugar and have coconut water with fruit."[11] Aminah Salah doesn't usually eat for suhur but "I drink a lot of water and eat just dates. It has fiber and it's easy and fast."[12] Tahir, who has a very hectic schedule, also gets by on water and dates. While many Muslims stay away from coffee or tea because it is dehydrating, for Tannaz Hannadi, a first-generation American Twelver Shi'a Muslim of Iranian descent who works as a policy analyst for the U.S. federal government, coffee is a must. "I usually eat leftovers. Sometimes breakfast stuff. Coffee for sure. Tons of water and watermelon. Food is not a big thing for us during Ramadan. We try to not overeat or overindulge."[13] Tea is also vital for Osman Aydas, a first-generation American Turkish Ph.D. candidate at the University of Wisconsin-Milwaukee. Every suhur for him is replete with a fresh pot of Turkish black tea from the green hills of the Black Sea region of Turkey that is made with two teapots atop each other.[14]

Eating suhur at twenty-four-hour restaurants is also a popular option on the weekends, especially because many observant Muslims stay up late to pray. For Rahaf Khatib, a second-generation Syrian marathon runner who grew up in Dearborn, Michigan, celebrating Ramadan in one of the most densely populated Muslim towns in the United States "is like celebrating Ramadan in a Middle Eastern country. There is really no difference. Fasting all day, *tarawih* [prayers] at night, *qiyam* in the masjid [mosque] . . . basically the grocery shopping and the atmosphere was very festive. Every day is like a holiday and shops were open 24 hours to accommodate the people who eat the early breakfast or suhur at about 4 a.m. It was very common to find shops open at that time for people who want to eat out for suhur or who want to grab something fast to eat."[15] Amjad Qadri, a second-generation Indian from Hyderabad with over three hundred relatives in the Chicago area, has a WhatsApp group with all his cousins who meet up for suhur after going to the mosque.[16] It is too difficult to call them all and arrange the meeting, so they send a group message to see who is available. One year, one of his cousins decided there should be a fajr, or morning, bus. His cousin would get up and pick up people to attend fajr prayers.

During Ramadan, many Muslim Americans spend more time than usual in the thousands of mosques that exist in the United States. Mosques feature various programs during Ramadan, including community dinners, food pantries, Qur'an programs, religious programs for kids, lectures for adults, and late night prayers. "Our lives are planned around the fast, everything revolved around it," said Aminah.[17] Tarawih (pronounced taraweeh), one of the most significant of Ramadan traditions for Muslim Americans, is a supererogatory prayer held after *'isha*, or night prayer. For Aminah, attending tarawih is a must: "It really adds to the spirit of Ramadan, allows me to do extra prayers, visit the mosque. I feel the sense of community that I don't get year round." Aminah's favorite part of the tarawih is the du'a that the imam makes in the last *rakat* of the night. This is a series of emotional prayers that last ten minutes or more. "It is one of the most beautiful portions of the evening because the imam prays for everyone around the world and we respond with 'Ameen' [Amen]," recounted Aminah. "He prays for the Muslims suffering from Syria to Darfur. He prays for us all to have good health, [be] content, blessed, and free from greed, envy, jealousy, hardship, and any other difficulty that can [be]fall a person. Sometimes people are even crying or the imam cries."[18]

For Fatima Khan, an assistant professor of Arabic at Northwestern University and a second-generation Indian, Ramadan is a time to turn the television off and focus on reading Qur'an and going to tarawih prayers.[19] Tahir, an African American Muslim who converted to Islam in 1996 in Oakland, California, amidst a rich hip-hop culture that embraced Muslims through music and activism, has spent much of his time arranging iftar and tarawih for Muslims on the University of Chicago campus or near it. "So last year, I organized tarawih here at the University of Chicago every night during Ramadan, which was one of the most taxing things I've ever done."[20] Planning and organizing such events requires a lot of energy and often goes into the late evening, which can be challenging when you need to wake up early the next day for work. For Tuscany, tarawih is important "because any extra prayers can stand on my behalf on Judgment Day and I feel like I need that. It's also a good time to see people I don't get to see the rest of the year."[21] Her husband Drew, a red-haired physics major of French Canadian descent, is Shi'a and doesn't pray tarawih. Shi'a Muslims tend to believe that while the Prophet Muhammad did pray tarawih during Ramadan, he did not do so in the manner that many Sunni Muslims do today—a tradition that was established later by his son-in-law, good friend, and third Caliph

Umar al-Khattab.[22] But Drew still stays up to pray with his wife and later eats suhur with her.

Another tradition that marks the month of Ramadan is dinner parties. It is customary and encouraged for Muslims in the United States to invite their family and friends over for iftar dinner. This is one of the many good deeds a Muslim might do during Ramadan. Eman Hassaballa Aly, an Egyptian American who works in health care, has been part of her mother's weekly iftar dinner at their local mosque for two to three hundred people during Ramadan for years. "For the last thirty years, my mom has been doing iftars during Ramadan. We would get there early and we would put out food and we would serve the community. There would be hundreds of people there, anybody in the community. It's still going until today, even though she's older and had knee replacement surgery. . . . Our Ramadans have been centered around service for most of my life."[23] Eman described a very busy Ramadan schedule with her family hosting or attending iftar dinners almost every day among the Egyptian community. Her mother became famous for her rice pudding, which everyone knows and requests. But as their families grew, community members began to focus on their own children, grandchildren, and great grandchildren.

Turkish Americans have also been hosting iftar dinners throughout Ramadan through a community program called Abraham's Tent. As Osman Aydas, a Turkish American Ph.D. student at the University of Wisconsin-Milwaukee, described it, "They send out emails to their database, which includes more than 10,000 people living in the Chicago metropolitan area, and they ask them if they would be willing to join a Muslim family during their iftar dinner. I heard last year they hosted more than 150 dinners and volunteers in their own houses. . . . Although iftar is typically late for these American families, many of them say they fasted for the day to share the experience. They had just water and no food. Or they didn't have meat or something like that. . . . Mostly the feedback has been very, very positive."[24]

For Tuscany, iftar dinners at the local mosque are what keep her going when Ramadan becomes lonely. Since Ramadan is a time for family and close friends, some Muslim Americans forget that converts to Islam come from non-Muslim families who don't understand the month or its significance.[25] Tuscany doesn't get any dinner invitations from friends because they are often focused on their families. There is a place at her local mosque for people to come, eat dinner for free, and socialize with other Muslims. But Ramadan can be quite challenging for those without a supportive community. Tuscany's Ramadan experience has not been easy. Iftar dinners can be taxing, but their participants feel the spiritual benefit of breaking fast with and serving others during Ramadan.

Going to work during Ramadan is problematic for many Muslim Americans who cannot change or arrange their work schedule to accommodate the month. Families often have to juggle a hectic schedule. Drew, born and raised in Indiana, recently started a new job at the Subaru Car Company with a work schedule of 4 p.m. to 1 a.m., which means he will not be able to break his fast and have dinner with his wife Tuscany throughout Ramadan.[26] Tuscany admits this will be difficult for her, but she remains positive.

When Ramadan falls during summer, it can also be challenging to take care of the kids. For example, Fatima Khan juggles a full-time job at Northwestern University and raising her five children. Her husband Yousef Abdullah, a half-Yemeni and half-Indian *hafiz*—one who has memorized the entire Qur'an—with a degree from the prestigious Dar al-Ulum in Deoband, India, serves the community throughout Ramadan as an imam at the Muslim Education Center in Morton Grove, Illinois. For fifteen years, he has led the tarawih prayers for the community. "It's really hard because he works full time and the days are long. He doesn't get to spend too much time with the family. . . . He comes home [after work] and he has to review the portion [of Qur'an] he has to recite for that evening to make sure he is error free. The prayer itself is about two and half hours because they do twenty *rakat*s [prayer cycles]. . . . So when he comes home, he eats and falls asleep."[27]

Aminah can only attend tarawih a couple of times a week because of her kids and work. She trades nights with her husband Iyad. When maghrib or sunset is early—such as in the winter time at 4:30 or 5 p.m.—the Mosque Foundation of Bridgeview holds two different prayers, one at 6:30 p.m. and one at 8:30 p.m. Maghrib during the Midwest summer can be so late—at 8:30 p.m. or 9 p.m.—that there is barely enough time for one tarawih at 10:15 p.m. or later. For Tahir, the chaplain at the University of Chicago, it is especially hectic during the month of Ramadan. "I'm fasting and I'm working. I'm not off just because it's Ramadan and

I'm not off just because it's the summer. . . . In the evening, I'm helping to organize an iftar the Muslim Student Association is doing. The MSA and our office collaborate together . . . we might have iftar dinners three times a week. Not every night but at least two to three times a week and I help them with that."

For Aminah, who works as a social worker with an agency affiliated with the University of Illinois at Chicago, fasting can be challenging while working the normal nine to five schedule. "It's hard. First couple of days are hard, working and not eating. And usually I end up telling my coworkers I am fasting and there is a lot of questions at work. They don't understand why, especially in the summer that I'm not drinking. I've noticed that some coworkers actually admire the fact that the only reason I'm not eating or drinking is because God is watching me."[28] In order to illustrate the difficulties of fasting during Ramadan at the workplace, the *Huffington Post* created a video entitled "The Struggles of a Ramadan Fast in a Non-Muslim Office" with Linda Sarsour, executive director of the Arab American Association of New York. Necva Solak, an attorney at the New York City Department of Housing Preservation and Development and a first-generation American Muslim of Turkish and Azerbaijani descent, said her colleagues have lots of questions, "Do you have to fast when you are sick? Do you drink water at least? Isn't it hard? Don't you feel tired?"[29] They would also make comments, "I could never do that, I get crazy when I'm starving. I get headaches when I don't eat."[30] Necva explained to them that it's not just fasting from food but from sinful acts as well, like gossiping, lying, cheating, and so on. The idea, Necva explained to them, "is to use your time wisely in Ramadan and maximize its blessings."[31]

While there are many questions and comments, coworkers can be very supportive as well. "I've noticed non-Muslims like to ask, 'Is that your Christmas?'" Amina told me. "'Yes, I guess, if you mean is this my most special holiday, yes.' People tend to be very sympathetic when I tell them this is my Christmas. I remember last year, I worked the day before and they just couldn't understand and said, 'Don't you have presents to wrap? Don't you have things to do?' They're very kind. I had a couple of coworkers who said, 'We had a couple of Christmas parties around the holidays, I think it's only fair that when it's your holiday that we have a holiday party for you.' It was nice."

The last ten days of Ramadan are especially powerful. Sunni Muslims believe that Layla al-Qadr, or the Night of Power, can take place any day during odd nights in the last ten days of Ramadan. Often, in deference to a prophetic tradition, it is marked on the 27th by Sunnis and on the 23rd by Shi'as. According to the Prophet Muhammad, a supplication made during this night is sure to be answered. Some Muslims pray throughout the night at the mosque, while others will visit the mosque a couple of different times during the night. Still others will simply pray at home.

Shi'a Muslim Americans also celebrate some distinctive rituals during Ramadan. According to Ali Naquvi, a first-generation Pakistani born in London but living in New Jersey, "on the 15th of Ramadan we celebrate the birthday of Imam Hasan, the son of Imam Ali and Lady Fatima, and we put out a feast before the actual iftar." This feast reenacts the occasions on which people would "come to Imam Ali at the masjid asking for food, [and] he would send them to his house. It was Imam Hasan [his son] who would make him give out food to the poor who were constantly coming to their home."[32]

Shi'a Muslim Americans also commemorate the death of Ali ibn Abi Talib, the Prophet Muhammad's cousin and son-in-law, and the fourth caliph, who died on the 21st day of Ramadan. According to Shereen, "those four nights from the 18th to 23rd, we tend to range between praying and mourning rituals. . . . One of the things we do is to recite, *Munajat*, a supplication Imam Ali used to make on this night. It's a beautifully constructed repetition of *Mawla ya Mawla*, 'Oh my Lord, Oh my Lord.' It says things like: 'Who can protect me but the greatest of protectors?' It puts you in perspective of who you are in relation to God and it is made all the more profound because days before we were commemorating the death of this person. Supplication in and of itself brings tears to my eyes."[33] During those commemorative nights, some Shi'as become very emotional as they reflect on the death of Imam Ali.[34] "Usually people participate in some form of beating of the chest. . . . It's part of the culture and the ritual forms of commemoration. . . . Any time there is a gathering where we are getting together to mourn or commemorate, it's generally called a *majlis*. . . . After you hear the story and people are crying, that's generally followed up with people standing, people just start hitting themselves, it's usually poetically done. There's usually some sort of rhythm and poetry that's recited and usually the beating of the chest is with the rhythm." Shereen feels it's an important tradition but emphasizes that in her view much of it is cultural, not religious.[35]

Eid al-Fitr: The Holiday Feast Celebrating the End of Ramadan

The month of Ramadan ends with what has become perhaps the most celebrated Islamic holiday in the United States—a huge feast called Eid al-Fitr, literally meaning "the feast of the breaking of fast." For Aminah's family, preparations for Eid al-Fitr begin days in advance of the actual holiday. She shops for all her children's clothing for eid day. She makes sure everyone has something nice and new to wear that is formal or fancy. She buys herself a new outfit. A few days before eid Aminah takes Sereen, her daughter, to Aunt Maisun's home for the traditional preparation of *ma'mul*, date- or nut-stuffed cookies made out of semolina or flour. They spend hours preparing the dates and nuts, and mold over a hundred round cookies with little geometrical designs that are dusted with powdered sugar.[36] On occasion Aminah makes *gharyaba*, an "s"-shaped cookie made out of butter and flour with a pine nut placed in the center. Her house is decorated with lights, lanterns, balloons, and signs wishing visitors *Eid Mubarak*, or "blessed eid." During eid mornings, every sleep-deprived family member rushes to take a shower or at least make ablutions by rinsing their face, arms, head, and feet so that they are ritually clean for the eid day prayer. Then the kids rush down for a light breakfast of oatmeal or cereal.[37] Aminah lays out the new clothes she has purchased for each of her three children on their beds. With her husband, Iyad, she has prepared and wrapped eid presents. The kids put on their finest dresses, shirts, pants, ties, and jackets, and eagerly rush to the family room to open their gifts from their parents.

Then everyone must hurry out the door to avoid the traffic and find a spot at the Mosque Foundation of Bridgeview, Illinois. If it is raining or snowing, they hold two different eid prayers at the mosque and the nearby Aqsa School and the Universal School. If the weather allows, the Mosque Foundation rents Toyota Park to accommodate the more than 15,000 people who attend the celebration.[38] Whether they are observant Muslims or not, whether they pray or do not, everyone in the local Muslim community seems to come out to celebrate this holiday together. As the Muslim community in the Chicago area has grown, the normal prayer facilities can no longer accommodate the burgeoning eid crowds. Muslims have started to gather for eid in soccer stadiums, parking lots, auditoriums, convention centers, hotels, and state parks. The Mosque Foundation of Bridgeview rents the soccer stadium and also arranges pony rides, animals, inflatables, train rides, clowns, balloons, goody bags, and food vendors to cater to the large number of children in attendance.

Aminah and her family wait in the long traffic lines on Harlem Avenue to park and enter Toyota Park. Lines and lines of cars can be seen as far as the eye can see. Cars and crowds are converging on this one location and creating chaos in the traffic patterns. Local non-Muslims who venture out in the direction of the mosque or Toyota Park are often unaware of the day or its impact on traffic. Iyad, dressed in his finest suit and looking like he just got his hair cut by the local Muslim barber, parks the car. Everyone disembarks in their finery and makes the trek to the entrance. Once they enter with the crowds, Aminah and her husband separate as he heads to the men's section with his son Yousef, and she heads to the women's section with her girls, Sereen and Emily. She sees passing friends and old acquaintances. As she waits to pass to the prayer space, Aminah observes all the people modeling their new eid fashions. Some are wearing makeup, matching shoes, and the latest fashions. The little girls are bursting with colors, patterns, and styles of dresses from floral to sequin and from silk to satin. The boys are dressed in gray and black suits, white shirts, ties, and dress pants. Some are dressed more humbly in a jean jacket and pants, and their hair is as it would be every day.

The soccer field is covered with cardboard so that people can pray and sit on a clean surface. Some people still bring prayer rugs to put on top or purchase them from vendors on site. Aminah texts her youngest sister, Maisun, or her friend, Heba, to determine where they will sit. Aminah is always early. She doesn't like to be rushed and likes to get there on time. She arrives at the women's section and anxiously searches for her family and friends. They usually sit together during the speeches, prayer, and religious leader's *khutba*, or sermon. Her daughter Sereen always looks forward to sitting with her "Abuelita," her grandmother, and Aunt Maisun. They all give each other hugs, lay out their prayer rugs on the cardboard, and then sit, talk in Spanish, and people-watch.

Eid al-Fitr prayer starts promptly at 10 a.m. The mayor of Bridgeview and the governor of Illinois come to highlight the significance of the

Muslim community to the city and the state, and they wish Muslims
"Happy Eid." When the speeches are finished, the imam, or religious
leader, tells everyone to stand for prayer. Conversations cease and quiet
descends onto the crowd as 15,000 people stand for prayer. The imam
commences the two rakats, or cycles of prayers, that include prostrations in the direction of the Kaʻba, the holiest place in Islam. Aminah
stands with her mother, sister, and daughters, and they cover their hair
with their hijabs, or head scarves. (While some Muslim women cover
their hair whenever they leave the home, others cover their hair only
to make their prayers.) Many people stand for prayer; others who are
not praying move to the back of the lines. The imam repeats the words,
"Allahu akbar," or God is great, seven times. After the prayer is finished,
the imam gives a khutba discussing the life of the Prophet Muhammad, the necessity of gratitude for all our blessings, and his concerns
for how various political events affect the Muslim community both in
the United States and abroad.[39] Aminah and her family sit quietly and
listen. Some people start talking to their neighbors. When this twenty-
minute sermon finishes, the imam asks the crowd to join in a communal
duʻa. Every supplication ends with the crowd saying, "Ameen." When the
imam finishes, people in the crowd stand up, puts their shoes on, and
slowly gather all their kids and belongings. Aminah searches for other
friends, catches up with old acquaintances, and chitchats while the kids
run and play with their friends. She makes sure she takes pictures of all
the kids in their finery with family and friends.

Aminah heads out to the parking area to try to find Iyad and Yousef.
One of the most important family traditions for Aminah's family on eid
is father and kids' nachos time—a practice that begins to indicate just
how different one family's celebration of eid can be from another's. The
Mosque Foundation of Bridgeview has been selling nachos and cheese
after eid prayer for many years. Aminah's kids love it. Aminah, Sereen,
Emily, Yousef, and other family members head to the play area where all
the vendors are selling nachos, ice cream, toys, prayer rugs, and Palestinian falafel, the fried chickpea balls now popular in American cuisine.
There is also a jump house, clowns making animal-shaped balloons, pony
rides, train rides, and someone giving the kids free goody bags and balloons. Aminah tries to convince her children to get on a pony ride or play
in the jumpy house every year but admits, "My kids are not very inter-

ested in the children's activities there. Sometimes I try to push them to try it. But they just say, 'I wanna go to Abuelita's house.' To them, that's eid. They are anticipating that, eating together, seeing their cousins." After finishing their ice cream, Aminah and her family say their good-byes to friends and head over to her parents' house, which is ten minutes away.

The family didn't always gather for eid brunch at Mahmoud and Blanca Salah's house. Living near the Mosque Foundation shaped their Ramadan and eid activities over the years. As the Mosque Foundation expanded, Aminah's eid celebrations were transformed. Initially, eid consisted of visiting her elder sister, Nathira, and having dinner at a restaurant with her uncle Muhammad's family. But "once we started living closer to the Mosque," she recalled, "our house became the central house in our family. We started a tradition. . . . Everyone in my family—and I mean my uncle, my married brothers and sisters, everyone—would pray after seeing friends at the mosque. Everyone would walk over to my parents' house and we would have a traditional Arab breakfast. Our house became a gathering place for nieces, nephews, and sometimes even family friends would stop by."[40] "Everyone" now includes Aminah's nine brothers and sisters and over twenty nieces and nephews.

Blanca, affectionately known as "Abuelita," begins to prepare well in advance for the family and friends coming to visit. Every room in the house is cleaned in preparation for a bustling day. Cash is withdrawn from banks to give to eager kids waiting for their *Eidiya*, or cash gifts. Presents are also wrapped for those kids who choose toys or clothes instead of cash. "My mom and older sister would buy gifts for the children in our family. The kids would open one present, sometimes two together. That tradition still continues until now."[41] The dining table is filled with traditional Palestinian foods like falafel, hummus, eggs, baba ghanoush (roasted eggplant with tahini sauce), *waraq dawali* (stuffed grape leaves), kibbeh with meat, triangle spinach pies, meat pies, cheese pies, and much more.

As the family arrives, everyone exchanges greetings in Arabic, saying "Eid Mubarak," a blessed eid, or "*kul sana wa antee salma*," literally meaning "every year may you have peace and good health." Or they simply say, "Happy Eid." The kids run into the house and greet their Sido, an Arabic word for grandfather, and Abuelita, the Spanish word for grandmother, and wish them an eid mubarak. They run to play with their cousins and jump in the bounce house set up in the backyard. All Aminah's brothers and sisters and their children slowly pile into the house. Brunch begins and everyone is talking and laughing, gathering food around the table, then sitting all over the house. After filling up on savories, they partake of the home-made ma'mul and other desserts available with tea or coffee. In the evening, Aminah goes to visit her in-laws for tea or dinner.

The types of foods and even some of the particular holiday greetings in Aminah's family reflect their Arab ethnic roots. Because Muslim Americans come from every racial and ethnic background, such traditions vary from family to family. For example, Turkish Americans might eat *borek* (dough with cheese or spinach), *sarma* (stuffed grape leaves), *dolma* (stuffed peppers or zucchini), and *poja* (bread stuffed with cheese or potato).[42] In South Asian families, the table may feature *samosa* (puff pastry stuffed with meat), lamb *biryani*, chicken, lentils, and rice. But some Muslims, of whatever background, might choose to eat a vegetarian feast, meat and potatoes, or Italian foods. It just depends.

Eid al-Adha: The Holiday Commemorating Abraham's Sacrifice

The other major holiday of the Islamic religious calendar is Eid al-Adha, which means the "feast of sacrifice." It represents the Prophet Abraham's ultimate trust in following God's directive to sacrifice his son Ishmael. It is four days long, though the first day holds the most significance. As Fatima described it, "When it came time for Prophet Ibrahim [Arabic for Abraham] to sacrifice his son, God replaced him with a sheep. So, Muslims must sacrifice a sheep or animal in commemoration of Prophet Ibrahim."[43]

Eid al-Adha marks the end of the ten days of the month during which the Hajj, or pilgrimage to Mecca, occurs. Like Eid al-Fitr, this eid is based on a lunar calendar, and it occurs on a different day of the solar calendar each year. Every year the holiday is ten days earlier than it was the year before. Traditionally, Eid al-Fitr is described as the "little Eid," while Eid al-Adha is considered the "big Eid." Fatima feels that Eid al-Fitr should be categorized as the "big Eid" because Muslims work hard to worship and fast during the month of Ramadan, considered a feat and accomplishment.[44] In some cases, Muslims in America celebrate these holidays by observing traditions from their native countries or new traditions they established in the United States.

Many of the traditions observed during Eid al-Fitr can also be found during Eid al-Adha, including communal prayers, a family dinner, charitable contributions, gifts to children, communal fairs, and other celebrations. As with Eid al-Fitr, homes are decorated prior to Eid al-Adha, often during the beginning of the Hajj season. People might put up lights around the house or display a glowing crescent moon in their window. Homes sometimes feature signs wishing their visitors Eid Mubarak or Happy Eid.

As Rahaf described it, in Dearborn, Michigan, the feeling of eid is everywhere and it is very festive. All the stores sell food, sweets, and decorations for eid. Stores like Shatilla, which sells traditional Arab sweets like *kunafa* with cheese, baklava, *qatayif* with nuts or cheese, and ma'mul, are very busy before, during, and at the end of eid.[45] Stores throughout the area wish their customers Eid Mubarak inside and outside their stores. In Bridgeview, Illinois, Walgreen's puts Eid Mubarak under their street sign and Walmart puts up eid signs and sells products for Muslim consumers with special advertisements for dates, ma'mul, candy, and other important foods for eid.[46]

Celebrating Eid al-Adha also becomes an opportunity for the creative expression of Islamic religious themes and symbols. Heena Musabji, a Shi'a Muslim raised in upstate New York, has made cookie baking part of her family's celebration of the holiday. She bakes cookies that look like sheep to symbolize God's merciful decision to spare Abraham from having to sacrifice his son. She makes a candy that looks like the Ka'ba in Mecca by wrapping a gold ribbon around Ghirardelli chocolate squares.[47] Heena also makes muffin baskets for distribution to friends and neighbors. Heena wants her children as well as their teachers and friends to understand the importance of giving during the Islamic holidays, and so her gift baskets often include a little note explaining the meaning of Eid al-Adha.[48]

At the communal celebrations sponsored by the Next Wave Muslim Initiative in the Washington, D.C. area, Eid al-Adha activities for children include face painting, balloon making, popcorn stands, moon bounces, carnival rides, and cookie baking. One cookie is shaped to look like the Ka'ba, an important part of Eid al-Adha since the activities during Hajj center around it (or near it).[49] Families can donate $20 and bring a dish to share if they like, but everyone is welcome.

Eid al-Adha differs from Eid al-Fitr somewhat because of its emphasis on the slaughtering of an animal and the sharing of meat with those in need. Some Muslim Americans may order a large quantity of meat—beef, mutton, or perhaps goat—and following the tradition of the Prophet Muhammad, give a portion to family, friends, or the poor.[50] Some Muslims want to continue their family's tradition of slaughtering the animal themselves, and there are small farms in the United States that permit people to buy and butcher their own meat on the premises. Procuring and preparing the meat at home is important. Eman, for example, called it "a day of meat. We take the meat and make specific dishes like *rua* [crispy pastry with meat] and *fattah* [chickpeas, yogurt, and pita bread] with meat."[51] In Osman's family, the Turkish dish of *kawerma* (pieces of meat) is always consumed on Eid al-Adha. For some, the purchase and sometimes the actual slaughter of the meat represents the sacrifice that all Muslims must make for Eid al-Adha, whether they do it themselves or pay to have it done on their behalf.

But another tradition that has developed among U.S. Muslims is eating out at restaurants for eid. In Eman's family, for example, they buy new clothes for eid, attend the mosque in the morning for eid prayer, visit their local cemetery where many family members are buried and give their respect for an hour, and then have lunch. There are usually 150 to 200 people participating in Eman's eid day celebrations.[52] One year they arranged for a party of two hundred people at Texas de Brazil, a Brazilian-style steakhouse and churrascaria or barbeque restaurant. The event sold out.

But of course, not all Muslims in the United States go to steakhouses or even consume meat for Eid al-Adha. As outlined by Magfirah Dahlan later in this book, Muslim Americans' food practices express enormous variety. Some Muslims avoid meat because they are vegetarians or because they have ethical concerns about the treatment of animals or the environmental impact of meat consumption.

Conclusion: Eid as an American Holiday

Eid al-Fitr and Eid al-Adha have now taken root as part of the multiethnic and religious heritage of the United States. News channels regularly cover the start of Ramadan and the two eid holidays. In certain metropolitan areas, stores such as Walmart and Walgreen's cater to their local populations with signs of Happy Ramadan or Eid Mubarak. While Islamic holidays are only now coming to be known as part of American popular culture—stoked no doubt by the desire of businesses to capitalize on yet another marketing opportunity—they have always been celebrated in the United States. Thomas Jefferson was the first U.S. president to have at least a de facto White House iftar during Ramadan on December 9, 1805. After discovering that Tunisian ambassador Sidi Soliman Mellimelli was fasting, he invited the ambassador to break his fast at the White House.[53]

It was not until 1996 that First Lady Hillary Clinton held what was probably the next White House eid celebration. "It is only fitting," she said. "Just as children and families of other faiths have come here to celebrate some of their holy days, so you too are all here to mark this important Islamic tradition."[54] Presidents Bill Clinton and George W. Bush continued the tradition, turning Eid al-Fitr into a regular White House holiday. On July 1, 2016 President Barack Obama's daughter Malia posted a video on Facebook of her father, sister, and mother distributing food to the fasting crowd at the Islamic Center of Washington, D.C. That same year President Obama's White House eid invitees included sabre fencer Ibtihaj Muhammad, the first American Olympian to wear a headscarf, as well as Muslim scholars, activists, politicians, and athletes.

Also in 2016, actress Angelina Jolie, Special Envoy to the UN High Commissioner for Refugees, and U.S. Secretary of State John F. Kerry highlighted the global refugee crisis on World Refugee Day on July 20, 2016 at an interfaith iftar hosted by the All Dulles Area Muslim Society (ADAMS).[55] Jolie urged people to reconsider how the United States and other countries view the 65.3 million people displaced by conflict: "We are at our strongest . . . when we draw on our diversity as a people to find unity based on our common values and our larger identity. We are not strong despite our diversity; we are strong because of it."[56] Refugees to the United States from all parts of the world attended the event, from newly arrived Syrians to Eritreans.

The city of New York too has officially recognized Eid al-Fitr and Eid al-Adha as holidays. "Earlier this year, a nearly decade-long campaign to add two Muslim holidays—Eid-ul-Fitr and Eid-ul-Adha—to the New York City public school calendar finally paid off. . . . An estimated ten percent of the city's total public school enrollment is comprised of Muslim students." This marks a major turning point for Muslim Americans. Activist Linda Sarsour "described it as 'the biggest political victory that the Muslim community has seen in the last 20 years.'"[57] It might have sounded hyperbolic to some, but the public recognition of a group's religious holidays is an important step in the history of ethnic and religious empowerment in the United States.

NOTES

1 Aminah Salah, interview by Jackleen Salem, March 27, 2016, transcript.
2 Jackleen M. Salem, "A History of a Muslim Community in Chicago: Religion, Ethnicity, Women, and Citizenship," Ph.D. dissertation, University of Wisconsin-Milwaukee, 2012.
3 Salah interview, March 27, 2016.
4 Salah interview, March 27, 2016.
5 Joan Elovitz Kazan, "Ramadan Fast Makes Food Special," *Journal Sentinel*, May 31, 2016, accessed May 31, 2016, www.jsonline.com.
6 Tuscany Bernier, interviewed by Jackleen Salem, February 15, 2016, transcript.
7 "Fiqh Council of North America Announces Dates for Ramadan and Eid al Fitr 2014," Islamic Society of North America, accessed February 20, 2016, www.isna.net.
8 Tahir U. Abdullah, interview with Jackleen Salem, April 25, 2016, transcripts.
9 Shereen Yousef, interview with Jackleen Salem, March 23, 2016, transcript.
10 Yousef interview, March 23, 2016.
11 "Ramadan Fast Makes Food Special."
12 Salah interview, March 27, 2016.
13 Tannaz Hannadi, interview with Jackleen Salem, December 14, 2015, transcripts.
14 Osman Aydas, interview with Jackleen Salem, May 25, 2016.
15 Rahaf Khatib, interview with Jackleen Salem, March 24, 2016, transcripts.
16 Amjad Qadri, interview with Jackleen Salem, May 21, 2016, transcripts.
17 "Ramadan Fast Makes Food Special."
18 Salah interview, March 27, 2016.
19 Fatima Khan, interview with Jackleen Salem, January 7, 2016, transcripts.
20 Abdullah interview, April 25, 2016.
21 T. Bernier interview, February 15, 2016.
22 Drew Bernier, interview with Jackleen Salem, February 15, 2016, transcripts.
23 Eman Hassaballa Aly, interview with Jackleen Salem, May 25, 2016.
24 Aydas interview, May 25, 2016.
25 T. Bernier interview, February 15, 2016.
26 D. Bernier interview, February 15, 2016.
27 Khan interview, January 7, 2016.
28 Salah interview, March 27, 2016.

29 Necva Solak, interview with Jackleen Salem, February 18, 2016, transcript.
30 Solak interview, February 18, 2016.
31 Solak interview, February 18, 2016.
32 Ali Naquvi, interview with Jackleen Salem, May 10, 2016.
33 Yousef interview, March 23, 2016
34 Yousef interview, March 23, 2016.
35 Yousef interview, March 23, 2016.
36 Salah interview, March 27, 2016.
37 Salah interview, March 27, 2016.
38 Ray Hanania, "Muslims Gather in Bridgeview to Celebrate the End of Ramadan," *Arab Daily News*, July 29, 2014.
39 Salah interview, March 27, 2016.
40 Salah interview, March 27, 2016.
41 Salah interview, March 27, 2016.
42 Aydas interview, May 25, 2016.
43 Khan interview, January 7, 2016.
44 Khan interview, January 7, 2016.
45 Khatib interview, March 24, 2016.
46 Salah interview, March 27, 2016.
47 Heena Musabji, interview with Jackleen Salem, December 10, 2015, transcripts.
48 Musabji interview, December 10, 2015.
49 Hannadi interview, December 15, 2015.
50 Aydas interview, May 25, 2016.
51 Hassaballa Aly interview, May 25, 2016.
52 Hassaballa Aly interview, May 25, 2016.
53 "Thomas Jefferson Iftar," U.S. Embassy, accessed July 15, 2016, iipdigital.usembassy.gov.
54 Megan Meyer, "Obama Not the First President to Host Ramadan Dinner," *Muslim Voices*, September 4, 2009, accessed March 1, 2016, muslimvoices.org.
55 Shaarik H. Zafar, "Welcoming and Celebrating Refugees: An Interfaith Iftar in Honor of World Refugee Day," *White House*, June 24, 2016, accessed July 27, 2016, www.whitehouse.gov.
56 "Welcoming and Celebrating Refugees: An Interfaith Iftar in Honor of World Refugee Day."
57 Farah Akbar, "New York Muslims Mark Eid Holiday and Celebrate Strides," *NBC NEWS*, July 17, 2015, accessed March 2, 2016, www.nbcnews.com.

5

Ashura

Commemorating Imam Husayn

MICHAEL MUHAMMAD KNIGHT

While an elderly uncle retold the story in Urdu, barely able to get the words out as he wept at each detail, his voice trembling, the assembly of men sobbing and occasionally provoking shouts of "Ya Husayn," six boys walked into the room, carrying a coffin on their shoulders. The white shroud covering the coffin bore splatters of red stains. We lowered our heads. There was not a body inside, and the stains came from red dye. The coffin represented a death that had taken place nearly fifteen centuries ago, though the men grieved as though it had happened yesterday—or it was presently happening right in front of their faces and would happen again tomorrow and the next day. And we knew that his mother was still crying, all these centuries later.

The men formed two rows facing each other. To the crying of the elegist, we turned our bodies into drums, swinging our arms and bringing them down hard upon our chests in sync with the recitation—sometimes slow, sometimes fast, matching the rise and fall of the story being told. As we beat our chests, remembering that the stings of our slaps were nothing in the face of his suffering, we called out to him: "Ya Husayn, Ya Husayn. O Husayn, O Husayn."

With the grief and its release, there was also a sweetness. The boys who brought out the coffin provided desserts and tea. Crying for Husayn brought a community together; like a real funeral, the crying was softened by miniature family reunions, friends comforted by seeing each other. When conversation turned to the subject of the chest slapping, one man explained that the practices varied by region: he had seen different things done in Africa. "Everyone observes it their own way," he said.

In another time and place in the United States, a young girl wearing a black cloak and a black headscarf sits at the front of a room crowded with people.[1] Behind her, several large metal symbols shaped like the palm of a hand rest atop wooden poles. They hover at her back, seemingly standing guard over her. In Shi'a Islam, these palm-like icons represent the Prophet Muhammad and his family. People draw close to them in remembrance of the Prophet and his family, and drape them with flower garlands in gestures of devotion. A large poster of Ali, the cousin and son-in-law of Muhammad, hangs on the wall to the side of the girl. The image of his face is larger than her body, and that difference in scale heightens her youth but also gives her an air of authority: she is the one who sits between the audience and these powerful representations of Muhammad and his closest family. She is all of eleven years old. Sitting on a chair, she faces those in the audience who are crowded side by side on the floor. Like the girl, they are all wearing dark clothes. She is the orator in this gathering, a *zakira* who recounts to those assembled a narrative that they already know and hold dear, the account of the death of the Prophet Muhammad's grandson Husayn on the battlefield of Karbala in 680 C.E.

The young zakira opens her oration with a single imperative "*Salawat!*" to call forth blessings, and the audience responds in unison: "O God, bless Muhammad and the family of Muhammad." This blessing signals the opening of her narration. As she recounts the battle of Karbala, she weaves the story together, and then pulls out a single strand from the larger narrative, the moment when the camp of those loyal to Husayn ran out of water. The children were parched and thirsty in the desert camp, she tells her audience, so Abbas, the half-brother of Husayn, went down the Euphrates River to fetch water for them. On the way back to the children with water, he was attacked from behind. The zakira reminds the assembly of Abbas's ethical action and self-sacrifice. "Abbas was coming back so that the innocent children could have water. Regardless of his own wounded condition, he wanted the water to reach the children so that they would be saved from thirst. He wanted to save the children from thirst." She strikes her leg as she speaks, the sound of her hand accenting Abbas's desire to act to protect the vulnerable children.

The zakira speaks in the context of a *majlis*, an assembly that has gathered to commemorate the death and martyrdom of Husayn in 680

C.E. In Shiʻa communities around the world, these majlises affirm the importance of the Prophet and his family, bridging their lives and the lives of those present. The zakira attempts to tell the story of Karbala with such passion and poetry that the audience will be moved to tears. To commemorate the martyrdom of Husayn is to mourn, once again, the way in which those who are just and righteous suffer at the hands of the powerful. This mourning also implicitly affirms the possibility of justice-seeking in human history: the audience is reminded of the resistance of those who have stood up against unjust power and have protected, at all costs, those who need protecting. When the zakira strikes her leg to stress Abbas's efforts in the past, her gesture emphasizes the embodied reality of the immediate moment, and the way Abbas stands as a model for acting in the here and now.

This young zakira, entrusted to coordinate the special "blessings and power" of a ritual assembly, continues a centuries-old tradition of commemoration and mourning, yet she is also the product of a distinctly modern approach to the ritual obligation of giving alms.[2] When not serving in the role of zakira, she is a student in a school that was built with donations given by Shiʻa communities in the United States and Canada, under the auspices of an international organization called the Imam-e Zamana Mission, described in depth by Danielle Widmann Abraham in her chapter on social giving and philanthropy. She is in the singular position of having the authority to remind a Shiʻa assembly of the ethical responsibility of caring for vulnerable children *and* being herself a recipient of the fulfillment of that obligation, as a student in a school funded by those in the diaspora. Her presence in the majlis thus marks a unique nexus of contemporary history, one in which changes in global politics, religious reform, transnational migration, education, and ritual practice conjoin to enable an eleven-year-old girl to stand before an audience and authoritatively speak about a model of social ethics for the world today.

What Is Ashura?

Ashura derives from the Arabic word for the number ten. It was on the tenth day of the Islamic month of Muharram in the year 680 C.E., in the desert of Karbala in what is now Iraq, that an Umayyad army overwhelmed and destroyed Husayn's rebellion. The Umayyad soldiers—outnumbering the rebels 100,000 to a mere 72, according to some narrations—slaughtered Husayn and his supporters, leaving their bodies decapitated, mutilated, stripped naked, and robbed, to rot in the sun. Husayn's head was carried from Iraq to Damascus on the point of a spear. The children in Husayn's camp were murdered or enslaved, and women such as his sister Zaynab were marched through the streets while in states of exposure. Beyond its sheer brutality, the massacre became a religious crisis for two reasons: first, Husayn was the last surviving grandson of the Prophet Muhammad; second, the army that tortured, murdered, and degraded Husayn, his supporters, and family acted on orders from the caliphate, which presented itself as a righteous Islamic regime upholding the commands of God and legacy of the Prophet. According to narrations accepted by both Sunni and Shi'a Muslims, Husayn and his brother Hasan would climb on Muhammad during his prayers when they were small children, and Muhammad named the two brothers as leaders of the youths in paradise. Accounts of Muhammad's tender affection for his grandsons amplifies the heartbreak of what would come years later. For Muslims to have acted so viciously toward the Prophet's own family marked a crisis in the nascent Muslim community's understanding of itself and contributed to the development of separate Sunni and Shi'a articulations of Islam, informing its ritual, legal, theological, and even mystical dimensions.

The ways in which Muslims responded to the events at Karbala defined communal and sectarian divisions. Sunnis, who today constitute a sizable majority of Muslims, would conceptualize the battle of Karbala as an unfortunate political event without special religious consequences, and generally engage in observations of Ashura as a significant day without an explicit connection to Husayn or the battle of Karbala. Many Sunnis perform a voluntary fast on Ashura, though this relates to a personal practice of Muhammad without relation to Karbala. In contrast, Shi'a Muslims, who constitute roughly 10 to 15 percent of the global Muslim population, represent Husayn's martyrdom as the central event in God's destiny for humankind, a moment in which oppression and salvation intertwine in ways that have informed comparisons to the significance of Christ's redemptive suffering for Christians. As Husayn's gruesome suffering became the "center of gravity for Shi'a religious emotion,"[3] the remembrance of his death at Ashura developed as a crucial marker of Shiʻa identity, communal consciousness, and personal piety. In American Muslim contexts, Ashura remains salient to constructions of identity and religious authenticity as Shiʻa Muslims contend not only with complex relations with Sunni communities but also with American anti-Muslim prejudice at large.

Historical Background

The events that inspired Shiʻa observances of Ashura took place roughly fifty years after the death of Muhammad, emerging amidst the power struggles and factional divisions that gripped the Muslim community in Muhammad's absence. When Muhammad died in 632, he left his community with no clear instructions as to how a nascent state, led by a divinely guided prophet, could continue to function in that prophet's absence. It was not even clear how the community could find new leaders in its postprophetic condition. Abu Bakr, Muhammad's father-in-law and close friend, was elected to lead the community, though a minority preferred Ali, Muhammad's cousin and son-in-law. Though it does not appear that Abu Bakr used the term in his own lifetime, he was retroactively designated the "caliph," suggesting that he functioned as a successor to Muhammad's authority.[4] Abu Bakr in turn was succeeded by Umar and then Uthman, who became controversial for alleged favoritism toward members of his own clan, the Umayyads. When Uthman was assassinated in his home by an angry mob in 656, Ali ascended to the caliphate. For Ali's supporters, who had waited over two decades to see him in power, justice had finally arrived; but not all Muslims supported his claim to leadership. Muhammad's widow Aʼisha, daughter of the first caliph Abu Bakr, led a failed revolt against Ali. Though Ali emerged victorious over Aʼisha's coalition, he faced continued resistance from Muʻawiya, the Umayyad governor of Syria. When Ali agreed to arbitration with Muʻawiya's forces, a number of Ali's disillusioned supporters split from him and formed their own sectarian movement, the Kharijiyya. In 661, a member of the Kharijiyya assassinated Ali, whose remaining supporters then looked to Hasan, son of Ali and Muhammad's daughter Fatima, as their rightful leader. Hasan, however, renounced his claim, ceding to Muʻawiya, and retired from politics for a quiet life in Medina. Despite Hasan's apparent removal as a threat to Mu'awiya's power, Shi'a tradition asserts that Mu'awiya nonetheless arranged for Hasan to be poisoned.

Mu'awiya himself died in 680 and was succeeded by his son Yazid, whom historians characterize unfavorably for a variety of impious behaviors such as drunkenness, arranging animal fights for his entertainment, and loving young boys. With the ascension of Yazid to the throne, the Muslim caliphate operated as a conventional monarchy, with sovereignty being passed from father to son. For those who had supported Ali and Hasan, the possibility of a counterlineage survived with Ali's younger son, Husayn. In contrast to Yazid's image, Husayn was an exemplar of Muslim devotion, with his religious credibility bolstered by his status as the grandson of the Prophet and, almost as critically, the son of Muhammad's rightful heir.

The people of Kufa, which had served as the capital city during Ali's caliphate, offered their allegiance to Husayn, but Yazid's forces intimidated the Kufans into submission and intercepted Husayn's small camp en route to the city. The confrontation between Husayn and the Umayyad caliphate was to take place in the desert of Karbala. Tradition remembers the date of the battle as the tenth day of Muharram, which seems to have had religious significance prior to Husayn's last stand. Even the month's name, *Muharram*, refers to a sacredness with which the month was invested in pre-Islamic Arabia.[5] Early sources on Muhammad report that he had recognized the tenth day of Muharram as Ashura and fasted on that day; some sources depict this voluntary fast too as one predating Islam, having been a norm for the people of Mecca and connected to Jewish practice.[6]

While historians agree on the basic outline of Husayn's rebellion against Yazid, which concludes with the massacre of Husayn and his supporters by a much larger army at Karbala, pious retellings have elaborated upon the story to fill every narrative gap with heartbreaking details of devotion, suffering, and sacrifice. Husayn is remembered for his charity and chivalry toward the enemy soldiers, even offering them water. Various members of his family are illuminated as paragons of faith and dignity in the face of merciless evil and oppression; even Husayn's horse, Zuljannah, becomes a saintly character, revered for its unwavering loyalty and noble service to Husayn in his final moments.

In one of the most poignant moments of the Karbala narrative, Husayn presents his infant son Ali-Asghar (literally "Smallest Ali") to the enemy soldiers who have cut off the water supply from his camp. Husayn, as mentioned above, had previously shared his camp's water with the soldiers. Husayn pleads that as his son had not wronged them and poses no threat to them, they should provide some water to save the baby's life. One of Yazid's soldiers responds by shooting a blowdart through Husayn's arm, piercing Ali-Asghar's neck. Husayn carries the dead baby back to his camp and then picks up his sword.

Yazid's soldiers beheaded Husayn and his supporters and trampled their bodies under their horses. In a parade of torture and degradation, the soldiers marched with the severed heads planted on their lances and forced the captured women to walk uncovered. The survivors from among Husayn's family and camp would spread the word of what they had seen and experienced, and the tragedy of Karbala came to be recognized by both sides. Though Sunni tradition had grown to be defined in part through its recognition of Abu Bakr and the early caliphs as legitimate and rightly guided successors to Muhammad's leadership, Sunni Muslims would also grieve for Husayn, and seminal Sunni collections of Muhammad's statements and actions (hadith) even portray the Prophet as mourning his grandson's future martyrdom. In fact, as Ali J. Hussain explains, the earliest Sunni writings on the events at Karbala are overwhelmingly sympathetic to Husayn and even "practically identical to the early Shi'a perspectives on the battle."[7] From numerous periods in history and into modern times, we find Sunnis joining Shi'as in the rituals of grief associated with Husayn's death. For Sunnis as well as Shi'as, Husayn was the beloved grandson of the Prophet and a hero of faith. Twentieth-century Sunni intellectual Muhammad Iqbal depicts Husayn as a mercy to the created universe and paragon of self-sacrifice in the face of tyranny, but skillfully dehistoricizes the context of Karbala to make Husayn's passion play accessible to Sunnis without conceding any points to Shi'ism. In Iqbal's Sunni retelling, Husayn and Yazid operate as archetypal representations of good and evil, higher and lower elements of human nature, without the sectarian problems of Sunni-Shi'a antagonism coming into play.[8]

The critical distinction between Sunnis and Shi'as in their assessment of Karbala and its significance came to be that for Sunnis, the first four caliphates—that is, the reigns of Abu Bakr, Umar, Uthman, and

Ali—constituted a golden age of just rulers and relative unity. For Shiʿa Muslims, there was no golden age after Muhammad's death, as Abu Bakr usurped the leadership position that had rightfully belonged to Ali and deprived Fatima of her property. While Sunni Muslims would conceptualize the tragedy of Karbala as an outlier in a period otherwise characterized by peace and righteousness, Shiʿa Muslims locate Karbala's significance within a broader narrative of the ongoing mistreatment and persecution of the Ahl al-Bayt (literally, "people of the house"), the immediate members of the Prophet's family and their descendants.

In Husayn's time, there were not yet "Sunnis" and "Shiʿas" in the ways that we presently understand these categories, but the slaughter at Karbala nonetheless marked a defining event in the division between Sunni and Shiʿa traditions. Schisms and factional infighting within the Muslim community, sparked by the initial crisis of Muhammad's death in 632, cost numerous lives, including that of Ali; in 680, these divisions reached a devastating apex in the slaughter of Ali's son and Muhammad's grandson, a moment from which the long-lost unity of Muhammad's movement never recovered.

Shiʿa Muslims would come to conceptualize an Imamate, a patrilineal chain of infallible and authoritative teachers, through whom divinely inspired guidance could continue to instruct humankind. These Imams were not prophets, since the history of prophethood was believed to have concluded with Muhammad's mission, but nonetheless had special access to transcendent knowledge. The first of these Imams was Ali, followed by his son Hasan. Husayn would be recognized as the third Imam. Husayn's son Zayn al-ʿAbidin, who survived the battle of Karbala, became the fourth Imam, Zayn's son Muhammad al-Baqir was the fifth Imam, and so on, the Imamate passing between fathers and sons, all tracing their descent to Ali and Fatima through Husayn. The Ithna ʿAshʿari tradition, constituting the largest Shiʿa community, recognizes twelve Imams in all. Keeping with the motif of Muhammad's family enduring repeated torment under governments entrusted with preserving Islam, Shiʿa tradition remembers each of the Imams as having been mistreated by ruling powers, jailed, deceived, and even poisoned. The twelfth and final Imam (Mahdi), who disappeared as a child in the tenth century, still lives in a metaphysical stasis and will return near the end times to fill the world with justice as it had once been filled with tyranny.

Between the martyred Imams and other members of the Prophet's family who suffered at the hands of rulers and their armies, the Shiʻa calendar is filled with holidays to mark the suffering of the righteous. Commemorating sites and events associated with Husayn, Ali, and the Prophet's family more broadly became a significant element of popular piety, particularly for communities at odds with the caliphate. As any act of oppression by the rulers could trigger memories of Karbala, the graves of the Prophet's family members and martyred Companions offered salient sites for devotion as well as protest. Mourning for Husayn became both a private act of reflection and a public expression of grief for a world in which such brutal injustice was even conceivable. As Husayn's great-grandson Jaʻfar as-Sadiq famously stated, "Every land is Karbala, and every day is Ashura." The Karbala paradigm, as described by Syed Akbar Hyder, offers a view of history in which injustice and oppression are the normative condition of the world, and the truest marker to distinguish the oppressors from the righteous is their degree of love for the Prophet's family.[9] To love God is to love the Prophet of God; to love the Prophet is to love the people whom the Prophet loved; to act on this love is to identify with the oppressed. The experiences of the Prophet's family are mirrored in the senseless violence enacted upon innocent people all over the world and in every era. Particularly in modern representations, Muhammad's persecuted family members become stand-ins for all those who suffer under corrupt power, and none of them more than Husayn, the paradigmatic hero who sacrifices himself while fighting to make a more just world. Those of us who become compliant witnesses to oppression, recognizing injustice in the world but taking no action that might risk our own safety, security, and comfort, however, reenact the cowardice and compromise of the people of Kufa, who initially pledged their allegiance to Husayn but ultimately gave in to the government's intimidation.

Karbala and Liberation

Karbala, Vernon Schubel explains, operates as "simultaneously the site of a particular historical tragedy and the location for a metahistorical cosmic drama of universal significance."[10] Karbala's significance as a central site for both the historical and metahistorical can be observed in the ways that Shi'a Muslims render its power "ritually portable," connecting to Karbala and the events of Ashura. One mode through which these linkages occur is the *turba*, the small clay disk used by Shi'a Muslims in prayer. During the *sajdah* portion of the prayer, in which Muslims touch their heads to the ground in prostration, a Shi'a Muslim would touch his/her forehead to a turba made from the soil of a holy site associated with the Imams, often Karbala. To participate in what many Muslims would regard as a foundationally Islamic act, the fulfillment of the five daily prayers thus becomes inseparable from consciousness of the blood that Husayn spilled at Karbala. To worship God and remember God's mercy and justice is to remember the brutalities visited upon God's beloveds and the suffering innocent.

The identification of Husayn with a universal, timeless resistance against oppression and tyranny finds instant resonance with modern struggles against colonialism and inequality. Mahatma Gandhi made reference to Husayn's courageous stand at Karbala during his first salt march, drawing from the Ashura narrative as a liberation mythology.[11] Makhdum Muhiuddin, a communist Indian poet, refers to Husayn in his elegy for Dr. Martin Luther King, Jr., following King's assassination. "This is not just the murder of one man," Muhiuddin writes. "This is the murder of truth, equality, nobility. . . . This is the murder of the alleviators of oppression." Muhiuddin goes on to recast King's martyrdom in both Christian and Muslim terms: "This is the murder of the Messiah, this is the murder of Husayn." In Muhiuddin's vision, every land indeed becomes Karbala—not only America itself, but also lands touched by American power: in opposition to the Husayn-like King, he depicts the hands of a sinister Yazid-like power at work in Sinai and Vietnam.[12]

The most prominent linkage of Husayn's impossible fight at Karbala and the ongoing struggle for liberation found expression in 1970s Iran, during which the symbols and narratives of Shi'ism fueled a mass uprising against the oppressive Pahlavi regime. As the Shah banned popular observances of Ashura, he unintentionally repositioned the performance of Shi'a piety as an act of resistance against the state. Moreover, the Shah's attempt to prohibit Ashura observances—while simultaneously producing a long record of human rights abuses and violent suppression of dissent—unwittingly played into established narratives of Shi'ism, in which the lovers of the Prophet's family are consistently targeted by tyrants and self-serving hypocrites. When the Shah sought to literally criminalize expressions of love for the Prophet's grandson, it only fed the Ayatollah Khomeini's comparison of the Shah to Yazid. As Khomeini naturally played the role of Husayn to the Shah's Yazid, intellectual Ali Shari'ati formulated a vision of Karbala that wove together the primary strands of resistance in 1970s Iran: popular Shi'ism and Marxism. In Shari'ati's articulation, Husayn became a hero of revolutionary class struggle in very modern terms, positioned comfortably among the likes of Che Guevara.

As a paragon of the righteous martyr who stands up to corrupt and unjust powers and knows that speaking the truth will cost him his life, Husayn has also been linked to a martyred icon of American Muslim history and the Black freedom struggle, Malcolm X. Some American Shi'a Muslims suggest that through his friendship with a Shi'a scholar, Malcolm became exposed to the story of Karbala and drew direct inspiration from Husayn's example.[13] In his masterful biography of Malcolm, Manning Marable speculates that Malcolm even anticipated his own assassination as a Husayn-like performance, "a passion play representing his beliefs."[14] Writing on my 2004 visit to Malcolm's grandson in prison, I described Malcolm as "America's Imam Husayn, so holy that his family tree could only be doomed to never-ending distress and torture, tragedy and atrocity one after the other until the Son of the Brilliant Fulfillers comes to set it right."[15] Reflecting upon the various tragedies that surrounded Malcolm's family both before and after his own martyrdom—his mother having fair skin due to her own mother having been raped by a white man, his father murdered for preaching Black nationalism, social services splitting up his family, his brother's descent into mental illness, his daughter's struggles, his widow's death in a fire set by their twelve-year-old grandson—the suffering of the Prophet's family appeared as an intuitive lens. Following his release, Malcolm's grandson, Malcolm Shabazz, later followed in his grandfather's footsteps with a pilgrimage to Mecca. While the elder Malcolm died as a Sunni Muslim, Malcolm Shabazz embraced Shi'ism, perhaps with a sense of his grandfather as America's Husayn. He died tragically in a street fight in Mexico City, reportedly while visiting the country to protest on behalf of Mexican laborers in the United States. For Malcolm Shabazz's ambitions both in political activism and Muslim community building, not to mention his family's history, some regarded him as an assassinated voice of resistance alongside his grandfather and great-grandfather. Whatever the circumstances of Malcolm Shabazz's death might have been, Ashura's significance as the timeless, transhistorical stand-in for all injustice provided an instant framework for giving meaning to his loss.

In one African American Muslim community, the suffering of the Prophet's family at the hands of unjust rulers connects directly to the modern Black freedom struggle. The Ansaaru Allah Community (AAC), originating in 1960s Brooklyn and proliferating throughout the 1970s and 1980s, portrayed Muhammad as a Black man whose message and power were appropriated after his death by "pale Arabs" under the leadership of Abu Bakr. In this retelling of Muslim history, Ali and Fatima are persecuted not only as members of the Prophet's family, but also as Black people subjected to a premodern "pale Arab" protoracism. The AAC, which constructed links to transnational Black Islam through ties to the Sudanese Mahdiyya tradition, claimed that Ali and Fatima fled persecution in Arabia and sought refuge in the Sudan. The oppression of the Prophet's family remains linked to the oppression of Black people, according to AAC pamphlets, as the "pale Arab" Sunni kingdom of Saudi Arabia promotes its own hegemonic vision of Islam among African American Muslim communities, who adopt Saudi-centered practices instead of aligning with global Black Islam and the love of the Ahl al-Bayt. Though not explicitly identifying as a Shiʿa community, the AAC wove the tragedies of the Ahl al-Bayt with the tragedies of modern white supremacy into a singular narrative: claiming a Sunni identity, denying the significance of the Prophet's family, and disdaining the heritage of Blackness for conformity to "pale Arab" norms and practices become triangulated as a single package of injustice and destruction.[16]

In the identification of the Ahl al-Bayt with the oppressed, modern Muslim intellectuals formulate Husayn's "political failure" as a "spiritual success," as Omid Safi explains: "Part of the ethical teaching of Shiʿism is to confront humanity with its failure to stand up: the failure to stand up not just for the historical Husayn but for all the Husayns of the world."[17] The spectacular theatricality with which Husayn offered his body to the spears, swords, arrows, and hooves of the caliphal army created a lasting critique of unjust state violence. Husayn, writes Safi, "understood the power of a soul force confronting the brute power of a cold military," and for his strategic sacrifice, achieved a "moral power" that has persisted throughout history.[18]

Husayn's life and death defy the impulse toward triumphalist narratives, in which victory on the battlefield would signal God's endorsement. The Sunni triumphalist narrative surrounding the early community, in which Muslims emerge as underdogs from a marginal region to not only achieve victory in their locale of the Hijaz but also build a world-conquering empire against incredible odds, falls apart at Karbala. Yet in the slaughter of Muhammad's grandson, God sides with the helpless and dispossessed, granting only temporary victory to the tyrants. Awaiting the arrival of the Imam Mahdi, Husayn's tragedy demands that we recognize the Ashuras happening all around us in our present age, acknowledge our ethical failures, and strive to make a better world.

Ashura Practices and Remembering Karbala in the United States

In Shi'a traditions, commemorating Ashura takes many forms. Shi'a Muslims perform dramatizations of the events or weepingly retell the story, visit the graves of Husayn or other Ashura martyrs or relatives of the Prophet, or perform in processions with elaborately constructed floats and replica coffins and tombs. Communities come together to hear sermons and lamentations, during which the grieving of both the reciter and audience become more vocal and intense as the narrative of suffering escalates.

The mourning and memorializing of Husayn's sacrifice take place not only on the date of Ashura itself, but throughout the first ten days of Muharram, with each day's observances highlighting particular events or heroic figures: it was on the second day of Muharram, for example, that Husayn's camp arrived in Karbala, and on the seventh day that Yazid's forces cut off Husayn's access to water. At an assembly (*majlis*) that I attended on the sixth day, attention was focused on Husayn's nephew Qasim, who was only fourteen years old when he was killed during the Ashura battle by a blow from behind.

Shi'a Muslims have also observed Ashura through public performances that involve embodied expressions of grief, including *matam*, the rhythmic slapping of one's chest, as well as acts of self-flagellation and cutting with chains and sharp blades. Debates over proper forms and limits for these practices became particularly prominent within Shi'a communities from the start of the twentieth century. An opponent of these acts, Sayyid Muhsin (d.1952) considered flagellation to be an unacceptable innovation that strayed from authentic Shi'ism.[19] The late nineteenth and early twentieth centuries were marked by the rise of modernist reformers in various religious traditions, who sought to distinguish what they regarded as the authentic cores of their religions—necessarily in harmony with particular notions of civilizational progress and scientific rationality—from what they perceived to be inauthentic, irrational, and superstitious distortions. In this context, some Shi'a Muslims found practices such as beating one's chest or whipping one's back with blades to be a source of embarassment for Shi'as in particular and Muslims more broadly; amidst modern reimaginings of "traditional" gender performance, even public weeping for Husayn was seen by some as a poor reflection of Muslim masculinities. As bloody images of Husayn's mourners wielding chains and blades proliferate in contemporary media, Ashura becomes an occasion for Sunni-Shi'a antagonism over what constitutes authentic Muslim practice. While some Shi'a Muslims articulate defenses of these practices against Sunni criticisms, others distance the cutting and whipping from their own notion of authentic Shi'ism. In answer to debates among Shi'as regarding the appropriateness of Ashura grieving practices, Ayatollah Ali Khamenei issued a verdict in 1994 that the use of weapons upon one's own body to draw blood was Islamically prohibited. In his ruling, Khamenei argued that when such behaviors were supported and carried out in public, they not only harmed the bodies of participants, but also threatened "great injuries . . . to the reputation of Islam."[20]

Controversies over the appropriate modes of expressing one's grief for Husayn also reflect what Frank J. Korom calls a "tension between so-called high and low culture on the level of ideology and practice," which finds expression "through interpretations of Muharram wherever it is practiced."[21] These tensions become particularly relevant in the American context, in which Muslims must contend with an Islamophobia industry that represents them as excessively violent, barbaric, and antimodern, and anti-Muslim media can use the images of Ashura observances to fuel a narrative of Muslims as fanatical and bloodthirsty. The tension between "high" and "low" culture also plays out in terms of the demographics of American Shi'a communities: Iranian immigrants to the United States prior to 1979's Islamic Revolution, for example, tended to come from upper-class families with varying educational and economic backgrounds and complex relationships to the state Shi'ism that would later take hold under Khomeini's Islamic Republic.[22] Meanwhile, Shi'a immigrants from Sunni-majority countries such as Pakistan or non–Muslim majority nations such as India, having experienced persecution for their religious identities, may relate differently to Ashura observances than exiles from a context such as Iran in which Shi'ism undergoes reconstruction as official state ideology.[23] Varying socio-economic contexts of diasporic communities likewise play a role in the gendered observance of Ashura, that is, the ways that Ashura constitutes a gendered performance that comes with different expectations for women and men, and the ways in which American Muslims construct these observances for themselves.[24] A number of factors, therefore, inform the possibilities for what will constitute U.S. Shi'ism and its marking of Ashura.

In U.S. Shi'a communities, it is exceedingly difficult to find a setting in which Ashura observances include the spilling of blood. My personal efforts to find such practices led only to uncommitted speculation about where cutting or flagellation might occur. At an Ashura observance in New York, I did witness two teenaged boys lightly flailing themselves with short chains in front of an assembly, but the chains had no blades and the boys were wearing thick sweaters. Outside the mosque at which the observances took place, some Ashura observers chose to donate blood at mobile Red Cross banks that had been organized by the community.

The practice of giving blood at Ashura, adopted by many Muslims not only in the United States but also internationally, reflects a reading of Ashura's performative actions—the loss of one's blood in recognition of Husayn—in conversation with the ethics of compassion and justice exemplified by Husayn's sacrifice. Community members were also encouraged to make charitable donations with the reminder that Muslims can contribute to charitable organizations even if non-Muslims are likely to be the recipients. Husayn, after all, did not ask people to confess their religious identities before he offered them charity, and he even shared with the soldiers who had been sent to kill him.

Ayatollah Muhammad Husayn Fadlallah, head of Hezbollah, suggested blood donation as an alternative practice; echoing Khamenei's ruling, a doctor at a Hezbollah-run hospital in Lebanon complained, the practice of ritual self-harm "gives a very backward image of Islam and we have to move away from that."[25] For James W. Wilce, these changes in discourse and practice call attention to what he calls "Shia modernity," a globalized Shi'ism in which transnational media drives ongoing negotiations over religious authenticity and authority.[26]

As illustrated by Ashura observances, American Shi'ism reflects a series of encounters and exchanges: points of intersection between Shi'as and Sunnis; between American Shi'a Muslims and a broader "Muslim world," specifically transnational Shi'a networks; and also between American Muslims and a broader American cultural landscape in which public expressions of Muslim identity are inevitably scrutinized by hostile media for evidence of Islam as essentially violent and incompatible with American life.

Attention to both the regional varieties and transnational networks present in observations of Ashura highlights the conceptual tensions between Islam as a "world religion" and notions of pluralized, distinct "Islams" such as an "American Islam." Neither the imaginary of a monolithic "world religion" nor the idea of isolated, self-contained, and utterly unique variants can adequately paint the full picture of Ashura in its global and local dimensions.

Conclusion

Practices surrounding Ashura become important expressions of identity, moments at which boundaries are drawn—or bridges are built—between Shi'as and other communities, both Muslim and non-Muslim. Though Sunnis have frequently taken part in Shi'a commemorations of Husayn's martyrdom (perhaps even calling into question the categorization of such practices in some contexts as distinctly "Shi'a"), modern revivalist trends often seek to more rigorously police the borders between Sunni and Shi'a practices. In the modern world, Ashura and other sacred days of the Shi'a calendar sometimes become points of conflict and communal violence between Sunni and Shi'a communities. Like-wise, in South Asian contexts, the participation of Hindu communities in Ashura observances meets opposition from voices on both sides that seek to uphold an impermeable barrier between Islam and Hinduism. Historically, that barrier has often proved permeable, perforated, and unstable. Scholar Syed Akbar Hyder recalls an Ashura commemoration in Hyderabad at which a Hindu man expressed his devotion to Husayn by walking on hot coals, and two Hindus present explained that Husayn and his brother Hasan were *devatas*, incarnated gods.[27] While expressing love for Muhammad's grandson within such a framework might offend many Muslims, this Hindu reformulation of Husayn demonstrates the capacity for the Ashura narrative to transcend religious boundaries and even the constraints of formal theological systems. However, as with the case of contemporary Sunni-Shi'a conflicts, modern Muslim revival-isms and Hindu nationalism often force intensified divisions between Muslims and Hindus, building new walls to purify each tradition from corruption by the other. While many Hindus continue to take part in Ashura observances, Ashura has also been an occasional site of hostility between Muslim and Hindu communities.

In the U.S. context, Shi'a communities articulate their identities not only in conversation with larger Sunni communities but with the land-scape of American religion at large, meaning that practices surrounding Ashura have to deal with prejudices from both non-Shi'a Muslims and America's non-Muslim majority. Inseparable from the political conflicts that contributed to the Sunni-Shi'a schism, Ashura calls attention to old wounds and long-standing tensions between Sunnis and Shi'as regard-ing the history of the earliest Muslim community. Ashura, therefore, can become an occasion for sectarian polemics and apologetics. Beyond debates between Muslim communities, Shi'a Muslims also contend with American Islamophobia. Images of bloody mourners or Shi'ism's popu-lar association with Iran can be employed by anti-Muslim media to de-pict American Shi'as (and Muslims in general) as violent fanatics who seek to destroy the United States from within. While Shi'as around the world engage questions of how to properly express their love for Husayn, the meaning of that love or at the very least its political consequences are inevitably influenced by the distinct setting of the United States.

NOTES

1 The following section on the zakira was written by Danielle Widmann Abraham. For more on the experiences of Shiʻa women in the United States, see Bridget Blomfield, *The Language of Tears: My Journey into the World of Shiʻi Muslim Women* (Ashland, Oreg.: White Cloud Press, 2015).

2 Diane D'Souza, *Partners of Zaynab: A Gendered Perspective of Shia Muslim Faith* (Columbia: University of South Carolina Press, 2014), 32.

3 Matthew Pierce, *Twelve Infallible Men: The Imams and the Making of Shiʻism* (Cambridge: Harvard University Press, 2016), 69.

4 Fred Donner, *Muhammad and the Believers* (Cambridge: Harvard University Press, 2010), 99.

5 M. Plessner, "al-Muḥarram," in P. Bearman et al., eds., *Encyclopedia of Islam*, 2nd ed. (Brill Online, 2016).

6 A. J. Wesnick and P. H. Marcais, "'Ashūra," in P. Bearman et al., eds., *Encyclopedia of Islam*, 2nd ed. (Brill Online, 2016).

7 A. J. Hussain, "The Mourning of History and the History of Mourning: The Evolution of Ritual Commemoration of the Battle of Karbala," *Comparative Studies of South Asia, Africa and the Middle East* 25, 1 (2005): 78–88.

8 Syed Akbar Hyder, *Reliving Karbala: Martyrdom in South Asian Memory* (Oxford: Oxford University Press, 2006), 140.

9 Ibid., 44.

10 Vernon James Schubel, "Karbala as Sacred Space among North American Shiʻa: 'Every Day Is Ashura, Everywhere Is Karbala,'" in Barbara Daly Metcalf, ed., *Making Muslim Space in North America and Europe* (Berkeley: University of California Press, 1996), 186–202.

11 Hyder, *Reliving Karbala*, 170.

12 Ibid., 162.

13 J. A. Morrow, "Malcolm X and Mohammad Mehdi: The Shiʻa Connection?" *Journal of Shiʻa Islamic Studies* 5, 1 (2012): 5–24.

14 Manning Marable, *Malcolm X: A Life of Reinvention* (New York: Penguin, 2011), 430–433.

15 Michael Muhammad Knight, *Blue-Eyed Devil: A Road Odyssey through Islamic America* (New York: Soft Skull Press, 2006), 211.

16 Isa Al Haadi Al Mahdi, *Hadrat Faatimah (AS): The Daughter of the Prophet Muhammad (PBUH)*, vols. 1 and 2 (Brooklyn, 1988).

17 Omid Safi, *Memories of Muhammad: Why the Prophet Matters* (New York: HarperCollins, 2009), 256.

18 Ibid.

19 Frank J. Korom, *Hosay Trinidad: Muharram Performances in an Indo-Caribbean Diaspora* (Philadelphia: University of Pennsylvania Press, 2003), 43.

20 James M. Wilce, *Crying Shame: Metaculture, Modernity, and the Exaggerated Death of Lament* (Hoboken: Wiley-Blackwell, 2008), 125.

21 Korom, *Hosay Trinidad*, 43.
22 Mary Elaine Hegland, "Women of Karbala Moving to America: Shi'i Rituals in Iran, Pakistan, and California," in Kamran Scot Aghaie, ed., *The Women of Karbala: Ritual Performance and Symbolic Discourses in Modern Shi'i Islam* (Austin: University of Texas Press, 2005), 200–227.
23 Ibid.
24 Ibid.
25 Wilce, *Crying Shame*, 125.
26 Ibid.
27 Hyder, *Reliving Karbala*, 172.

6

Milad/Mawlid

Celebrating the Prophet Muhammad's Birthday

MARCIA HERMANSEN

A group of Indo-Pakistani American women gather at a private home in San Diego, California. White sheets are spread on the floor and the aroma of fried and spicy cooking lingers in the air. Small booklets entitled "The Greater Birth Ceremony" (*Milad-e Akbar*) comprised of Arabic invocations and poetry and prose narrations in Urdu are distributed among the small group of about twelve women.[1] Some participants who have the vocal talent melodiously recite Urdu *na'ats*—hymns of praise in honor of the Prophet Muhammad as well as poetic verses that commemorate females in his immediate circle—his mother, "Bibi"[2] Amina, and his wet nurse, "Dai"[3] Halima. "Dai Halima—a moon is waxing in your lap" is just one line from a well-known religious song (*qawwali*).[4]

The booklets are opened and selected readings from the birth narrative of the Prophet are shared. "When she became pregnant with him his mother saw a light shining out of her by which she saw the castles of Busra in the land of Syria."[5] At the conclusion of the ceremony all the women stand in unison with hands folded across the chest and heads slightly bowed in reverence and chant the "salam," a performative mark of devotional Islam in South Asian countries such as India, Pakistan, and Bangladesh: "O Prophet, peace be upon you, O Messenger, peace be upon you, O Beloved, peace be upon you, peace and blessings be upon you." The women quietly embrace tenderly in the aftermath of this shared communal moment. A meal is spread out and the opening chapter of the Qur'an—"al-Fatiha"—is read over the food to be consumed with hands outstretched, palms facing upward in a gesture of supplication.

The terms "milad" and "mawlid" refer to birth celebrations and are originally Arabic words.[6] Public milad[7] festivals are held in many Muslim cultures to commemorate the birthday of the Prophet Muhammad. Since he is said to have been born on the twelfth day[8] of the third Islamic month, Rabi' al-Awwal, celebrations and ceremonies are generally held throughout that month. The Islamic calendar is about eleven days shorter than the solar calendar and therefore the date of the Milad month is somewhat earlier each year. In some Muslim countries the Prophet's birthday is a public holiday and at this time streets and parks may be decked with streamers, colored lanterns, or otherwise illuminated. During this period television programming in countries such as Pakistan may feature special performances of poetry and music in the Prophet's honor. In venues such as private homes, Milad sessions may take place any time throughout the year, as they are thought to convey blessings and protection upon hosts and participants alike. Thus Milads are "holy days"—in the sense of celebrating and marking sacred time, but they are not necessarily tied to specific moments or calendric periods. In this sense they span the genres of holidays and prayer.

A Milad ceremony is a focus of devotional piety and may be scripted or free form. The "scripts" for Milad rituals may consist of books of devotional poetry, biographical anecdotes of the Prophet and his family, and prayers prepared especially for use on these occasions. Milads may be segregated, convened exclusively for males or females, and female Milads may give special attention to remembering Amina, mother of the Prophet.

In public spaces Milads may entail processions. Muslims in some of the larger U.S. communities such as Chicago or Jersey City[9] may therefore celebrate Milads by marching in the streets of their towns or gathering in rented banquet halls where children and youth holding green banners or flags and emblems in the colors of various Sufi orders may process toward the stage. This is a time for males to don their special headgear, consisting of colorful caps and turbans, which perhaps signal respect and humility in sacred space. In some cases the colored turbans or special shaped caps may signal affiliation with a particular Sufi mystical order or to a contemporary Islamic movement such as Dawat-i Islami,[10] or they may even suggest that the wearer has some elevated rank in a Sufi order. In some cases female attendees have their own sessions and speakers convened in separate rooms, or they may join the collective assembly for all or part of the event while seated in a separate area or behind the male attendees.

In private homes a temporary ritual space may be created by spreading white sheets on the floors and burning incense so as to create a mood of sacredness. Special foods may be prepared and consumed and in larger public Milads these alimentary treats, designated by the Persian word for sweets, "shirini," are distributed at the conclusion to be taken home by attendees. They may consist of small packages of South Asian sweets such as laddus (sweet rice or gram flour balls) similar to those distributed when a baby is born, or they may contain small sweet rolls.

In the United States Milads may feature chanting and recitation of poetry and homiletic speeches, or they may resemble academic conferences. Some Milads may be mounted to promote intra-Muslim harmony by including Shi'a and Sunni guests and presenters or they may encourage interfaith understanding by inviting non-Muslims with the goal of providing positive information about the Prophet as a role model. Other Muslim groups such as the Isma'ili community or the Gulen movement in the United States have in the past convened intra-Muslim and interfaith Milads, possibly as part of a strategy to establish themselves among the broader constellation of American Muslims and also as a component of outreach to non-Muslim neighbors. In the context of recent controversies surrounding Muslim sensitivities about honoring the Prophet, Milads also offer the opportunity to educate non-Muslims about the positive aspects of Muhammad's character and actions.

The Prophet Muhammad is a central element of Muslim faith and along with the Qur'an—the divine word of God revealed through him—the Prophet is a primary shared element across diverse sectarian, regional, and historical articulations of the religion. At the same time, divergent appreciations of the figure of the Prophet and how to understand and practice Islam according to one's view of who he was may become litmus tests for internal differentiations and variations across Muslim piety. In summary, the content and performance of Milads are malleable according to diverse contexts and forms. They may be occasions for promoting unity within and across Muslim communities but may also be contested or received in divisive ways.

Who Is the Prophet?

Just as Christians vary in their appreciation of the significance and role of Jesus, Muslims likewise exhibit a range of approaches to appreciating the role of Muhammad. Among Muslims who espouse mystical or devotional attitudes to the religion the Prophet may be conceived of as a cosmic being whose existence is coeternal with creation itself or may have even preceded it, as in the hadith appreciated by Muslim mystics, "I was a Prophet when Adam was still between water and clay."[11] The Prophet is even on occasion presented as the cause for creation itself, as in the hadith reporting God's words: "If not for you (O Muhammad) I would not have created the universes," or he may be identified with an eternal cosmic Muhammadan Light (*nur Muhammad*).[12]

While Islamic theology certainly recognizes the exceptional nature of Muhammad's character, concepts such as the "sinlessness" of the Prophet or his role as an intercessor for Muslims and even for all of humanity may be embraced to varying extents and interpretations across cultural and sectarian differences. The more austere perspective among Muslims ranging from modernizing reformers to textual literalists such as Salafis and Wahhabis understands the Prophet to have been a great historical messenger who conveyed the divine word, reformed and established a religious community, and passed away having fulfilled his role. A major sin in Islam is known as "shirk" (associationism) which entails attributing to any person or object, powers or reverence that should rightly only be the purview of God. However, a more cosmic understanding of the Prophet as a being endowed with supernatural powers and knowledge and expecting the Prophet to intercede for believers on judgment day are views held by many Muslims. Other Muslims feel that such a level of veneration leads to a possible conflation of the Prophet with the divine and therefore reject all ideas and practices that might reinforce such understandings.

In many Muslim contexts these differences expand and harden from being individual proclivities to becoming sources of theological or ritual conflict. In Muslim South Asia, specifically the Indian subcontinent, over the past several centuries, differences about the scope of the Prophet's role and his religious significance have blended with other historical and sociological factors into what might be considered sectarian subdivisions within Sunni Islam. The major groups in this debate are known as the Barelvis,[13] Deobandis,[14] and the Ahl-e hadith,[15] representing the range from the most cosmic and devotional views of Muhammad to the more puritanical and austere emphasis on the historical Muhammad as a guide and example, but certainly not a supernatural being. Among new generations of American Muslims these distinctions have become less salient and are largely unknown. Within immigrant Muslim circles, however, celebrating Milads may constitute a visible way of expressing one's position along this spectrum of views.

History of Milads

In terms of the debates over legitimacy, both the concept of celebrating the birth of the Prophet and the details of the performance need to be anchored in some sort of "Islamic" precedent.[16] The Qur'an and the Sunna, usually defined as the practice of the Prophet himself, are the major criteria for this. Thus, opponents of celebrating Milads argue that such events do not have a qur'anic foundation and that neither the Prophet nor his early Companions commemorated his birth through any ritual.[17] The proponents of Milads, in response, cite the qur'anic verse affirming that "God and his angels send blessings on the Prophet" (33:56) and the historical incident where a Companion of the Prophet, the poet Hassan ibn Thabit, recited poetry honoring Muhammad during the latter's lifetime.

The "birth" aspect of celebrating the Milad, some scholars believe, emerged as Islam expanded to environments dominated by Christianity, under the influence of celebrations of the birth of Jesus. This, of course, would not argue for its Islamic legitimacy but simply explain its origin as a birth commemoration in cultures where this already existed. Other scholars trace the first public Milads to Shi'a communities, including the Isma'ili Fatimid dynasty in Egypt (969–1171 C.E.), among whom veneration of the Prophet and his descendants was an important component of piety and ritual expression.[18] In the Arab world today, Milads/Mawlids are primarily celebrated in societies where Sufism holds some popular influence and the birth of the Prophet may be celebrated as a public holiday.

Milad at Home

On auspicious occasions Milads may be performed in a celebratory way to acknowledge blessings received and to create an atmosphere conducive to further spiritual and material benefit. A young professional Pakistani American family had established itself and recently constructed an impressive home in a posh northern suburb of Chicago by the shores of Lake Michigan. Therefore the first Milad held in the new space also functioned as a house-warming ritual. There were about fifty persons in attendance, evenly divided between males and females.

The Milad was officiated over by a senior male immigrant from India who, like many others in greater Chicagoland, has ties to the city of Hyderabad. This individual and in fact his entire family profess a strong background in devotional and scholarly pursuits and are known for holding monthly Milads and *Burda sharif*[19] ceremonies at their residence. The family of the presenters also possesses a *mu'i mubarak*, a relic consisting of hairs (head or beard) of the Prophet which is strategically displayed during more important ritual occasions.[20]

Female attendees were accommodated in an upstairs living room equipped with a flat-screen TV and speaker connecting to the basement where the men were gathered. The males performed; the females observed and listened during the Milad ceremony. The evening ceremony began about ninety minutes after the announced time with a young teacher of Qur'an recitation at a local Islamic school reciting Qur'an and then offering some brief preparatory remarks. Many of the male attendees involved directly in the Milad performance were dressed in white *thawbs* (long Arab-style robes) augmented with tasteful, high-quality Kashmiri shawls and turbans.

The teacher presented some homiletic remarks taking off from a hadith, or saying of the Prophet Muhammad, that "Allah bestows but the Prophet distributes,"[21] which became the theme of his devotional oration. Such a statement would be highly contested by some Muslims since it presents a cosmic role of the Prophet in managing human affairs beyond his historical function as a guide and social reformer. The speaker also mentioned the benefits of the supplications of one's Sufi spiritual master (*du'a* of the Pir). This marks the intended audience as a group assumed to be at least familiar with, if not actual participants in, traditions of mystical Islam. Certainly not all supporters of Milads are Sufis, but Sufism in particular is amenable to devotional appreciations of Muhammad.

These remarks were followed by an exposition of the *salawat ayat* (verses about supplication for the Prophet) of the Qur'an that devolved into an argument that sending blessings on the Prophet (salawat) is a customary practice of God himself and thus a customary practice (sunna) of Allah. The Sunna (customary practice) of the Prophet Muhammad based on his preserved sayings (hadith) and actions is the second normative source for Muslims after the Qur'an itself. The concept that Allah also has a habitual and normative way of acting (sunna) is qur'anic, as in "You will not find any alteration in the Sunna of Allah" (35:43). Here the practice of sending blessings on the Prophet is further reinforced as legitimate by being associated with God himself.

The speaker next veered into a grammatical explanation, noting that the verbal form "yusalluna" in Arabic means that *all together* offered praises, as in the qur'anic verse "Allah and his angels send salutations" (33:56). Thus Allah is giving us the great blessing of following the same practice that He himself performs in praising the Prophet. This, of course, establishes the Islamic nature of praising the Prophet both generally and also specifically through celebrating the Milad. Anchoring this practice in the qur'anic injunction attempts to legitimize it against Wahhabi or puritan criticisms that a ceremony such as a Milad is a heretical innovation (bid'a).

The speaker then explained the history of a devotional poem in praise of Muhammad called the *Burda* (Ode of the Mantle)[22] that was to be recited as part of this Milad to an audience whose familiarity with that text was not assumed. In fact, there was a slightly apologetic or defensive element to the exposition, since the idea that the poem carried a special spiritual benefit needed to be established in Islamic terms. The historical background to the poem *al-Burda* (The Mantle) includes the life story of its composer, the Egyptian Sufi poet al-Busairi (d. 1294), in particular his illness in which he was afflicted by paralysis and had a dream in which the Prophet Muhammad appeared to him, cured him, and presented him with a cloak or mantle (burda). In Islamic traditions, dream apparitions of the Prophet Muhammad are taken very seriously. The speaker reminds the audience that while the Shaytan (devil) can take on almost any form in dreams, even God's form, he cannot take on the form of the Prophet. This claim, in fact, is itself established by a hadith.

How to recite the *Burda* performatively was also covered in the speaker's remarks, in particular with reference to specific verses in the poem recited for their curative powers.[23] The presenter explained that there is a special way to perform these verses, which is to recite them, then blow on one's hands and rub them over the body in order to effect internal and external purification and healing.

The collective recitation of the *Burda* was performed aloud by the males in the assembly who could refer to small booklets in Urdu, Arabic, and even transliterations into the Roman alphabet distributed among them. Some attendees knew the poem by heart although they did not understand the Arabic language in which it was composed and recited. Some of the women turned to a *Burda* app[24] on their cell phones that allowed them to follow along, mouth, or even chant the words as the recital progressed. A small drum (*daff*) was beaten to accompany the rhythm of the rhyming verses.

The recitation of one section of the *Burda* took about twenty minutes and was followed by a talk in Urdu explaining the Islamic legitimacy of venerating relics based on qur'anic proofs—in this case an example was cited of the Ark of the Covenant that, according to some Islamic accounts, was lost and desecrated and then returned. The other example given to explain the Islamic legitimacy and benefits, even curative benefits, of relic veneration was the use of the cloak of Yusuf (Joseph) to cure his father, Jacob's blind eyes (Q 12:93). These justifications functioned as a prelude to a special feature of this particular Milad ceremony—an opportunity for the visitation (*ziyarat*) of a relic, a hair of Muhammad himself.

The proper attitude and comportment (*adab*) of the visitation ritual (zirayat) can be explained through an idea of synecdoche—the part becomes as the whole so that when a person comes into the presence of the hair he or she can feel and behave as if the Prophet himself is present. In the presence of the hair one is to demonstrate reverence by remaining standing and acting as if one is in a royal audience (*darbar*). Because the back should not be turned to the hair at any time, one exits the room facing forward. The idea of proper comportment (adab) in Muslim tradition is both religious and cultural.[25] Muslim ritual practices such as prayer (*salat*) entail elements that are absolutely required for its performance to count, and other elements that are desirable or preferred. These desirable aspects of attitude or comportment are known as "adab," while more generally the concept of adab is also associated with politeness and propriety. For example, before performing religious rituals in Islam, entering a mosque, or participating in a ceremony such as a Milad, Muslims would be expected to ensure that they were in a state of ritual purity by performing the ablutions known as *wudu*. Visiting a relic of the Prophet is a way of connecting with his presence and embodied practices and attitudes are embraced by those who participate. The practice of visiting (ziyarat) sacred sites such as the Holy Cities of Mecca and Medina, Shi'a shrines, or the tombs of Sufis are part of Islamic ritual and are believed to impart religious and spiritual benefit. Which sites should be visited for religious purposes is not universally agreed upon. While there is consensus on the holy cities of Mecca, Medina, and Jerusalem, sites or shrines beyond these three may not be shared across sectarian and interpretive communities. In this case the practice of visiting the hair was augmented by ingestion—drinking holy water which had been brought from the Meccan well of Zamzam whose properties were enhanced by the immersion of a rose petal that had touched the hair itself. The water should be drunk while standing and facing Mecca, the direction of ritual prayer known as the *qibla*.

The men performed the visitation first. Then came the women's turn. The hair was displayed within a special glass case set on a large table in the study of the home; there was a small receptacle filled with what looked like hardened brown mud in which the hair had been embedded. Two magnifying glasses were provided because in fact the two hairs in this relic were very small and curved around near the surface in which they were embedded. They were very fine, more like hair clippings than beard hairs. The women all faced the front of the room and approached the hair one at a time, perhaps to give a sense of private communication or audience. There was silence, and some women quietly wept after seeing the hair because they were so moved by the experience.

On the left side of the room was suspended a flat-screen TV where a loop of images presented tasteful backgrounds consisting of abstract calligraphic renderings of religious phrases interspersed with photos of the Prophet's mosque in Medina. Meanwhile, in the background one heard a revolving track of phrases conveying blessings on the Prophet chanted in a soft modern style, thereby creating a devotional ambiance. The blessed water was served in clear little Arab style tea glasses and quietly sipped after visiting the hair.

The smell of Pakistani curries began to waft through the home as a meal was heated and brought out and served buffet style. Dinner was followed by open mic recitations of melodious poems in praise of the Prophet by the male attendees that were piped to the women upstairs through the video connection.

Milads with a Message

Many mosque congregations do not permit the celebration of Milads, either due to the theological opposition of the leadership or to concerns that holding the ceremonies might stir up division or controversy among members holding divergent interpretations of the religion. Alternative spaces for American Milads are therefore banquet halls, community centers, rooms rented in hotels, university auditoriums, and even chapels.

For the past several years, Muslim chaplain Tahir Umar Abdullah has convened a Mawlid at the University of Chicago Rockefeller Chapel. This space was also regularly used by the Muslim students on campus for Friday prayer services. In 2016 about two hundred persons, both Muslim and non-Muslim, with a preponderance of college-age participants, gathered in the chapel. For the last several years the Mawlid month (Rabi' al-Awwal) has fallen in the depth of Chicago winters, and participants may have had to navigate snow banks and freezing rain to arrive at the various sites. The gothic architecture and somberly shining pipes of the chapel organs conveyed an appropriate solemnity and spirituality, as did some lingering whiffs of frankincense. Many attendees were young couples seated together, including families with younger children. The crowd was ethnically diverse with many African American participants and even some Chinese students and other diverse Hyde Park community members.

The female Muslim university chaplain from Northwestern, Tahera Ahmad, opened the gathering with recitation from the Qur'an. This was followed by the guest musicians, the Firdaus Ensemble from Spain, who performed Andalusian style instrumental and vocal music, in this case songs in praise of the Prophet.[26] The audience held up cell phones and iPads to capture the moment. One number was especially introduced as a Mawlid song, "Nur al-huda wafana." Some lines in translation were:

> The Light of Guidance has come!
> His splendor, it revives us,
> Meeting him honors us,
> Lord lavish blessings on him.[27]

Despite the fact that the songs were in Arabic, the performers appeared to be Europeans who had converted to Islam.

The messages communicated by various aspects of this Milad were inclusion and interfaith dialogue, intercultural and interracial encounter and engagement, and social relevance. The flyer billed the event as "an evening of poetry, song, and salutation in honor of the birth of the Prophet Muhammad." The University of Chicago Mawlid programs over the past several years had consisted of diverse Muslim speakers reflecting on the meaning of the Prophet according to annual themes: the light of the Prophet, connecting to the Prophet, and "The Prophet: A Mercy to the Worlds!" and so on.

For example, a 2016 speaker, Ustadh Ubaydullah Evans, was a young African American teacher from the Chicago Muslim community. He began his talk with a reflection on love for the Prophet, which he described as "visceral." "What is the way of the Prophet, or sunna?" he rhetorically asked, asserting that it was "considering the other," in contrast to what he described as "sunnamania." This he illustrated by his recollection of "seeing a guy putting on eyeliner in the *masjid* (mosque) in order to imitate the Prophet." After all, Evans reflected, the example set by the Prophet was care for the forgotten and marginalized and Allah was not a "rigid taskmaster."

Along the lines of Sufi or Barelvi devotionalism to Muhammad, Evans recounted the belief that the Prophet physically returns the salutations (*salams*) of the believer even from the grave, for Muhammad is returned to his body in order to do this. He exhorted the audience, stating, "Understanding this is transformative. What we need to do is orient ourselves to the fact that he [the Prophet] is present and spiritually involved through our calling on him. The Prophet constantly implores God to forgive his community."

In summary, there was both a Sufi and an American quality to this Milad/Mawlid. The entertainment was multicultural and, Islamically speaking, liberal, in the sense that there were female performers, Qur'an reciters, and speakers, musical instruments were used, and the space in which the Milad was held was neutral, not specifically a mosque or Islamic center, while the seating was not gender segregated. The musicians used instruments, including stringed and wind instruments in their performance and one heard the female voice raised in song, prayer, and qur'anic recitation, in a public and authoritative way before a mixed-gender audience. This would not have been acceptable among more strict Muslim communities that shun any instrumentation other than the use of percussion, and consider female vocal participation in mixed public contexts to be forbidden.

The themes and messages conveyed at the University of Chicago Milad were the contemporary social relevance of the Prophet's life and teachings, his merciful nature, and intra-Muslim cultural and racial diversity, including prominent roles for African and African American speakers and, on some occasions, food. For example, in 2015 one speaker was Sokhna Rama Mbacke, great-granddaughter of the famous Senegalese Sufi Ahmadu Bamba, while the refreshments were catered by a local Senegalese restaurant. The University of Chicago Milad speakers and their messages were located in both an American and global political reality. For example, in 2014, shortly after the Charlie Hebdo killings in Paris, Muslim sensitivities about the Prophet could hardly be ignored, and the convener and several speakers condemned the attacks while emphasizing the merciful qualities of the Prophet.

Conclusion: Milads and Changes in U.S. Islam

As immigrant Muslim communities took root in various regions of the United States, ceremonies such as Milads were mainly held in private homes. During the 1970s global Islamization took hold and led some congregations to exclude local traditions such as Milads from their mosques since Islamist groups such as the Arab-based Muslim Brotherhood or the South Asian Jamaat-i Islami, which were influential in many large Islamic organizations in America, considered Milads to be heretical. As part of this trend ethnomusicologist Regula Qureshi observed the gradual

replacement in her community in Edmonton, Canada, of female virtuos-
ity and the performance of poems and songs of praise to the Prophet by
women silently participating in group readings of the Qur'an.[28]

During the 1990s a revival in the public celebration of Milads took
place in the Chicago area, spearheaded by the Naqshbandiya Foundation for Islamic Education,[29] a group of Indo-Pakistani immigrant professionals who favored Sufism and Barelvism. Participants in the revival
of Milads felt that these rites had been unfairly excluded from many
mosques dominated by ideological factions and imams who espoused
Deobandi or Islamist interpretations that rejected such rites as inappro-
priate innovations (bid'a). These new Milads were celebrated in banquet halls or neutral spaces such as the auditorium of the University of
Illinois.

Other groups such as Dawat-i Islami, followers of Pakistani Qadri
Sufi leader Muhammad Ilyas, have taken the Milad public with street
processions in recent years. For example, during one procession on
Devon Avenue, heart of the South Asian diaspora in Chicago, a group
of some thirty South Asian males of various ages dressed in white shalwar kameez and green turbans and carrying banners and placards in
English, Urdu, and Arabic marched while loudly chanting "*marhaba ya
Mustafa*" (welcome to the Prophet). This alarmed some passersby who
had no context for the ritual and might have understood it as an aggres-
sive political demonstration by Taliban-like figures. The signs in English
bore messages such as "What Is Islam: Justice for All," "What Is Islam:
Religion of Peace," "What Is Islam: Believe in All Prophets," indicating
that the purpose of the march also included a broader Islamic public
outreach, beyond its role as a Milad.

Some South Asian Muslim shopkeepers along the route seemed to
appreciate the boldness of this public display and spontaneously began
handing out water bottles and fruit juices to the marchers. A lone South
Asian female attempted to tag along behind the procession and I joined
her—to the chagrin of the leader of the group, who almost pleadingly
invited us to segregate ourselves by having a seat in a car that was slowly
driving alongside the group carrying some women family members.
After a few blocks the caravan descended into the basement of the
Bombay banquet hall where an exclusively male audience listened to
speeches in Urdu.

Quietly and gradually more devotional and Sufi-inspired practices such as celebrating Milads have returned to American Muslim communities in new forms in recent years. For example, the recitation of the *Burda* poem may be engaged in by children attending Islamic schools. The online social media initiative "Celebrate Mercy" that commenced in 2010 allows participants to log on in real time to participate in commemorations of Muhammad's life by well-known Islamic speakers.[30] A local initiative known as the Chicago Mawlid Committee[31] sponsors an Internet and social media campaign augmented by periodic events in private homes, auditoriums, and some Islamic centers where speakers focus on the role of the Prophet and performers chant *nashids*, poems of praise and supplication with no instrumentation. Rather than presenting poetry in the Arabic language only, there is an increasing tendency to incorporate English translations of these hymns of praise or to compose original English works, sometimes using genres such as rap, popular among youth.

In conclusion, Milads/Mawlids among American Muslim communities have proven resilient in adapting from smaller ethnic gatherings to broader public and social media events that engage a new, younger, and more multiethnic audience in the United States and globally. At the center of these developments is the figure of the Prophet Muhammad himself. Although maligned by Islamophobes and according to some opinions marginalized, at least in his spiritual dimension, by Muslim modernist reformers and puritans, his image continues to attract and unite new generations of Muslims with an evolving yet perennial appeal.

NOTES

1 *Milad-e Akbar* by Muhammad Akbar Warsi, Shaykh Ghulam 'Ali, Lahore, n.d. This work is briefly discussed in Marcia Hermansen, "Translation (from Urdu) and Introduction to *Milad-e-Akbar*, a Popular Religious Text from South Asia," in *Religions of India in Practice*, ed. Donald S. Lopez (Princeton: Princeton University Press, 1995), 367–372.

2 "Bibi" or "lady" is an honorific title in Urdu used before female names.

3 "Dai" literally means midwife in Urdu, although Halima's role was that of a nursemaid.

4 The poetic words of this song, translated, are found at www.oocities.org. Accessed July 23, 2016.

5 This miraculous narration is found in an early biography of Muhammad composed by Ibn Ishaq. While not accorded the status of hadiths, such popular

reports circulated in the texts developed to accompany Milad celebrations. See Marion Holmes Katz, *The Birth of the Prophet Muḥammad: Devotional Piety in Sunni Islam* (London: Routledge, 2007), 31.

6 In many Muslim societies *mawlid* is the term used for celebrations of local Sufi saints' death anniversaries.

7 *Milad* is the term more commonly used in South Asian communities and *mawlid* in Arab ones.

8 Shiʿa tradition holds the date to be the 17th of the same month.

9 Photographs taken at this Milad are available at "Milad Parade and Ceremony Held in Jersey City," www.nj.com. Accessed July 30, 2016.

10 Dawat-e-Islami is a pietistic movement that was founded in Pakistan in 1984 by Maulana Ilyas Qadri, a Barelvi, a Sunni scholar.

11 A longer discussion of this and other reports of this nature and their presence in the development of Milad/Mawlid traditions may be found in Katz, *The Birth of the Prophet Muḥammad*, 12–15.

12 A number of reports and traditions connected to the cosmic understanding of Muhammad are discussed in Katz, *The Birth of the Prophet Muḥammad*, 15–29.

13 The term "Barelvi" is derived from the name of a scholar considered to have laid the intellectual foundations of this school of interpretation, Ahmed Raza Khan of Bareilly (d. 1921), a city in northern India. This term is usually used by outsiders, those of this persuasion preferring the term "Ahl-al Sunna" which means "People of the Sunna," i.e., Muslims who follow the practice of the Prophet.

14 This group takes its name from a famous religious school, the Deoband madrasa of northern India, established in 1866. While allowing some more mystical interpretations, the Deobandis are critical of what they consider to be excessive veneration of the Prophet or the incorporation of practices that do not have an Islamic basis according to their views. Deobandi-trained scholars dominate many South Asian Muslim mosques and communities in the United States. For a Deobandi set of opinions that elements of Milad ceremonies do not have precedents in the practice of Muhammad and his Companions, refer to islamqa.org. Accessed July 23, 2016.

15 Literally, "the People of the Hadith," a relatively smaller group of South Asian Muslims who advocate a strict literalistic interpretation of the Qur'an and hadith. They eschew mystical elements and practices that they consider innovations or excessively devotional. In this way they resemble the Wahhabi and Salafi interpretations of Islam that originated in the Arab world but have global influence.

16 See a detailed discussion of this in Katz, *The Birth of the Prophet Muḥammad*.

17 See for example, "Why Mawlid-un-Nabi Is Bid'ah," www.youtube.com/watch?v=GPnh8tyxofy, accessed July 14, 2017.

18 Katz, *The Birth of the Prophet Muḥammad*, 1–5.

19 Recitation of an Arabic poem *al-Burda* (The Mantle) in honor of the Prophet. This poem will be discussed in more detail later in this chapter.

20 Ian G. Williams, "Relics and 'Baraka': Devotion to the Prophet Muhammad among Sufis in Nottingham, U.K.," in *Reading Religion in Text and Context: Re-*

flections of Faith and Practice in Religious Materials, Elisabeth Arweck and Peter Collins, eds. (Aldershot: Ashgate, 2006), 65–82. See also Y. Meri, "Relics of Piety and Power in Medieval Islam," *Past and Present* (2010) 206 (suppl 5): 97–120.

21 Al-Bukhari hadith collection, Volume 4, Book 53, Number 346.

22 A detailed source on the *Burda* in the context of the Arabic poetic tradition is Suzanne Stetkevych, "From Text to Talisman: Al-Busiri's Qasidat al-Burdah (Mantle Ode) and the Poetics of Supplication," *Journal of Arabic Literature* 37, no. 2 (2006): 145–89.

23 *Burda* Part V:
26. "Nor was any Prophet accused (of lying when) giving knowledge of the unseen.
27. His miracles are (completely) clear, not hidden from anyone.
28. Without it justice cannot be established amongst people.
29. How often has his hand granted freedom (cure) from disease by (his) touch.
30. And set free the insane from the chains (fetters) of insanity."

24 itunes.apple.com and for Android play.google.com

25 Barbara Daly Metcalf, ed., *Moral Conduct and Authority: The Place of* Adab *in South Asian Islam* (Berkeley: University of California Press, 1984).

26 The Firdaus Ensemble performs as part of the annual evening of poetry, song, and salutation in celebration of Mawlid. Based in Granada, Spain, the ensemble draws upon classical European style, with influences from Celtic and Flamenco traditions, and from the rich heritage of traditional Sufi music from Arabic, Andalusian, and Turkish sources (Mawlid flyer 2016). Pictures from the 2014 Milad are available at the University of Chicago. See also, firdausensemblesufimusicgroup. blogspot.com. Accessed July 30, 2016.

27 This translation of "Nur al-Huda" was located at jumacircle.com. Accessed August 1, 2016.

28 Regula B. Qureshi, "Transcending Space: Recitation and Community among South Asian Muslims in Canada," in B. D. Metcalf, ed., *Making Muslim Space in North America and Europe* (Berkeley: University of California Press, 1996), 46–64.

29 Apparently still one of the largest sources of Milad videos on YouTube. Jonas Svensson, "ITZ BIDAH BRO!!!!! GT ME??—YouTube Mawlid and Voices of Praise and Blame," in *Muslims and the New Information and Communication Technologies: Notes from an Emerging and Infinite Field*, Thomas Hoffmann and Göran Larsson, eds. (Dordrecht: Springer, 2013), 89–111.

30 This initiative may be followed at www.celebratemercy.com. Accessed August 1, 2016.

31 www.chicagomawlid.com. Accessed July 15, 2016.

PART III

Life Cycle Rituals

7

Birth Rituals

Welcoming a Child into the World

MARIA F. CURTIS

This chapter examines birth rituals practiced by Muslim American families living in the United States while focusing on various ethnic communities, some new immigrants and some not. The emphasis in scholarly literature tends to be on immigrant communities and to point out the strain of immigration and the longing for past traditions and places.[1] This contribution instead asks: What do Muslim American families do to welcome new children into the world, in what ways are they actively creating meaningful birth traditions, and how does taking part in the quintessential American baby shower blend with previously established and conventional Islamic birth rituals, practices, and traditions? These were among the questions asked via a survey and ethnographic interviews aimed largely at Muslims living in the greater Houston area, now considered America's most diverse city.[2] Muslim Americans appear to thrive in the celebrative traditions surrounding childbirth and child raising, enjoying those traditions that are "all American" as well as traditions that have been passed down from their families who may hail from all reaches of the globe. Furthermore, the traditions seem to go far beyond the mere materiality of objects collected at baby showers, as these celebrations become spaces where interfaith and intrafaith cultural exchanges occur. Whether it is sipping a chilled cinnamon and clove sherbet drink (*Lohusa Şerbeti*) spiced with toasted pine nuts from a tulip-shaped glass as one would on the Aegean coast of Turkey, or sharing a fragrantly spiced goat stew followed by a traditional coffee ceremony as one would in East Africa, or nibbling on lacey pink and blue French-inspired pastries from a Lebanese American bakery, Muslim Americans—despite their great diversity—all singularly uphold the

Islamic notion that raising a child is one of the most important things a human being might do in his or her short time on earth.

Between the Dugger clan's "19 Kids and Counting," America's most notorious megafamily, and the almost constant celebrity baby news seen at the grocery stand, Americans are presented with heteronormative models of family at every turn. The megafamily meets its megastore in places like Babies "R" Us where expectant parents are encouraged to ask for long lists of baby items in personalized baby registries. In this sense, Muslim Americans are no different from all other Americans in their pursuit of raising children and building families and feeling the subtle and not so subtle socialization that urges them to seek fulfillment in parenthood; the Abrahamic cultural logic of "go forth and multiply" is pervasive in American society. Whereas Europe has an overall decreasing population, American birth rates continue to stay constant and the idealized notion of an American family may not be so unlike an Islamic one.[3] While "the child" is highly sought after, how one celebrates its arrival may vary a great deal from family to family. Muslim Americans embarking on the sacred journey of becoming a parent often turn to the Qur'an, the Hadith, and of course their parents and elders when preparing spiritually, mentally, and financially for the arrival of their children.

Participants in the survey on American Muslim birth traditions were asked to comment on what traditions came to mind when they thought of how newborn Muslims are welcomed into the world by their families and communities.[4] Among the traditions[5] to which they were prompted to respond were the recitation of *adhan* and *iqamah*, the purchasing of special clothing, *ghusl* for washing newborns, shaving the newborn baby's hair as a measure for giving charity, giving *aqiqah* and *sadaqah* as forms of charity to one's community, the practice of circumcision for boys, the process of naming the child, widespread thoughts on breastfeeding, how to and from whom to seek knowledge about parenting, the social role of visiting and baby showers, forms of support given to new mothers, and how to handle miscarriage and preterm delivery. Lastly, participants were asked to reflect on how they thought traditions had changed over recent generations.

Preparing for Pregnancy

Islam is a religion based to a great extent on an awareness of *niyyah*, or intention. Many participants commented that preparation for parenthood began long before the birth of the child, even before conception, and that they had internalized their niyyah for wanting to become a parent and to take on the responsibilities, joys, and potential hardships that would unfold on their journey. Concentrating on sincere prayer and expanding one's Islamic knowledge and restraining from consuming non-halal foods were ways to prepare the body for conception and to ensure the best future life for the child. Like many non-Muslim Americans, many Muslim Americans too have deeply held beliefs about what foods should be consumed while the baby is in the womb and developing. Muslims strive to be more halal in all they eat and consume, hoping to improve the overall nutritional content of their diets and to be more mindful and aware of what they put into their bodies. This concept of halal extends beyond food, careful consideration being given to the ingredients in skin care products and household cleaners, and preference given to purchasing organic items free from harmful chemicals. For many, the first ritual may relate to creating a body that is healthy and ready to conceive a child.

Throughout the survey, participants echoed the sentiment that a compatible union between spouses was the most important step to becoming a successful parent. Mohammad, a Jordanian American, explained: "Being a great parent starts from choosing the right life partner. This is the most important responsibility for every single man or woman from the start. Following the Qur'an and the Sunnah to build a family will lead to a healthy family structure." Similarly Mehmet, a Turkish American father of four children, explained,

> People go through a lot of pain and years of dedication to be doctors, teachers, engineers but they hardly take any time to learn to be mothers, fathers, or parents. This is very unfortunate and creates many of our social problems in our communities. That's why parenting doesn't actually begin with the birth of a child but rather while seeking a suitable spouse. My wife and I believed the preparations of having a child started even before the marriage.

He went on to say that how one earns a living, or "sustenance" as he called it, also impacts the health of the marriage and the development of children. When one is right with the world, interacting with others in a fair and just manner, one's social interactions come back to reward one, blessing the family with happiness and serenity. Choosing a pious and devoted spouse was like investing in an "insurance policy" and ensuring a successful marriage and happy and pious children. He added that even in the most intimate exchanges with a spouse, one is enacting God's will, and intentions and devotion will manifest in the family.

A Turkish American professional working mom of four children, Ebru, described the preparations for becoming a parent as follows:

> We should read parenting books in the American way and in the Islamic way go to seminars or training sessions on this topic before being a parent, even get educated about marriage before getting married. We should always get opinions of other parents that have more experiences with the same kind of family backgrounds and beliefs.

Echoing Mehmet's sentiments, she said, "How you behave to your children will automatically be reflected from your children. They gain everything from the people they live with automatically." She explained that it is in loving interactions with our children that they are taught to love and respect their parents, and that the cycle of caregiving will shift from parent to child as the children will ultimately look after their aging parents. She concluded with a small prayer, saying, "May Allah not test us with bad experiences with our children and family."

Erin, a convert to Islam of French Canadian Louisiana Creole background, commented most directly on the physical preparations needed for Muslim pregnancy and childbirth: "I read American parenting books, attended prenatal classes, and read about breast-feeding. I also recited passages from the Qur'an, read/repeated special recommended prayers for a healthy and pious child and easy childbirth, and listened to the Qur'an so the baby could hear it in utero." Taken together, these comments from Muslim American parents demonstrate that marriage, childbirth, and the ongoing attainment of Islamic knowledge are three important pillars that support their understanding of the meaning of family.

Beliefs about Managing the Birth Experience Itself

In hospitals today, new parents have multiple ways to let doctors, nurses, and staff in medical settings know about their religious preferences and there are ways to easily bring Muslim American ideals and practices into the delivery room. Just as all American couples consider to what degree they want faith and medical intervention to guide their birth experiences, so too do Muslim Americans meditate on what is most healthy for both the mother and the newborn. Meryem, a white American convert, described her experience of preparing for birth and motherhood:

> We read books about labor and aftercare. I decided that I wanted to have as close to an intervention free birth as possible, I took the example of Mary [the mother of Jesus]. I ate lots of dates, attended natural birthing classes with my husband, and did my research. I had two kids born at home, one with a midwife, one without. One hospital birth with a midwife. No drugs and all natural with all of them. I prayed a lot during labor and recited certain Duas over and over. I imagined Mary. I would have loved to have had a Muslim doula or midwife. I did have one Muslim midwife at my first homebirth.

Meryem's comments are not surprising given that there is a chapter of the Qur'an dedicated to the miraculous birth of Jesus; indeed the chapter is dedicated to Mary herself. Mary, or Maryam as she is called in Arabic, is seen as an ideal mother in the Islamic tradition, strong and self-sacrificing. One of the most common names for Allah found in the Qur'an is "ar-Rahim," or "the beneficent," a name derived from the Arabic word for womb.[6]

Aliya, who grew up in Texas and is of East African, Persian, and Indian Isma'ili background, commented further on the multiple forms of Islamic devotion that can be relied on to manage the pain and fear that accompany childbirth: "I didn't request a Muslim Chaplain for guidance in the hospital. However, my family was praying for me and I supplicated to Allah during labor and delivery prep and before going in for a C-section." Further reflecting on her own birth experience vis-à-vis those of her ancestors, she told me that her maternal great-grandmother had been from Mombasa, and that she was a midwife, a doula. She had been a healer tending to all those in her village and specialized in delivering babies. Aliya said, "She used astrology, herbs, prayers, and her hands as a midwife. She would follow the Islamic lunar calendar, and used the new moon cycles to pray for *barakat* [blessings], health and happiness, as well as to assist with the healing of someone's ailment." Parallel to Meryem's desire to have a birth free of medical intervention, Maria, a mother of six children, said, "My parents are from Bolivia, and they are very proud of natural labor and breast-feeding and natural medicine is widely practiced. Natural birth is growing within the Muslim community whereas before even my Muslim doctors thought I was an extremist for not wanting to use drugs during labor."

Adhan and *Iqamah*: The Newborn's First Sounds

Despite the far-ranging ethnic, racial, economic, and educational backgrounds, and the varying sectarian perspectives of those who took part in this study, there was wide consensus on most topics, most notably on the importance of the adhan and iqamah at birth. The adhan is the Muslim call to prayer that is issued from the minaret of the mosque five times a day, and the iqamah comes after the adhan, instructing Muslims to line up in congregational prayer. In addition to the adhan and iqamah, new parents may also recite important passages of the Qur'an into the newborn baby's ear. New parents hope that hearing foundational passages from the Qur'an along with the call to prayer right after birth helps put the infant on the right path in life. Of all those who participated in the survey, only one sought out the Muslim chaplain in the hospital where her children were born. All others said the father or an elder family member recited the adhan, iqamah, and passages of the Qur'an. Most often it was the father who did this, because other male family members were unlikely to be near the mother so soon after delivery. Some also said they purchased fresh, not dried, dates and let the newborn suckle on them momentarily with the idea that the baby was breaking its fast just as Muslims break their fast during Ramadan. After the baby is cleaned up and bathed, like ghusl ablutions taken before praying, they are immediately suckled, as breast-feeding is another foundational birth and child rearing practice.

Meryem said that when her four children were born their father recited the adhan and iqamah, along with their chosen name for the baby, and followed up with the taste of a date in the baby's small mouth. Rebecca, a white American convert of Quaker background, noted that she herself did the research and informed her Turkish Muslim husband about the recitation of the adhan and iqamah for their two daughters' births. Aysha, originally from Central Asia, also concurred, "Adhan is an absolute must." Seher, an Indian American medical doctor, further articulated, "The recitation must be done in the right ear." Mehmet elaborated on his experience with his children's births, "In our case I did the adhan and iqamah in the room where our children were born every time facing the *qiblah* direction [the direction toward which all Muslims pray]. We requested from the doctor to hand him/her [to me] as soon as they finished their first checkup so this is done right away and the first sound the child hears in this world is the Greatness and Oneness of God." Although considered an important rite, only one participant elaborated on the ghusl, or the washing of the baby after birth. Sukaina, a convert of mixed European and American Indian descent, explained,

> In our birth plan that we gave to the doctors, nurses, and staff in the hospital before the birth we explained that we were Muslim and that ablutions are very important and symbolic for us. We explained that my husband would assist in washing our daughter after birth and he would be doing this along with the nurses. It was a very beautiful thing to watch, and also funny as my poor tired husband had no idea how to manage a newborn! It is one of my most favorite memories of him from our marriage. He was so tired after my long twenty-six-hour labor, but he did a great job. Later we went back to the hospital with our baby daughter to thank the nurses for their support and to give them little thank you cards and gifts.

Purchasing Special Clothing for the Newborn

Several participants commented on the importance of having special clothes for the newborn. Some new parents simply wanted the baby to be comfortable, while others wanted handmade items from their parents, and some commented on what not to wear. Meryem insisted that newborns should not be dressed in yellow or red. This caution is found in both Sunni and Shi'a sources and is understood to be a means of protecting the baby. However, Sukaina remembered her Turkish mother-in-law draping a yellow gauzy scarf around her sleeping daughter's head when she was suffering from colic. Others commented that yellow cloth might be placed around the head of babies with jaundice. Zeynep, a grandma whose grandchildren were born in Texas, claimed that for the first six months the child should only wear clothes purchased by family members to ensure the wealth of the child in the future. She said it was a tradition of her ancestors in the Caucasus that she wanted to pass on to her children and grandchildren. Aliya commented that she was not at all interested in clothes, and that she took baby books to the hospital to symbolize the passing on of wisdom to her newborn daughter. Maral, a Turkmen American who had lived in the United States since high school, noted that there were no special clothes, just something clean and new, fresh like the new baby.

Shaving the Newborn Baby's Hair

As a means of showing gratitude for the birth of a new baby, some Muslims shave the hair of newborns, weigh it, and convert the weight of the hair into the weight of gold. Once the value of the gold is determined, that precise amount is given as sadaqah, or charity to the poor. The "poor" can be defined as someone less well off than yourself. For Meryem, it was important that she did this for all four of her children. There was a wide range of opinion concerning when to do this. Some said it should be done on the seventh day, or the fourteenth, or the twenty-first day after the birth of the child. Maral said it was done on the fortieth day, a day when the baby's family and greater Muslim community typically have a communal feast to celebrate the birth. Seher said the head must be shaved by an uncle on the occasion of the large feast day, or aqiqah. Some parents claimed that shaving the head ensured a full head of strong hair which was a sign of health, and that they wanted to keep the hair of the newborn to cherish it. Mehmet explained, "We actually loved shaving the hair. It feels so unpredictable as all my children had a different amount of hair and sadaqa that was due was different as a result. I feel that this is one way Allah makes the family give thanks differently for each child," as a reminder that each child is a unique individual and therefore no one tradition or ceremony will ever be identical to the others.

Giving *Aqiqah* and *Sadaqah*

Like the practice of reciting adhan, nearly all who took part in the survey said they offered some form of aqiqah, a communal meal from the meat of a flock animal, and sadaqah, some form of charity, after the birth of their children. There was an emphasis on having large groups of guests, as the Islamic preference is to feed as many people as possible as a sign of generosity. Sometimes these festivities are held in mosques and in homes, and all those who offered their thoughts for this research said that Muslims and non-Muslims were invited to attend. Although visitors might bring gifts, they are not required to, as their attendance and participation are seen as an important expression of welcome and recognition of the new baby. Here the thinking is that the family is expected to extend the blessings of their child symbolically to the larger community, itself a public act of accepting Allah's hand in the miracle of birth and an acceptance of the seriousness of raising a child.

Lady G, a Nigerian American, said, "We had an aqiqah for each of my three children. It was a huge celebration, we fed about a hundred to a hundred and fifty people at the *masjid* [mosque]." Rebecca said, "I wanted to perform aqiqah. We did do it later, after the baby's fortieth day, as a donation and not a celebration/party." Maral explained that the "aqiqah should be given according to a family's financial possibilities," and that such festivities should not be extravagant. She continued, "My parents and my husband gave aqiqah for my daughter's birth. My parents had a small sadaqah back in Turkmenistan where they fed the needy," and a second more social event was held in Houston where friends were invited to officially meet the new baby in public for the first time. In addition to these two public occasions, Maral welcomed individual visitors to her home. She prepared special Turkmen food such as *manti*, a cross between ravioli and dumplings, which she served with Turkmen green tea. Visitors in turn arrived with gifts of food for the family in order to alleviate their need to cook for themselves.

Sister Zynab, originally from East Africa, said, "I have three children and I had aqiqah for all, Alhamdulillah [thanks be to God]." Melvin, an African American convert to Islam, explained, "We had no baby showers for my three kids, we had the aqiqah for them." An imam from a W. D. Muhammad mosque indicated that among them the welcoming ceremonies were less formal, the most notable event being when the new parents brought the newborn to Friday prayer to introduce him or her to the community. He explained that this could occur whenever the parents wanted it to, and that food may or may not be served at the mosque, while friends and relatives would certainly make home visits to take gifts and food for the new family. Saadiya, a Pakistani American from the Ahmadi community, stated, "I have two children. We don't have birthday parties but we celebrate religious events such as aqiqah and Qur'an completion [the Ameen ceremony] in a very big way."

Adding to the possible ways in which the aqiqah and sadaqah can be undertaken, Mehmet explained, "Aqiqah can be cooked to be served as a meal like aqiqah dinner or the meat can be donated uncooked to neighbors and friends. This traditionally should be done on the seventh day after the child's birth." Again explaining that each of the aqiqahs for his four children was different, he stated that a ram was the ideal animal to offer at an aqiqah because it served as a reminder of the story of the Prophet Abraham and his son Isma'il from the Qur'an.

Mehmet's wife, Aynur, was considered something of a saint among the Muslims in Houston. In addition to tending to the spiritual needs and development of her own four children, she organized countless baby showers, home visits, and prayer circles, and helped organize women's groups to systematically deliver meals for several weeks to new parents both to feed them and to interrupt any instances of postpartum depression. She taught Qur'an lessons to small girls until the end of her short life without letting on that she had been doing all this community work while privately battling cancer. At her funeral on a very gray and bitterly cold day in Houston, those of us women who had benefited from her quiet efforts stood arm in arm with each other, and hand in hand with our small children, looking on as she was lowered into the ground. Aynur was the first person with whom I left my own daughter so I could attend a community interfaith dinner when she was just three weeks old, and later Aynur recited Qur'an at her "fortieth day celebration," as we called it. My daughter always knew her as "the aunty who fed us and sang for me when I was a baby." As all the adults walked away, stunned to have lost such an important person in our lives, my daughter pointed out to us that Aynur had been buried next to the grave of a small child. It comforted all of us to think of her there, as if the presence of that small child next to our dear friend somehow made the day less sad, less gray, and less painful.

The Circumcision of Boys

In addition to the practices mentioned above, participants in this research with sons commented on the importance of the practice of circumcision. For the American Muslims surveyed here, circumcision for boys carries health benefits and is seen as a religious obligation. In countries outside the United States, a circumcision ceremony might typically occur later in a boy's life, and be a very festive occasion in which extended family members and friends are expected to participate. The procedure itself is mostly very private, while the festivities and celebrations are very public. In Morocco and Turkey I witnessed families of elementary-aged boys whose parents proudly feted the occasion in traditional clothing and held parties in public parks and public places, inviting community members to come and eat and dance and celebrate their son's first steps toward manhood. In the United States, however, circumcision appears to be done for the most part when a boy is very small and preferably still a newborn in the hospital. Most parents who shared their thoughts for this research explained that they wanted the procedure to occur in a hospital and their child to not remember the pain he had experienced. They felt that other celebrations are an inevitable part of the Muslim child's life, and that there would be other opportunities to celebrate the child when he was a bit older, around milestones such as memorizing portions of the Qur'an, or when he had finished reading the Qur'an in its entirety for the first time, or on the first day of school. While circumcision may not have been a birth tradition in previous times, it does appear to have become one in the American context. These were the sentiments of all American Muslims who commented on this study, regardless of age, the number of children, or ethnicity.

Naming the Child

Numerous Islamic traditions for childbirth among Muslim Americans span the Shi'a-Sunni spectrum, and agreement on the vital importance of selecting a sound and proper name for one's child appears to be among the most agreed upon of all. Names are chosen in consultation with community elders in the hope that offering a child a well-thought-out name bearing some connection to the greater Islamic heritage will place the new child further down the road to becoming a productive member of society. Indeed, it is hoped that one's children will live up to the full potential of their names. Meryem said, "Names should be something with a great meaning or related to a great person in Islam, given within the first seven days or on the seventh day." Aliya said she "put quite a bit of thought" into her child's name because she "believe[s] in the power of [the] word." Michelle, a Hispanic convert to Islam, underscored that the real reason selecting a name is of such great consequence is because "naming the child an appropriate name pleases Allah." Maria emphasized the importance of identity: "We chose blended names that honored both cultures, Latin and Muslim." Maral explained that in Turkmenistan "the whole family partakes in the selection and narrowing down the name," and the child might have several names, each one given by a different relative. Khadijah, a white American convert, said that "naming the child after a pious person or a name with a positive attribute" was paramount. Nene, whose mother was West African and whose father was African American, said in her family a name should carry "a good religious meaning from any of the Abrahamic faiths, and [be] selected by the time of birth." Saadiyah said she found names for her children by searching for Muslim baby names online. While most of this study's participants were women and most claimed that they had an important role in choosing their children's names, Mehmet offered a slightly different perspective:

> Giving a good name to the child is considered a father's duty and usually is done in consultation with the mother and elders in the family. When there is a disagreement usually multiple names are given. It's fairly common to ask a known religious scholar to name either the middle name or first name or sometimes the family names the child after a respected scholar. For girls usually the prophet's wives, daughters, women companions, or names and places in paradise as well as flowers are common. My father told me he named me after a well-known scholar of his time.

Breast-Feeding

Across all ethnic groups and ages, breast-feeding was seen as extremely important. Indeed, if medically possible, mothers are highly encouraged to breast-feed their children for long periods of time as long as it does not pose a threat to their health. Besides agreeing on this, there is a variety of opinions about how long a mother should breast-feed. The most common answer was two lunar years. Most Muslims agree that boys should be breast-fed longer because they are slower to develop. Most women said they had breast-fed their children for two years or more. All concurred that mothers could continue to nurse beyond the two-year period if they so chose.

Sukaina recounted a story about her difficulties breast-feeding her first child, a daughter who had severe acid reflux and colic, and whom she had a hard time nursing despite her determination and obvious interest in trying. Sukaina had been given some basic tips by nurses and lactation experts while in the hospital, and by a steady stream of friends who came to bring her food and gifts before she went home. She developed mastitis after being home for a few days, and she unexpectedly found herself in the middle of two very different conceptions of women's space and maternal rights. As a first-time mom, she received a lot of calls from Muslim moms wanting to visit and offer help. In between these calls she received a follow-up call from the hospital nurses who wanted to know about the breast-feeding. When she mentioned to the nurse that she thought she had mastitis, the nurse immediately sent over a lactation specialist who made house calls with medical-grade equipment that could be left in the home until the situation was resolved. Sukaina described the lactation expert as something of a superhero, an athletic figure reminiscent of both Billie Jean King and Inspector Gadget, quite literally wearing combat boots and a long black coat that flapped in the wind like a makeshift cape, and carrying breast pumps and other healing paraphernalia of the womanly arts over her shoulders. She entered quickly, not at all winded by the three flights of stairs she'd just climbed to get to Sukaina's door. She took Sukaina's temperature and diagnosed her problem as an advanced case of bilateral mastitis, and said that if Sukaina did not make progress soon she might need to be admitted to the hospital for more serious treatment.

Just as the lactation expert was unpacking her equipment and saying that Sukaina should not receive any guests for several days until she felt better, a large group of excited and determined Muslim moms appeared at the door with their small kids in tow and with enough food to feed Sukaina for the next three weeks. The lactation expert quickly shifted to zealot mode and began telling the women that they needed to come back at another time. This prompted Anessa, a Russian Turkmen former professional judo champion, to step forward. Sukaina could not contain her laughter when describing these two strong women facing off and asserting their respective ideals about maternal well-being and what one should do with oneself during this crucial postpartum moment. It was a contest between creating a quiet reflective healing maternal space in isolation with modern gadgetry or drawing on a large group of experienced moms with a network wide enough to provide ongoing daily support visits to see this situation through.

The judo champ prevailed, and within a few minutes the crowd was in the kitchen, scarves were loosened, overcoats and *abaya*s discarded in a mound, and sleeves rolled up. Then commenced a furious unpacking of food as saran wrap and aluminum foil flew, and the unpacking of a variety of home remedies from at least three continents where Muslim women had battled mastitis and won. All this in the name of getting Sukaina through her mastitis quickly to ensure that breast-feeding would not end prematurely as the result of this setback.

The lactation specialist demonstrated techniques, nursing positions, gadgets, and brochures for helplines and literature on why "breast is best," while the Muslim ladies looked on and nodded in approval and inserted an occasional setting-the-record-straight sort of comment into Billie Jean Gadget's well-rehearsed and well-meaning shtick. The judo champ and her crew took the said articles and wrapped them in stories of hope and persistence, served tea and lent Sukaina their shoulders to cry on. Sukaina went on to breast-feed a baby that weighed twenty pounds by the age of four months and was literally off all growth charts in terms of height and weight until she was a toddler. She continued to nurse until the day her seventeen-month-old daughter decided it was time to do something else.

Seeking Knowledge and Advice about Pregnancy and Child Rearing

Sukaina's story illustrates the strong bonds of friendship and the ways information is passed on from generation to generation, and from mom to mom. In addition to purely Islamic frames of reference regarding the family, Muslim American parents also reach for American classics such as Dr. Spock and those like him, and *What to Expect When You're Expecting*, to name just a couple. Muslim Americans create their own authentic emotional and spiritual frames that blend Islamic traditions from not only their own ethnic groups but from multiple Muslim cultural traditions. American mosques are often highly cosmopolitan spaces where congregants are literate in the traditions of their ancestors as well as the traditions of the families with whom they spend time within their larger congregations. Support and advice flow naturally in various contexts. All participants agreed that they pursued knowledge about being a "good" parent because they considered it a religious duty to perform their parental duties in the best possible way.

Fajarini, the Indonesian American daughter of a diplomat who had lived all over the world and later married a Mexican American with whom she had two beautiful daughters, said she "[m]ostly consulted with family members and close friends, Muslims and non-Muslims alike, and read up on all the popular parenting books." Atousa, an Iranian American married to an Azeri husband who had raised her daughter in Oman, Libya, and Sugar Land, Texas, explained that she was often "[r]eading American and Persian parenting books and sometimes consulting with family." Aliya said she read all the books she could, and particularly the Hadith (sayings and practices) of the Prophet Muhammad. She particularly loved his saying that Muslims should "seek knowledge even in China," which she understood to mean that when faced with a difficult task one should be open minded and look far and near until the right solution emerges, not always taking the easiest or most obvious path. When seeking advice on a particular matter she alternated between different forms of worship, hoping to receive knowledge from God through "prayer, *zikr, du'a, tasbih*." Dina, an Egyptian American married to a Syrian American doctor who lives near NASA, explained, "I saw my parents trying to educate themselves from both kinds of books, so I did as well." Michelle said that in addition to reading a variety of American parenting books along with Islamic books on parenting, she also felt it critical to teach her daughter about her and her husband's heritage. More than teaching their daughter about Islam, they also taught her about her maternal grandmother's Catholic faith and read her nursery rhymes and stories in Spanish, English, and Turkish in the hope that she would be multilingual and would be comfortable in all scenarios in her mixed American, Mexican, and Turkish family. Similarly, Maral explained that everyone blended knowledge in their own way depending on their own family situation and ethnicity: "I think everyone finds their own balance. I read books from different cultures: American, Russian, Turkish, and Turkmen." Mehmet echoed a similar interest in blending streams of knowledge, and emphasized that it was up to the Muslim parent to bring together both Islamic and scientifically sound parenting practices and medical decisions.

Supporting New Mothers and Infants in the First Forty Days of Life

According to prevalent Muslim tradition, the first forty days of a newborn child's life are its most vulnerable. Similarly, American pediatricians underscore the importance of the first six weeks of life. To protect the newborn baby from illness and harm, Islamic societies across the globe have well-developed beliefs and traditions that aim to protect both mother and baby as they adjust to their new lives. In previous times and in other geographic locations where women were less likely to work formally outside the home, staying at home under the care of elders and women neighbors and friends might not have seemed unusual. In the United States this practice appears to be taking on new shapes and forms, still prevalent but in slightly different ways. There was a great deal of ambivalence about this topic, some women longing for an idyllic all-woman space full of support and nurture, something they longed for as they returned somewhat reluctantly to work after giving birth. Other women felt isolated at home and needed more social interaction in order to overcome postpartum blues. First-time parents seemed to feel particularly strongly about this topic, while more seasoned parents tended to take things as they came. Fajarini said, in "Southeast Asia, the birth traditions are very communal, the mother is never left alone and would always have someone nearby to help." Meryem explained that "the forty-day *lohusa* phase [was one for] saying a lot of du'as [prayers] and praying against Nazar [evil eye, bad luck] on the baby." Rebecca said, "My husband firmly believed that I must stay inside for a full forty days after the birth and I had to do research to 'prove' to him that full seclusion was not religiously required." Yasemin, of mixed Turkish, Bulgarian, and Albanian ancestry, who grew up in Germany, said, "When the baby is born and at home, we invite family members and friends of the mom and have Qur'an recitation. The guests bring gifts for the baby and enjoy treats and beverages. Chilled cinnamon sherbet is a beverage specially prepared for this occasion."

Erin explained what she understood as the logic of forty days of seclusion from the Islamic tradition as being close to an American ideal of staying home "to rest, recuperate, and get the hang of being a new parent." She thought the two approaches shared a great deal in common, particularly that breast-feeding seemed to be so central to both. She explained that it was hard to establish strong breast-feeding habits if one did not have the time and space to devote to it, and that it was important to breast-feed for the sake of the baby's developing immune system.

Fajarini described the ways in which female kin viewed the recuperation of moms after birth: "On the island of Java, traditionally the women are encouraged to drink *jamu*—a medicinal herb drink with turmeric and honey to cleanse your system, and they also do belly binding or *bekung* to help moms gain their figure back. Sometimes this lasts up to forty days." Similar belly-binding practices were described by women from other backgrounds, particularly Latinas. Furthermore, this was something the elder women would help the new mother with, and it was to help her feel loved and cared for, an important aspect of self-care when early motherhood could be so demanding. Aliya discussed an Islamic practice also recommended by most Western medical doctors: "There were other cautions mothers were urged to take such as not to bathe [or be submerged in the bathtub] for seventy-eight hours after your child was born."

Karla, a Mexican American convert with a daughter and a son, described birth practices in her own culture, obviously longing for the female-centric spaces of her country:

My parents and relatives are all from Mexico, some from Spain that is what I know and I think our birth traditions were very American with a pinch of ancient Mexican culture. My favorite ancient tradition will be for moms to take care of themselves during forty days after the delivery, you only drink water that has been boiled in advance, you don't eat anything cold like ice cream or even watermelon. You could walk and go outside but only with someone else to assist you. You wrap your stomach tightly and eat very healthy food and this goes for the baby as well who is losing the cord blood and getting used to being "outside." All friends and family members take turns to help you [with] cooking, cleaning, and taking care of the baby so you do not have to do it.

FZ, from Tunisia, detailed specific foods that were eaten and offered to guests during visits to meet the new baby, "We have basically open house for many weeks for people to visit and congratulate. We make special desserts to serve for childbirth, usually a nuts, butter, and honey mix. And we drink coffee and tea, of course."

Two participants offered their thoughts on the more tragic side of pregnancy, the experience of losing a child. Miranda recounted that when she was several months pregnant she miscarried in her husband's family home in Palestine. There, if a baby dies after the fourth month, it is considered to have had a soul and to have been a fully developed person in the sense that it needed to be bathed according to Islamic funerary traditions (ghusl), given a name, and celebrated and mourned with an aqiqah meal. Women surrounded her and she recuperated as she might have done after a normal full-term birth. She recovered from the physical and emotional trauma of losing a child while also taking part in the funeral tradition, and finally burying the child in the family cemetery in Palestine. Aliya said, "The women in my family have a history of complicated pregnancies and stillbirths. Women were encouraged to play music, *qasida*s, read poetry, and pray for their unborn children" as a way to prevent miscarriage. She also said that similar exercises would continue after the birth of the baby to encourage plentiful breast-feeding. Sukaina mentioned miscarriages as God's way of giving mercy to the child and parents when the child might have been too ill from an unknown medical condition.

The Baby Shower and First Events to Celebrate the Life of a Child

Of the ten questions on this survey, no other question elicited as strong a response as did the question, "What are your thoughts on baby showers?" Some more recent Muslim American immigrants are uncomfortable with the idea of asking for items in a baby shower, as they fear it implies that their child will arrive in the world according to their expectations, with or without God's will. There is also a wide range of opinion on how early a baby shower should take place. "In sha' Allah [God willing], I would have my baby shower with the forty-day celebration after we read the Qur'an" was a common response and a commonsense blending of multiple traditions. The baby shower is largely for women, and organized by women who are already mothers, as a way of welcoming them into the experience that is motherhood. Religious studies scholar Gisela Webb reminds us that studies on Muslim women demonstrate a strong need to aid and support other Muslim women in a "Muslim way" (xi–xii).[7] As young girls become women, they want to help other young women by participating in the cycle of support from one generation to the next, which resembles the mutual-aid model of support that relies heavily on a multigenerational community presence.[8] The idealization of traditional female support and caregiving is applied broadly both within, and notably outside, the nuclear and extended families. Thus, a very traditional Islamic understanding of motherhood where women are largely in control of the homesphere[9] emerges in discussions of the "baby shower." Women described baby showers that seemed to be cross-pollinations of a women-only aqiqah and group visitations during the first forty days.

Mehmet, commenting on the childbirth choices he and his late wife had made for their four children, said, "I didn't know about the baby showers in American culture until I started working. My wife had some experience with her friend circle where we used to live before me. We actually liked it. But we didn't feel doing it before or after is mutually exclusive, rather they complement and complete each other." Meryem, who explained that talking about childbirth was "her passion," said, "I don't have strong feelings about it [baby showers]. I like the idea of a 'mother blessing' for motivation before the baby is born.

Baby showers are good with friends. I had a gathering after the birth and they read Qur'an, which was nice too." Lady G said, "We do baby showers before birth, and lots of other parties as well at other times." Each child is celebrated multiple times in multiple ways, some secular and some religious. Aysha enthusiastically said, "I am absolutely okay with a baby shower. It is just a support of your close friends and family before the baby is born. Moreover, it is sometimes more convenient to have things before the arrival of a baby. You have more time to arrange things needed for a newborn. And of course you can enjoy your time with friends."

Those who were not accustomed to baby showers in their home countries offered different reasons for how they came to appreciate them. Maria said, "I didn't have a baby shower until my fifth child because I used to think it was *haram* [forbidden]. But now I feel like it is no big deal. I have six kids. We make a big deal about Eid after Ramadan. We throw a party like a birthday party. Balloons, piñata, bounce house. Birthdays are very low key. Cake and that is it." Maral explained, "I did have a baby shower which is not a practice in my culture. I think baby showers are great and help the couple with getting ready. It is sometimes culturally considered to be a bad omen to celebrate the baby before it is born. However, like with everything in Islam, intentions are important. So if the intentions are to help out the young parents to get ready for the baby I think it's a great and practical thing." Friends with shared cultural traditions can have very different opinions, as is evidenced in Maral's friend Adilya, a Russian Tatar who studied in the United Kingdom and later settled in the United States. She said, "I don't support an idea of a baby shower prior to birth, and I think it's fine to have it after giving birth, giving an opportunity to see the baby and celebrate with friends and read some chapters from the Holy Qur'an and pray for the well-being of the baby and his/her family." Erin emphasized the need to make becoming a parent easier and expressed her support for baby showers: "I follow the American custom of a baby shower prior to the baby's arrival. By giving items like a crib, stroller, high chair, bedding and clothes, it removes the financial burden from the shoulders of the expecting parents and allows family and friends to participate in the pregnancy."

FZ (Tunisian) described how her perception of the baby shower had shifted in the twenty-five years since she had left Tunisia to live in the

United States, and also described additional festivities she organized beyond the birth of her daughters. "When I think of celebrations first of all I think of joy, family gatherings, love, food, gifts, sweets, blessings from God, giving sadaqa." She said that she was initially uncomfortable with having a baby shower but later came to understand it as a practical and helpful thing, even saying that "some of our Arab traditions and fears may actually contradict Islamic beliefs." She talked about other important firsts for babies that included the baby's first bath and tooth, saying, "We put gold in the tub to bring him wealth. When they get their first tooth out, we have a celebration where we hold a scarf over their heads and pour candies over the scarf."

Conclusion: How Traditions Change and Evolve

In conclusion, most participants in this study agreed that changes have occurred with regard to Muslim American childbirth traditions. There were multiple lines of thinking about why changes occur and what these changes signify. Because of the diversity of American society, Muslim Americans have become increasingly diverse as well. Some said that just as our workplaces and public spheres have become more diverse, so too are our innermost spheres: "The diversity of our public lives leaves an imprint on our internal circles as well." People appreciated both "the old" and "the new." Some claimed that we live in an increasingly commercialized world where our every experience may fall victim to a marketing scheme, and we might have a day dedicated to some rare, odd holiday or thing nearly every day of the year. Some, like Ebru, were skeptical about the impact American commercialization has on Muslim American childbirth rituals: "I believe young generations nowadays don't give large meals and read Qur'an and make du'as as much as before. People now usually exaggerate these celebrations, and too much money is spent. I see in Turkey they celebrate a baby's birth as if they have a wedding almost."

Others like Fajarini explained the shift in traditions as a consequence of the change in the social roles and status of working women. A working mom of two small daughters herself, she said, "Mothers are more independent now, they prefer to do things on their own and not rely heavily on other family members or friends." If we compare this statement to her earlier description of the women-friendly communities she had experienced in Java, we sense ambivalence in her thought. Meryem explained that she thought families relied more on their own ability to access multiple forms of information: "More information, videos, classes, stories, new research, trends, money, and the particular location of the mother." All these new sources of information made it easier for Muslim American moms to imagine realities that supported their own notions of what it means to be part of a family in today's world.

Aliya's comments about diasporic traditions are most telling. She reminds us of the forced diasporas experienced by some smaller groups such as the Isma'ilis. Whereas we tend to think of the diaspora as something new, she reminds us that people have always moved around and they have always carried their traditions with them, keeping what they can and keeping what serves them on their journeys. She said that she "practiced yoga, saw an acupuncturist, who helped align my meridians, or *nadis*, provided me with herbal connections to strengthen my uterus and help balance my hormones. I believed in his ability and our connection, I also said du'as and tasbihs, and took blessings from the elderly."

Participants also had varying theories about the "Islamic" nature of traditions. Dina, for example, said that people today are "not as adherent to Islamic practices. They became more traditional than religious." Conversely, Lady G said with great vigor, "We do ALL the traditions. . . . Recitation of adhan and iqamah, special clothing, ghusl, shaving the hair, aqiqah and sadaqah, circumcision of boys, piercing the ears, naming the child, and breast-feeding. We do all of the above." In contrast to Dina's comment that people were becoming less Islamic in their birth practices, Lady G thought that younger generations tried harder to incorporate more Islamic ideals and traditions, turning thoughtfully to their faith as a source for conceptualizing how to welcome their children into the world.

Two different views from women who were influenced by Russian culture in different ways can be seen in Maral's and Adilya's points of view. Maral asserts, "The newer generation picks and chooses the traditions they want to follow unless their families are very conservative. Some things that are required by the Islamic tradition will probably stay the same. Everything else is open to interpretation." Adilya said, "Almost all of my parents' siblings [in Russia] were home born, and my siblings and their kids were born in the hospital. I don't think there were any special religious traditions observed apart from circumcision, adhan, and possibly aqiqah in the mid-twentieth century when my parents were born. Nowadays it's more widespread to perform these and other religious duties."

Seher, an Indian of South African ancestry, commented on the questioning of the rationale of the overmedicalization of birth. She says, "I believe that traditions change quite a lot by going back and forth between traditional and modern medicine. For example, when I was born a lot of mothers were having C-sections as it was widely promoted. However, nowadays more and more people are having natural births at home as they did two generations ago. I believe these things are also advancing with modern medicine, however natural ways are often proven to be the best way to go." Perhaps Seher's comment encapsulates the newer possibilities that are open to Muslim American families as they face childbirth in the United States. They have the option of customizing a birth space with traditions that belonged to their ancestors, *and* of adopting whatever else makes them feel comfortable as they embark on their journey as parents. Her allusion to a "return to what's natural" seems to leave room for more Islamic women-centered knowledge at the same time that it parallels feminist critiques of the loss of women's rights to her body in the childbirth process.

NOTES

1 Ayşem R. Şenyürekli, "A Profile of Immigrant Women from Turkey in the United States, 1900–2000," in *Turkish Migration to the United States: From Ottoman Times to the Present*, A. Deniz Balgamiş and Kemal Karpat, eds. (Madison, Wis.: University of Wisconsin Press, 2008).

2 Stephen Klineberg, "Public Perceptions in Remarkable Times: Tracking Change through 24 Years of Houston Surveys," Rice University, 2005.

3 Ayşem R. Şenyürekli and Daniel F. Detzner, "Intergenerational Relationships in a Transnational Context: The Case of Turkish Families," *Family Relations.* 57, 4 (2008): 457–467.

4 See Earle H. Waugh, Sharon M. Abu-Laban, and Regula B. Qureshi, eds., *Muslim Families in North America* (Edmonton: University of Alberta Press, 1991).

5 These traditions were outlined in Gholamreza Khademi, Maryam Ajilian Abbasi, Abbas Bahreini, and Masumah Saeidi, "Customs Desirable after Childbirth in Islam," *International Journal of Pediatrics* 4, 1 (2016): 1195–1204, http://ijp.mums. ac.ir.

6 For an extended conversation on the association of God with the womb as evidenced throughout the Qur'an, see Asma Barlas, *"Believing Women" in Islam: Unreading Patriarchal Interpretation of the Qur'an* (Austin: University of Texas Press, 2002).

7 Gisela Webb, "May Muslim Women Speak for Themselves, Please?" in *Windows of Faith: Muslim Women Scholar-Activists in North America*, ed. Gisela Webb (Syracuse, N.Y.: Syracuse University Press, 2000).

8 Xiaolin Xie and Yan Xia, "Co-Residence in Chinese Immigrant Families," in *Strengths and Challenges of New Immigrant Families: Implications for Research, Education, Policy, and Service*, eds. Rochelle L. Dalla, John Defrain, Julie Johnson, and Douglass A. Abbott (Lanham, Md.: Lexington Books, 2009).

9 Hinna Mirza Upal, "A Celebration of Mothering in the Qur'an," *Journal of the Motherhood Initiative for Research and Community Involvement* 7, 1 (2005): 86–97.

8

Weddings

Love and Mercy in Marriage Ceremonies

JULIANE HAMMER

Oh Humanity! Be conscious of your Lord who created you from a single soul, and created from it its mate, and out of the two spread a multitude of men and women. And remain conscious of God in whose name you demand your rights from one another, and of the ties of kinship. Verily, God ever watches over you.
Qur'an 4:1

And among His Signs is this, that He created for you mates from among yourselves, that ye may dwell in tranquility (*sakinah*) with them, and He has put love (*mawaddah*) and mercy (*rahmah*) between you: verily in that are Signs for those who reflect.
Qur'an 30:21

Every wedding is its own story. We might think that once we have attended a few weddings, we know the basics: a ceremony, a celebration, the bride in a dress, food, and music. Watching American weddings in movies and on television deepens the feeling that once we have seen a few we know what they are all about and we know what to expect. American Muslim weddings are a combination of religious and cultural practices and norms and as such, they might or might not conform to our expectations. It is equally flawed to try to judge the Americanness of American Muslims or their Islamic authenticity by their wedding practices. Both assume a standard or a norm against which we measure human practices and actions. After attending quite a few American

Muslim weddings I have chosen here to tell three of the wedding stories I encountered in my research. They are each unique and specific to the couple, and they are also part of the communal fabric of Muslim religious practices in the United States. My three stories are held together by two things: references to two verses from the Qur'an on marriage which were referenced at each of them, and the creation of an American Muslim family through marriage.

A Muslim wedding is many things: a celebration, a legal contract, a ritual, a ceremony, and an announcement to families and communities. The basic requirements for a *nikah*, the Muslim marriage ceremony, to be Islamically legal are simple: the consent of both parties, a *mahr* (an agreed upon gift from the groom to the bride), and the presence of two witnesses at the ceremony. It is possible and recommended to also agree upon a marriage contract that stipulates ethical as well as practical terms for the marriage. This contract does not have to be in writing but most often is these days, and it is signed either before or at the ceremony. Many American Muslim couples are married by a person who has both Islamic legal authority and state authority to perform a marriage ceremony, which in turn makes the ceremony legal according to the laws of a particular U.S. state and Islamic law. The former requires a certification process and the latter basic knowledge of the form and function of Islamic legal requirements for a marriage—but not extensive legal training or recognition as a general religious authority for Muslims.

I have found that a wedding is not always one event but rather that many Muslims, for many reasons, divide the different components of ritual, ceremony, and celebration along different lines into more than one event. Weddings are sites for discussing and embodying gender roles, and they are spaces for American Muslims to negotiate what they consider American culture, other cultural backgrounds, and religious norms. In what follows we will see these negotiations play out in a variety of ways.

The *Nikah* at the Mosque: Patricia and Collin

On a rainy day in October, I am on my way to a mosque in the Northeast of the United States. I arrive at the specified location before anyone else does. A few minutes later, two African American men arrive, one, as I find out, the father of the bride, the other the imam (here this means he is a religious authority figure) who will conduct the *nikah* ceremony. We are welcomed by a man present at the mosque and shown into the *musallah*, the main prayer space of this small mosque. As more guests arrive, a spatial division by gender becomes apparent. There is no one telling women to go to one side and men to the other, but a side-by-side arrangement emerges. This is likely due to the fact that most Muslims are familiar with and used to such arrangements in their own mosques. I realize at this point that there is a separate entrance for women at the side of the mosque, which I did not see when I first arrived.

About half an hour later, the bride, Patricia, arrives, out of breath, in a white, sequined wedding dress and a wrapped scarf turban covering her hair. She was stuck in traffic and feared she would not make it, and she worried that the thunderstorm we all encountered on our way here was a bad omen. She clearly is the one responsible for organizing this event and quickly recovers her wits as more people arrive.

Patricia and Collin met at their workplace, a social service agency. Patricia is part of an African American family and grew up as a Muslim. Her parents joined the community of Warith Deen Mohammed[1] in the 1980s and raised their children within that community. Collin is the son of white Methodists and converted to Islam about six months ago. He is committed to his new religion but apprehensive about knowing all that is required in terms of ritual practice and other rules. Collin and Patricia have met for coffee, then later for dinner, and have talked, but they have not dated and have certainly not consummated their relationship or lived together. Rather, they have spent time talking about their values, histories, families, and expectations. Collin proposed to Patricia by coming to her parents' house for dinner and asking her father for her hand in marriage.

Closer to the scheduled time of the ceremony, a group of folks arrive in fancy dresses and suits. Many are dressed for a party—these are Collin's family members. They are looking a bit perturbed by the need to take off their shoes at the entrance and the suggestion that they join the women's and men's sides respectively and sit on the floor. Chairs appear from somewhere and some of them sit at the back of the prayer space, at least a little more comfortable than they would have been on the floor. After the Muslims in the room perform their *maghrib*, or sunset, prayers, they rearrange themselves side by side for the imam to perform the ceremony. The bride is sitting on a chair at the front of the women's section and several men, the groom, the imam, and the father of the bride are sitting on the floor at the front of the room, facing the audience. Then the imam begins to speak.

It is perhaps unusual but perfect for the audience that he begins his speech by welcoming the coming together of families, expressing his gratitude to Allah, and explaining that an Islamic wedding is perhaps a little different from what non-Muslim Americans are used to. He addresses Collin's family directly when he begins with the fact that there are negative ideas about Islam in public discourse and then presents a picture of God as the Creator and the human need to obey God. He points to a history of revelation and a succession of prophets sent to what he calls mankind/womankind and thus to the connection of Islam to other faith traditions. He appeals to them to respect and support Collin in his journey in the faith, and prays that more people will join the fold of Islam.

He begins the "official part" of the wedding ceremony with a *du'a*, a supplication in Arabic, appealing to God and his messenger, honoring the prophets, and emphasizing the importance of family for Muslims. Next he recites the first verse of chapter 4 in the Qur'an, also in Arabic, pertaining to God's creation of spouses and the significance of kinship, both signs of God's omnipotence and infinite wisdom. Then he recites Qur'an 30:21, the verse about spouses having been made to live in tranquility, love, and mercy, and paraphrases the supplication and Qur'anic verses in English. Then he continues:

> We want to concentrate on what is really important, which is the coming together of families. We are grateful to Allah, our Creator and Lord, for bringing us together in this moment. The marriage really starts with people seeking a mate. . . . What matters is character, the right kind of person, looking for the right kind of character that will bring about a wholesome family and develop well-adjusted children who are ready to be a productive member of the society. They learn what their responsibilities are. Both Collin and Patricia have studied, have sat and listened, and then decided on an agreement. They have a contract. There were no such written contracts in the Prophet's time but now we have the paper to print them. But what is more important is that they understand the contract

that is in their hearts. . . . For married people the first obligation is to the Creator. They need to know that the purpose of their coming together is to please the Lord. Marriage is about others, not ourselves. . . . You were "I" for a long time, in the womb, then mama's me, your teenage me, but in marriage it becomes "we." You are still individuals but looking for reward from Him.

The imam mentions that the bride and groom have met with him for premarital counseling and to agree on the marriage contract. They have fulfilled the three conditions: they consent to the marriage, they have provided a bridal gift which has been accepted, and witnesses are present. Then he explains that the actual ceremony will go as follows: the *wali*, or representative/guardian of the bride, which in Patricia's case is her father, is the agent for the woman. He is looking out for her interest and needs her approval for the marriage to be valid. He will make an offer to the groom and then Collin will accept. "That is really the marriage: no aisle to walk down, no flower girl, no ring boy, no big kiss at the end. These things are reserved for their privacy."

The father gets the microphone and says in English: "I offer you, Collin, my daughter, Patricia, in marriage." Collin takes the mic and says, clearly nervous: "Yes, I take her." When people snigger a little, he corrects himself: "Yes, I accept her." The imam speaks one more time: "Alhamdulillah, this concludes the wedding. You are now one family and we ask the Creator to bless these two people, and to bless their families, and to give them the strength really, in these times, to put Him first, to please Him, and in doing so they will please each other and they will make their children happy and they will be good to their parents. We are all here for both of you, the community, and the family." He closes with another supplication, this time in English, for God to bless the marriage and the children coming from it.

The women walk over to Patricia, offering hugs, kisses on both cheeks, and congratulations. The men do the same with Collin. The imam approaches first Collin and then Patricia to sign the required documents for the marriage to be legal in their state. People are milling about the mosque for a few more minutes. From the imam's first sentence to the supplication at the end, this event has lasted less than twenty-five minutes.

Patricia and Collin have invited their families, friends, and coworkers for a reception at a nearby library and community center and everyone files out to drive there. The room is set up with ten tables, eight chairs each. Each table is covered with a purple tablecloth and decorated with candles, books, and fresh flowers. Each place setting is marked by a metal plate and a napkin with cutlery. The invitation called it a reception with refreshments but the buffet actually consists of catered dishes constituting a dinner menu, including baked fish, mashed potatoes, salad, and cheesecake. The drinks table contains a variety of sodas in cans and water in bottles. Several of the women are helping in the small kitchen and serve the food when the guests line up at the buffet table. Collin's family congregates around two of the tables while many of the Muslim guests, family, friends, and coworkers fill the other tables, most of them divided into men and women. Patricia and Collin are seated at the same table but seem to be spending their time directing the buffet, talking to their guests, and receiving more congratulations and hugs. There is no music but the low hum of friendly conversation and the occasional shrieks and giggles of the younger children roaming the space between mouthfuls of food from their mothers. I spend most of the reception at a table with female friends of Patricia asking about my research and in turn telling me their stories of marriage, finding spouses, and having children.

Collin and Patricia are planning an official wedding party in a few months and Patricia protests when I say that this was already like a wedding. She admits that they are trying to find enough funds for a more elaborate celebration of their marriage but she hopes that this will resolve itself sooner rather than later. The couple will move in together after today, so they consider this ceremony and celebration their legal and Islamic wedding and a first public announcement of their union.

Interlude I: Marriage and Islamic Law in the United States

Marriage is often taken for granted as a timeless societal institution and it is only on closer inspection that its historical embeddedness in religious discourses on sexuality and gender is discovered. Islam is no exception in this regard. Muslim marriage norms regulate sexual access and practice and provide Muslims with guidelines for sexual and gender

norms. Like other religious norms and practices, marriage, divorce, cus-
tody of children, and sexual access are regulated by Islamic law, itself an
institutional framework for the legal interpretation of sacred sources,
including the Qur'an and Sunna of the Prophet Muhammad.[2]

Because American Muslims live as a religious minority community,
the application of Islamic law to their lives, including marriage, is limited and increasingly combined with, if not replaced by, direct references
to the Qur'an and the prophetic example. American Muslim scholars
and leaders have contributed to the development of Islamic legal frame-
works for minorities (*fiqh al-aqalliyyat*) and have tended to emphasize
the obligation of Muslims to follow the laws of the countries they are
citizens of and/or live in, which is especially relevant for family and personal status law. Muslims with the requisite Islamic legal training can act
as legal advisors and decision makers for other Muslims. Many efforts
have been underway to develop organizational structures which offer
American Muslims legal advice, fatwas on issues raised in their specific
context, and recommendations for how to address the challenges of contemporary life.

There are specific challenges to navigating the application of Islamic
law—because it is a set of interpretations and not an immutable legal
code—to the particular life cycle rituals and practices related to marriage. If and when weddings are recognized as regulated by Islamic law,
couples and their families approach religious scholars and leaders for
more specific knowledge and/or they search for information available
in other forms such as online resources and marriage advice literature.[3]

American Muslim organizations, leaders, and activists have recognized the significance of marriage for the preservation of Muslim communities and Muslim identity. There are initiatives and programs that
have helped produce guidance materials in two specific areas: premarital
counseling to ensure compatibility between the prospective spouses in
their values and expectations, and templates for the Islamic marriage
contract that recognize mutual rights and responsibilities and at least
attempt to be legally enforceable in U.S. courts. The issue of Islamic
marriage contracts as legally valid in U.S. family courts is a significant
one. The Islamic marriage ceremony is only recognized in U.S. courts if
it has been carried out by a certified civil celebrant—this certification
can be acquired through an application, and many imams in Ameri-

can mosques are qualified to perform a marriage ceremony recognized in state courts.[4] The marriage contract as a legally enforceable contract becomes relevant in case of a divorce, which needs to be channeled through the U.S. court system. Provisions made in the marriage contract such as alimony and spousal support can only be enforced if the contract abides by the standards of U.S. law.

In addition to offering sample marriage contracts, Islamic marriage advice literature relies heavily on anecdotes and stories like the ones told here to illustrate challenges and solutions to Muslim matrimonial issues and trends that are specific to U.S. Muslim communities.

The *Nikah* at the Hotel

As I get out of my car on this unseasonably warm December morning, I wonder whether my outfit is fancy enough (long black skirt, teal tunic, and colorful pashmina scarf around my shoulders) for this South Asian American Muslim wedding. It is the fourth such wedding I am attending for my research and I am always hard-pressed to come up with anything to wear that can compete with the splendor of South Asian wedding outfits. Women and girls wear *shalwar kameez* and *saris* in all the colors of the rainbow which sparkle even more with beads, sequins, and tiny mirrors. Gold jewelry, elaborately braided hair, and especially glamorous scarves covering the hair of some women complete the picture. Men appear in shalwar kameez as well, in more muted colors, or wearing formal suits.

As I enter the hotel lobby I am directed by a sign toward the ballroom. This wedding is both the official nikah ceremony and a celebration/reception, in one evening. There is a lobby area outside the ballroom where people are beginning to arrive. The parents of the bride are standing in the front, welcoming guests as they enter the space. It is a widely practiced custom for American Muslim weddings, though not a requirement, to have two separate wedding events: First, the nikah, sometimes with a reception built in, and at other times later in the same day, often in a different location. The parents of the bride often organize (and finance) this part of the wedding. There is then a second event, the *walima*, which is a celebration to announce the wedding of a couple to the community and society. The walima is organized and paid for by the groom's family. It also usually takes place in a different location. This practice helps accommodate geographically distant families and friends: some will come for both the nikah and the walima, and some will only attend one or the other. Nor is it uncommon for the walima or nikah to take place in another country—often the place from which the family or one of the spouses originated. Both the walima and nikah are also a reflection of economic ability and thus class.

Rabia and Mohsin are both of Pakistani American background and Rabia made sure to tell me that their union was not arranged by their parents or families. Instead, they met at a matrimonial banquet at an Islamic Society of North America (ISNA) convention. Such matrimonial banquets have taken place for several decades and ISNA is not the only organization that organizes them in conjunction with its annual convention. Muslims interested in matrimony can sign up for these events in advance and meet potential spouses in a banquet hall over food and in a completely chaperoned environment. Mohsin is a graduate student in public health and Rabia is completing her residency program to become a pediatrician. She told me in an interview that she was not sure how she felt about Mohsin at first and that it was only thanks to his insistence that they continue talking on the phone that they stayed in touch and eventually decided there was a future for them. Rabia had tried an online matrimonial site for Muslims—I suspect Mohsin did as well but would not admit it—and had found the experience frustrating. She said that the matrimonial banquet allowed for a first impression of the person that online exchanges preclude. She was worried, as was Mohsin, that both online matchmaking and the banquet would make people think they were desperate to get married. They weren't but there was pressure, especially from Rabia's family for her to get serious about getting married as she approached thirty.

When things started getting serious, both sets of parents got involved. Informal checks on the respective families did not uncover anything worrisome and the families even found common friends and connections in Pakistan, a plus in their quest to make sure that their children would marry into "good families." Mohsin's older sister is divorced and Mohsin had been worried about what he called "making a mistake" in choosing his future wife. Divorce, while legally possible, is still considered a stigma in many South Asian Muslim families and communities.

In interviews it often becomes clear that young Muslims consider their marriage and family histories carefully and that the experiences of family members inform their own matrimonial choices. Rabia was adamant that for her the most important consideration was that she and Mohsin had similar levels of religious commitment and practice. It did not hurt that they were both of Pakistani heritage—there would have been family debate otherwise—but she had been open to marrying a Muslim man from a different background, at least in principle. Muslim families have long expected that their children continue to practice endogamy, marrying within one's community, the argument being that cultural compatibility and the preservation of cultural norms and identities are an important part of marriage.

Mohsin suggested the person who is performing the nikah ceremony. Walid is a friend of his and well-known in the local Muslim community for his efforts to work within the mosque setting to attract more young Muslims to lectures, workshops, and community activities. Rabia and Mohsin both met with him, separately, and then together, for what I would call premarital counseling even though they did not use that term. They discussed expectations and the possibility of a marriage contract. Rabia wanted the contract to include several stipulations in her interest: that she would be able to work as a physician if she wanted to, that she would not have to share a house or apartment with her in-laws, and that she could initiate a divorce, a right that in Islamic legal terms is the husband's alone unless otherwise spelled out in the marriage contract. All these conditions are common in such contracts but also reflect the specific concerns of individual couples and spouses. Perhaps the hardest for Rabia, she said, was to discuss divorce stipulations before getting married.

A buffet with appetizers is arranged in the center of the lobby and about fifty guests are already milling about. Conversations are a mix of Urdu, the national language of Pakistan, and English. Guests and family hug, shake hands, and greet each other as they move around the room. Servers offer appetizers on trays and along a wall guests can pick up water, soft drinks, and chai. The appetizers are distinctly South Asian: vegetable pakoras, small chicken kebabs, and vegetable samosas, complemented by spicy, tangy, and yogurt-based sauces.

The ballroom is set up with a stage in the front that contains a white and gold couch and chairs, draped red curtains, and flowers on the sides.

A three-level wedding cake, decorated in white and red, adorns the right side of the stage. Guests will be seated at round tables for ten people each. They are covered in white and gold tablecloths and decorated with flowers as well. There is a table on the side with wedding favors: small red boxes containing chocolates and small bags of fennel seeds and candies. There is also a table for the wedding gifts: as is customary at many South Asian Muslim weddings, guests are asked to offer cash gifts (the invitation said: "no boxed gifts"), so the table contains a large box to deposit the envelopes in. There is also a wedding register where guests can sign in and write out congratulatory messages to the couple.

As the guests file in they arrange themselves at the various tables. I see the wedding photographer and her assistant, two Muslim women in hijab, who specialize in Muslim wedding photography. They start taking pictures in the ballroom and then call select family members for more staged photos in the adjacent rock garden. When everyone seems to have settled in, the bride's uncle announces the beginning of the ceremony. As the guests stand up and congregate around the door of the ballroom, a Sikh man wearing the traditional Sikh turban and beating a drum appears at the door. To the sound of the drum, the bride and groom enter the ballroom followed by parents, siblings, and their children. Smart phones and cameras capture the moment and two small girls throw rose petals before the couple's feet. Rabia is wearing an elaborately decorated dark red South Asian silk dress with long white sleeves, heavy gold embroidery, and sequins. Her hair is partially covered with a similarly decorated scarf, which is very heavy and large, and she wears a gold ornament on part of her forehead. Her hands are covered in the complicated lines of henna flowers and ornaments.[5] She wears a large amount of gold jewelry, including bracelets and several necklaces. Mohsin's outfit consists of white shalwar pants and a black knee-length kameez shirt with gold embroidery on the collar and sleeves as well as a white flower pin on his chest. He also wears pointy black leather slippers and a red and gold turban. The couple walks toward the stage and settles on the white and golden couch, their parents in the chairs on both sides. By now there are at least three hundred adults and quite a few children in attendance.

Walid walks up to the stage and takes the microphone. He outlines the structure of the ceremony as follows: he will read some verses from the Qur'an and some hadith, or sayings of the Prophet Muhammad, then he will offer the wedding *khutba* or sermon, followed by the official wedding ceremony. The couple will then exchange rings, followed by a supplication which will mark the end of the ceremony.

In a melodious voice and beautiful *tajweed* (qur'anic recitation) style he proceeds to intone several verses from the Qur'an in Arabic. As he begins his recitation, many of the women in the room who are not wearing a *hijab* pull their *dupattas* to cover their hair in a sign of respect for the Qur'an and its recitation. The first verse is from Sura al-Imran, the third chapter of the Qur'an, verse 102. It tells Muslims to be conscious of God. Walid will later translate this God-consciousness (*taqwah*) as fear of God. The second verse is the already familiar Q 4:1 which we encountered in Patricia and Collin's ceremony. It speaks of God's creation of a single soul, then of a pair from that one soul, which becomes a multitude of men and women. Muslims are called to be conscious of their Creator and honor the bonds of kinship. The third verse is Q 33:70, another verse imploring Muslims to speak out for justice and truth. Together these verses establish the connection of the ceremony to God and to faith and the God-given institution of marriage as a natural pairing of men and women. Walid translates all three verses into English and explains that these three verses are part of the traditional wedding khutba. He expounds the significance of God-consciousness as the single most important dimension of a marriage: the responsibility for one's actions in the eyes of God and thus accountability in worldly affairs such as marriage.

The qur'anic verses and explanations are followed by three hadith in which the Prophet Muhammad emphasizes the significance of marriage as part of Muslim practice, as important as prayer, fasting, and giving charity; represents himself as the example of a Muslim husband to his community; and—ironically, given the setting—describes the best wedding as one that is modest and within the family's means. As Walid explains, this nikah ceremony is the wedding, and what needs to be stripped away is the layers of South Asian cultural practice of six-day wedding proceedings and the excesses of consumer culture. I read it as his simultaneous critique of both Pakistani culture and American capitalism in one sentence.

From there he moves on to a story of Mullah Nasreddin, a figure in Muslim lore famous for his wise as well as funny actions and rebuttals in which Nasreddin begs for money to buy an elephant and, as he is questioned by a passerby about the stupidity of his plan, says that he is asking for money, not advice. So here is Walid, sharing his wedding khutba and there will be some advice! People chuckle here and on several other occasions. Later I will hear comments about this being the most "modern" and entertaining wedding khutba ever.

Walid's advice comes in three stories and revolves around three central values: gratitude, selflessness, and simplicity. Gratitude to God is connected to companionship in the story of Adam and Eve, whose Arabic name, Hawwa, means "the living being." Walid explains that Adam was not really living until God created Eve to be his companion. After the fall from paradise for transgressing God's command to not eat from the tree of knowledge, Adam and Eve were separated for two hundred years, finding each other again at Mount Arafat in Arabia, a place that Muslims visit during the *hajj* season. It is thus innate to human beings to yearn for companionship and to only be fully human through the family. At the same time God is due eternal gratitude for creating humans with that yearning and giving them the possibility to fulfill it through marriage.

Selflessness is exemplified in relationships like a mother's care for her child or love between siblings that do not involve selfish gain. Walid mentions Richard Dawkins's book *The Selfish Gene*, only to disagree with Dawkins that all human acts are ultimately selfish. According to Walid, true faith and truly faithful acts come from true selflessness. He quotes a famous saying by a Sufi, or spiritual master, claiming that every spiritual seeker is a product of his time. Walid takes this saying to mean that in our time the more trying life is the more the true Muslim needs patience and grace, in daily interactions as well as in relationships with people. He suggests that each of us should surprise people, perhaps buy someone coffee, and that Muslims in the room lead the charge in interpersonal relations. This reference to the political climate in the United States and the particular challenges to Muslims, as much as the earlier stories, is clearly addressed to all the people in the room, not just the bride and groom: "And this is very true for marriage: don't always worry about your rights. Be consumed by your responsibilities. Just as Adam was the caretaker of this planet, we are by extension caretakers of this planet. So be simple, be consistent, be filled with empathy and compassion. Be filled with mercy and draw strength from your daily prayer."

Walid's third message is to embrace simplicity. Islam is not complicated. Perhaps if one is looking at it from the exterior it looks very complicated, but it is not. What matters is being mindful, honoring one's elders, not cheating, being grateful for all blessings—this is what Islam is teaching us. "The Prophet, Peace Be Upon Him, ate very little meat and he looked at everyone he met as a potential friend." While God instilled in people a thirst for knowledge, he also gave us a yearning for order and simplicity, which is the only way to find meaning and guidance in a world that seems like total chaos at times. "The little things in life are truly the big things in life. . . . We focus so much on our brain and on logic that we forget to listen to our hearts. Listen to your heart, this is also the message of Islam."

Walid then turns to the bride and groom and recites this poem attributed to the well-known Sufi woman, Rabia al-Adawiyya, the bride's namesake:

> In love nothing exists between heart and heart,
> Speech is born out of longing
> True description comes from taste
> The one who tastes knows
> The one who explains lies
> How can you describe the true form of something
> In whose presence you are completely blotted out
> And in whose being you still exist
> And who lives as a sign for your journey.

This is followed by another poem, this one about the internal and external beauty of the Prophet Muhammad. Walid recites the poem in Arabic and then translates it into English. He wishes for the couple that they may always be a gift to each other, to live in companionship, and to recognize the possibility of miracles. He turns to the families and recites an Urdu saying about the possibility of miracles and who can see them— the audience murmurs in affirmation. "A family from one coast is connected to a family from the other coast through a city in the Midwest and here we are acting like that is completely rational and not a miracle!" Everyone laughs as he continues to speak of marriage as a journey, as a connecting of souls and families, as gaining sons and daughters, and as he explains that each person in the room is a veil to God and a door to God. With this he concludes the khutba and moves on to what he calls the formal ceremony.

According to Walid, five things need to occur in the ceremony. The first is the establishment of guardianship for the bride—Walid asks the father of the bride for permission to proceed, which is granted verbally. The second condition is the presence of witnesses. Only two are needed, but as Walid points out, there is a roomful present at this ceremony, so the condition is more than met. God is the greatest of witnesses. In addition, there is a list of three official male witnesses, whose names he reads aloud for confirmation. The third condition is the *mahr*, a gift agreed upon between the families or the parties which can be paid upon the wedding or delayed, but it has to be honored for the marriage to be valid. Walid mentions that it has been agreed upon, so the condition is met. The fourth condition is the marriage contract which the parties have agreed upon and which has already been signed by the groom. Rabia will sign the contract which lists the witnesses, the *mahr*, and the conditions, as part of the ceremony. The fifth and final condition is the ceremony itself, which he describes as the offer and acceptance of the offer of marriage.

Walid recites the *basmallah*, a phrase that prefaces every action of a Muslim to be carried out in the name and under the blessing of God. He continues: "Here is how we are going to do this. I will offer Mohsin to you and you accept. I will ask you three times and you have to accept three times." And now Walid sets up the crowd for a joke. "But because you can say, 'I do'—he skips a beat and whispers unders his breath—'not,' I want you to [also] say in Arabic, '*qabaltu*,' which means I accept you wholeheartedly, and no fingers crossed, okay?" People begin to snicker halfway through Walid's instruction and at the end they are laughing out loud. "And then after the third one I will ask you to sign the paper." After clearing his throat, he proceeds in a serious voice: "I ask you Rabia, daughter of Afzal and Ambreen, in accordance with Islamic law and according to the tradition of our noble Prophet, Peace Be Upon Him, and according to the contract and the mahr agreed to, do you accept Mohsin, son of Faisal and Zahra, as your husband?" Rabia answers "qabaltu" in a quiet voice. He repeats the question two more times and she answers the same way two more times. He then thanks her and asks her to sign several papers. Some shuffling of papers occurs and he again recites the basmallah as she signs the papers.

Walid then turns to the groom's side and asks whether he accepts Rabia as his wife. He answers in the affirmative, also in Arabic, and the question and answer are repeated two more times. Mohsin also signs the papers, followed by the signatures of the three official witnesses. Walid then prays for their union to be blessed. He asks Mohsin to place a ring on Rabia's hand and he does, followed by applause from those present and murmurs of "*mashallah*," which literally means "what God wills," an expression of acknowledging God's power over everything that happens but also an expression of amazement at something beautiful, which in turn always comes from God. The final du'a, or supplication, recited by Walid in Arabic, asks for God's blessing, honors the prophets from Adam to Muhammad and their families, and expresses gratitude for all the blessings already bestowed. As is the custom, after every specific blessing those in attendance murmur "ameen" to support the supplication. The ceremony ends with Walid translating parts of the supplication into English.

Both bride and groom are then hugged by their parents and new parents-in-law. Family and friends file onto the stage to congratulate them. Hugs and kisses are followed by picture taking, official and amateur. And then there is the food! The buffet consists of more excellent South Asian food including haleem, tandoori chicken, beef biryani, chicken curry, basmati rice and naan, complemented by green salad. As guests line up and get their food, waiters bring soft drinks and juices as well as chai, South Asian tea with milk and spices, and coffee. After about half an hour, they cut the wedding cake and lay out pieces of it on the dessert table.

This could be the end of the evening, but we have not yet encountered our verse from the beginning of this chapter. After dinner and dessert, there is a speech by an older bearded man who turns out to be Rabia's former Sunday school teacher.[6] He begins his speech by quoting Q 30:21 and takes its focus on tranquility, love, and mercy as the central points in his reminder to the couple of what matters most in a marriage. He explains the love meant in the Qur'an as more than the romantic English notion of infatuation and describes it as a lifelong commitment that comes from wanting to serve God through the family just created through this wedding. He emphasizes the wife's need to be obedient to the husband and that of the husband to protect his wife.

After his speech, the father of the groom tells me that he did not like this speech and that he does not understand why it was necessary to bring up obedience in it. He would have preferred a more traditional and "less religious" after-dinner entertainment. Some of this does happen in the form of male family members producing stand-up poetry in Urdu, some serious and some humorous. This is a wedding tradition in some parts of Pakistan and people seem to enjoy it. It becomes quite apparent which guests and family members understand enough Urdu to get the jokes— this time there is no one translating into English. I do not understand Urdu so am not in on the poetic prowess of the men; instead I observe the reactions of the audience. The bride and groom have managed to eat something and are back on the couch on the stage. They look tired but content and seem to enjoy the poetic performances and short speeches.

The evening ends with the bride and groom being walked to a waiting stretch limousine outside. The bride's family can be seen hugging, kissing, and crying because she is now moving to the husband's family. After more tearful goodbyes, blessings, and good wishes Rabia and Mohsin disappear into the back seat of the car and drive off into their new life as a married couple. After a breakfast with family members—with at least some innuendo about the wedding night—they will move in together. Their walima is already scheduled to take place in the city in the Midwest they both live in and will take place about a month after the nikah, followed by a two-week honeymoon.

Interlude II: Muslim Communities, Cultures, and the American in American Muslims

American Muslim communities are diverse in terms of their ethnic and national background, their religious affiliation and levels of practice, their economic status, education, and locations within the social fabric and geography of the United States. Not surprisingly, this diversity is reflected, at least to some degree, in matrimonial selections and practices, and in American Muslim weddings.

For much of the twentieth century, communities of Muslim immigrants and their descendants favored endogamy, the practice of marrying within one's ethnic or cultural community, often on the grounds that cultural and linguistic compatibility were a precondition for marital success and contributed to the preservation of the communities in question. Other American Muslims, including African Americans from Muslim families, and white and Latina converts, have intermarried across community lines. Consequently, it is safe to assert that American Muslims have always married from within their communities and other Muslims from very different backgrounds. It is worth mentioning that there have always been marriages between Muslims and non-Muslims as well.[7]

While the idea of marrying for love is a relatively recent ideal, for Europeans and Americans as much as Muslims, American Muslims find their partners on their own and expect compatibility as much as mutual affection turning into romantic as well as lasting love. In attending weddings, discussing them with guests at the events, and interviewing couples, I have perhaps been most fascinated with the public nature of private life. Something as personal as who one wants to share one's life with has turned out to be embedded in the larger contexts of family, community, and society. As a result, the weddings I have studied and written about are all continuous sites of negotiation; they display the diverse ideas American Muslims have about their religion, their culture(s), and perhaps equally important, gender roles and sexuality. Rather than defining and categorizing the couples I work with and their families, I expect them to tell me how they conceive of their own weddings and marriages. This makes for a lot of fluidity, which is a better reflection of their experiences than the insistence on clear labels and boxes to put them in.

It is quite common, even in academic literature, to create a distinction between the Muslimness of American Muslims and their Americanness. Being part of the fabric of American society means both shaping and being shaped by attitudes, values, and practices identified as "American." In the process, dimensions of culture and religion are also continuously shaped and negotiated. In a small way, the complications of these identity descriptions become apparent in the story of Noura and Abdullah.

The *Walima* at the Wedding Hall

The entrance to the wedding hall is surrounded by lovely flowering bushes and two lion statues. It feels a little like walking into the palace for Cinderella's ball. The spacious foyer leads into a large room which is set up with large round tables and chairs around a circle of open space in the middle. The tables are covered in lavender tablecloths and feature chandeliers and floral arrangements in matching tones. There is a buffet waiting to open on the left and a table for gifts and cards on the right.

Noura and Abdullah met and fell in love with each other while in college. They were both active in the Muslim Students Association on campus and through many shared activities got to spend time together. They discovered their shared political commitments and academic interests. After college they both enrolled in graduate programs, in different cities, but managed to maintain contact. They refuse to say that they were dating in college and insist that their romance was rekindled when they spent time together at a friend's wedding almost a year ago. From talking all night on Skype to meeting each other's parents, their relationship accelerated to the point where they decided to get married. Noura is Palestinian American and comes from a family of proud activists on behalf of Palestine. Abdullah's parents are from Egypt and his father came to study in the United States. He stayed and brought his wife from Egypt and they grew their family to include four children.

Noura and Abdullah's nikah ceremony was a small affair at the house of Noura's uncle. Only twenty of their closest family members attend. They did not call it a nikah either, but rather used the Arabic term *katb al kitab*, literally the writing of the book or contract. It involved the same conditions we have seen in the nikah ceremonies earlier: agreement, mahr, and witnesses. Their families considered the *kitab* closer to an engagement ceremony even though it legally married them. There was *mansaf* at the kitab, a traditional dish with rice, thin bread, and lamb in yogurt sauce, popular in Palestine and Jordan.

The walima for them is the big public announcement of their marriage and they are expecting at least four hundred guests. They arrive in smaller groups and settle around the tables. Noura's family seems to be settling on the left side of the room and Abdullah's on the right. There are tables with families and others with only women and children or only men. Some guests are friends, classmates, and colleagues of the couple. Many of the women are wearing party dresses, jewelry, and heels, while others, both older and younger, are attending the wedding in long traditional embroidered Palestinian dresses of a black or beige fabric, covered in mostly red, some gold, and blue embroidery. The patterns are intricate and hand-embroidered and represent an important part of and pride in Palestinian national culture. Some women have their hair covered and others do not.

People stand up and applaud as the bride and groom are carried into the room on chairs which are carried by four young men each. They are settled at the edge of the open space and the festivities begin. Noura is wearing an elaborate white wedding dress and a tiara in her beautifully styled hair. Abdullah is wearing a light grey suit and matching tie. The arrival of the couple is accompanied by the women in the room ululating, a familiar sound of celebration in Arab cultures. People talk in Arabic and English and children run around the room.

Noura's uncle, a leader in his Muslim community, takes the mic to give a short speech. He welcomes the couple and guests, in Arabic and English, and talks about how Noura and Abdullah met—this is the official version. He speaks on behalf of both families when he says that they are very happy about their union and that they wish them the best for their new life together. He then beautifully recites our now familiar two verses from the Qur'an and reminds the couple of the significance of God consciousness in all they do, especially in their marriage, and of the centrality of building a relationship based on tranquility, love, and mercy. In a nod to Egyptian wedding traditions, he then offers the bride and groom a glass of hibiscus tea, and servers around the room carry trays with the same tea for the guests.

When he puts down the mic, music begins to play over the speakers and the bride and groom are urged into the circle for the first dance. They have hired a professional *dabkeh* dance group to accompany them and perform this traditional Arab/Middle Eastern dance. Abdullah was at first reluctant to include dabkeh in the walima, as it involves men and women dancing together, but he has been practicing with Palestinian friends and manages quite well. Noura has performed as part of a dabkeh group since high school and presents a flawless performance despite the unwieldy wedding dress. Surrounded by the dance troupe, the two are joined by others who feel comfortable participating. Many of the guests have gotten up to line the circular space and clap along to the traditional rhythm of the music. Some of the Egyptian family members of the groom seem a bit scandalized by the gender-mixed dance and stay at their tables.

The music and dancing are interrupted by the dinner buffet being opened and attended to. The food is Middle Eastern, with chicken kebabs; minced meat skewers; tabbouleh, a parsley and semolina salad; *mujaddara*, a rice and lentil dish; succulent pieces of lamb on a bed of rice; *fattoush*, a green salad topped with fried pita bread and sumac; and large baskets with pita bread. There are overloaded trays of baklava and other sweets. Later, the couple will cut the three-layer white wedding cake and feed each other the first piece. It is a joyous occasion and the icing around Abdullah's mouth elicits lots of laughter from all involved. The celebration, which started around 6 o'clock, does not wind down until almost midnight.

Conclusion

These three stories are my recollections of the wedding events, and additional information from interviews and conversations. They narrate the particular and tell us how these three couples found each other and created their families. Hundreds if not thousands of American Muslim weddings take place every year, and they are as diverse as the couples that celebrate and mark their marriages through rituals, ceremonies, and feasts. These weddings, including our three, share basic features such as a religious ceremony, the nikah or kitab, the presence of witnesses, and the agreement on a mahr, as well as the announcement of the marriage through a celebration or feast. Specific features such as dress, food, guests, music or not, and venue vary widely and reflect the many facets of American Muslim communities and families, from ethnic and racial background to class and gender norms.

Not all American Muslim weddings take place in the United States and not all weddings involve two people who are both Muslim or who identify as a man and a woman. And it is hard to believe from our three stories that not all American Muslims who get married are young or have never been married before. I wish there were room here for the story of the Muslim-Hindu wedding, or the Pakistani-Syrian wedding, or that of a Sudanese American man and his Indian Muslim wife, not to mention the older woman convert who was getting married for the fourth time, or the gay Pakistani couple's wedding a friend told me about.[8]

There are stories of complicated paths to even having a wedding, the heartbreak of canceled weddings and broken promises, and the supportive and unsupportive reactions of families and communities. At times, weddings bring a foreboding of future troubles; at other times they set the tone for new and challenged gender relations and family norms. There are debts to be paid for expensive weddings and relationships to be mended when things did not go according to plan or everyone's expectation. And although the marriage is more important than the wedding, an analysis of the who, where, when, and how of a wedding provides a fascinating framework for understanding the marriage it creates.

NOTES

1 Warith Deen Mohammed (1933–2008) was the leader of the African American Muslim community organization that emerged from the Nation of Islam after the death of its leader, Elijah Muhammed (1897–1975). The organization had various names over the years, including American Society of Muslims and The Mosque Cares.

2 See Debra Majeed, "Sexual Identity, Marriage, and Family," in J. Hammer and O. Safi, eds., *The Cambridge Companion to American Islam* (Cambridge: Cambridge University Press, 2013), 312–329; Juliane Hammer, "Marriage in American Muslim Communities," *Religion Compass* 9, 2 (2015): 35–44.

3 See, for example, Salma Abugideiri and Mohamed Hag Magid, *Before You Tie the Knot: A Guide for Couples* (No Place, 2013); Munira Lekovic Ezzeldine, *Before the Wedding: Questions to Ask for Muslims before Getting Married* (Irvine: Izza Publishing, 2009); Ruqaiyyah Waris Maqsood, *The Muslim Marriage Guide* (Hicksville: Goodword, 2014).

4 There is a book that contains sample contracts: Hedaya Hartford and Ashraf Muneeb, *Your Islamic Marriage Contract* (Amman: Al-Fath, 2007), as well as online resources for marriage contracts, such as iman-wa.org, hijabman.com. For an example of premarital counseling materials, see this questionnaire developed by the ADAMS Center in Virginia and widely used in other mosques: www.adamscenter.org.

5 The mehndi or henna party is technically also part of wedding practices among many Muslims. It revolves around the application of henna paste, in intricate designs, to the hands and feet of the bride and women present at the celebration. Henna parties are usually gender segregated and men have a party as well but usually do not apply henna. The application of the henna designs is part of the preparation and beautification of the bride for the wedding and wedding night.

6 Many American Muslim children attend classes, usually on Sunday, to learn about their religion.

7 A specific dimension of marital selection and discussions of it in Muslim communities are explored in Zareena Grewal, "Marriage in Colour: Race, Religion and Spouse Selection in Four American Mosques," *Ethnic and Racial Studies* 32, 2 (2009): 323–345.

8 See also two wonderful collections of first-person narratives about love and marriage: Ayesha Mattu and Nura Maznavi, eds., *Love, Inshallah: The Secret Love Lives of American Muslim Women* (Berkeley: Soft Skull, 2012); Ayesha Mattu and Nura Maznavi, eds., *Salaam, Love: American Muslim Men on Love, Sex, and Intimacy* (Boston: Beacon Press, 2014).

9

Funerals and Death Rites

Honoring the Departed

AMIR HUSSAIN

The King Fahad Mosque (KFM) in Culver City is one of the largest mosques in southern California, with over a thousand people gathered together every Friday afternoon for the congregational prayer.[1] Following the *khutba*, or sermon, and the *salah*, or daily prayer, come the usual community announcements about upcoming events, and then an unusual request for those remaining to perform the funeral prayer, called the *salah al-janaza*, for a brother who passed away the night before. The request is unusual in that this mosque, like the large majority in North America, does not have a mortuary attached to it. However, bodies are sometimes brought to the mosque if someone died in the vicinity. In this case, the person was an elderly man who died as he wanted to at home, surrounded by his family who prepared his body in an appropriate Islamic fashion.

A few minutes later, a hearse pulls up and negotiates the usual chaos of cars and people that is the crowded parking lot at KFM. A simple wooden coffin—really no more than a rectangular rough plywood box—covered by a cloth embroidered with qur'anic verses is brought out on a trolley, and wheeled up to the front of the main prayer area. This mosque is gender segregated, with the men praying in the large main prayer area on the first floor, and the women praying upstairs in a balcony that overlooks part of the men's prayer space. What strikes me first as a witness to this scene is the number of men who rush to help move the coffin from the hearse to the main prayer space. Most of them, like me, don't know the deceased since the KFM congregation is so large, but we are all willing to help. We know that by definition, this is not something that the deceased will be able to do for us. Instead, it is his last right on us as members of the Muslim community. We will pray for him, perhaps out of the hope that someone will pray for us when our time comes. Technically, there is an obligation on some in the KFM community to perform this ritual—what is known in Islamic law and ethics as *fard kifaya*—a duty that is obligatory on some members of the community, but one for which all members of the community will be held responsible if the duty is neglected.

The salah al-janaza is unique in that the congregation remains standing without the bowing or prostration that is characteristic of the daily prayers. Since the performance of this prayer is uncommon, the imam reminds us of the steps involved in the way that he will lead the prayer according to the Hanafi school, including not raising our hands up to our ears any time after the first *takbir* or call of *Allahu akbar*, "God is greater." With the short funeral prayer completed, the body is placed back in the hearse and taken to a cemetery in Westminster. This is the closest cemetery to the KFM that has a section for Muslim burials.

I am a Muslim and also a scholar of Islam. For twenty years, I have lived in Los Angeles and worked with various Muslim communities here. I have created and taught courses on death and dying in the world's religions. I have prayed the salah al-janaza several times at mosques in Los Angeles. Yet until I began doing the research for this chapter, I had never been to a Muslim burial service. I had never visited a Muslim mortuary, nor spoken with a Muslim funeral director or anyone who was involved in the rituals of Muslim funerals or burials. In this chapter, I discuss Muslim funerals and burials, and in so doing illustrate the issues that are important for Muslims in the United States about death rites and funerals.

Islamic Understandings of Death and Resurrection

The Islamic understanding of death, introduced to seventh-century Arabia by the Prophet Muhammad, represented a dramatic shift from pre-Islamic Arabia. In pre-Islamic Arabia, there was a notion of fate, with time (*dahr*)[2] being the determining agent of a person's life and death. This is reflected in the Qur'an, where the pre-Islamic Arabs say: "There is nothing but our life in this world. We live and we die and nothing destroys us but Time" (45:24).[3] To this, Muhammad is commanded to say: "It is God who gives you life, causes you to die, then gathers you together for the Day of Resurrection, of which there is no doubt" (45:26).

In the modern United States, there is a significant change in the rites and rituals of death and dying for Muslims. In the premodern world, the majority of people died at home, and so family members by necessity had to be familiar with the rituals surrounding the dead. In that way, the prayer service described above is anomalous, since the person died at home of natural causes and his family members were able to prepare his body for burial. In the modern world, the majority of people die in hospitals or other institutions, creating a distance from traditional rituals since they are now usually handled by funeral professionals or volunteers and not family members. In addition, American Muslims live as religious minorities and have to negotiate U.S. laws about the disposal of the dead.

When a Muslim dies, the corpse is treated with great respect. Ideally, the dying person will have asked for God's forgiveness, prepared a will, performed the ritual full-body ablution before prayer, and recited the *shahada* or profession of faith before his or her death.[4] The body is then washed (a ritual known as *ghusl*). Traditionally, this would be done by members of the family, with males washing the body of males, and females washing the body of females (spouses are allowed to wash the bodies of their partners). In the contemporary world, where family members may have no familiarity with this washing, or the deceased may die in a hospital where washing is not possible, the washing is usually done by volunteers in a funeral home or mortuary. These volunteers can also guide family members who wish to do the washing themselves. Rkia Cornell has a moving description of doing this washing as a volunteer at the Islamic Center of Southern California.[5]

Once the corpse is cleaned, it is wrapped in a shroud consisting of five pieces of clean white cloth for a female, or three pieces for a male. The pieces of cloth contain no sewn seams or knots, and if the person has performed the Hajj or pilgrimage, his or her Hajj garments may be used for the shrouding. As noted above, there is a special funeral prayer for the deceased (salah al-janaza) which is unique in that the congregation remains standing without the prostration that is characteristic of the daily prayers. The corpse is then buried, ideally within twenty-four hours of death and without a coffin. A grave is dug deep enough to cover the body (usually at a level of six feet), which is buried lying on its right side with the head facing in the direction of Mecca (as in salah, or daily prayer). The grave is then filled in with earth, usually resulting in a mound that is above ground level. A simple headstone may be erected, but elaborate memorials are not recommended.

For most observant Muslims, the physical death of the body is not the end of existence. There is a developed understanding of judgment in the grave, a waiting period until the Day of Judgment, and a final reward or punishment in heaven or hell. The Qur'an is clear about the idea of a resurrection after the end of this life. This is expressed succinctly in 22:66: "It is God who gave you life, will cause you to die, and will again give you life: Truly the human being is ungrateful!" Another verse from the Qur'an, 22:7, was popular on tombstones as early as the ninth century in Egypt: "And because the Hour (of judgment) is coming, there is no doubt about it; and because God shall raise up those who are in the graves."

The Salah al-Janaza in Sunni Islam

One evening, I came back to my office from teaching a night class to find an email from a friend that the father of a mutual friend had passed away that afternoon while on a business trip. Instead of driving home, I drove to the King Fahad Mosque. It was after the *'isha*, or night prayer, but I was hoping some people would be around, so that we could pray the funeral prayer for my friend's father. Unfortunately, when I got to the mosque, it had already closed for the night, and the security guard had finished his shift and locked the doors, so I couldn't enter the building.

In the Hanbali and Shafi'i schools of Islamic law and ethics, one can pray the funeral prayer in absentia, making the prayer without the actual body being present.[6] In the Maliki and Hanafi schools, this is not permitted, and the corpse must be present for the prayer to be valid. Since my friend's father had died on a journey and might not be returned to his Muslim community for several days at least, I thought it was important to offer the prayer for him. However, I could not enter the mosque to do the prayer. Instead, I performed it outside, on the marble floor that leads to the main doors of the mosque. This was the first time I had performed salah al-janaza outdoors, and it made me appreciate a benefit of there being no prostration in the prayer. To perform the regular prayer on a cold outdoor marble floor, without a prayer mat, would have been difficult. But the salah al-janaza has no prostration, and one remains standing throughout.

I thought of the funeral prayer that I had performed a few months earlier, which I noted at the beginning of this chapter. There, once the coffin was brought to the front of the men's prayer space, the imam told us the name of the deceased and we lined up to pray the funeral prayer. Over half the congregation had left by that point, since it was after the conclusion of the Friday afternoon prayer. However, several hundred of us remained to perform the prayer.

The imam reminded us of the requirements of the prayer, that there would be four takbirat, or recitations of "God is greater," with no bowing or prostrations in between, no call to announce the prayer, and only bringing our hands up to our ears on the first cycle of prayer. The imam led the prayer according to the Hanafi school of Shari'a; had it been performed in accordance with the other schools there would have been slight differences, such as raising the hands up after the first cycle of prayer, or the wordings of the prayers recited in the last two cycles.

The prayer began with the intention to make the salah al-janaza for the deceased, who was named by the imam so that we could remember him by name in our prayers. The imam raised his hands to his ears and recited aloud the first takbir, which is the phrase "Allahu akbar," literally, "God is greater." We followed him, and then with our arms folded in front of us, recited silently along with the imam the first chapter of the Qur'an. This was followed by a short prayer in praise of God: "Glory be to you, O God, and all praise is due to you, and blessed is your name and exalted is your majesty, your praises are elevated and no one is worthy of worship but you." This ended the first cycle of prayer.

The second cycle began with the imam again saying the takbir aloud. This was followed by the silent recitation of the praise of the prophets Muhammad and Abraham which typically come at the end of the daily prayers: "O God, shower your mercy on Muhammad and the family of Muhammad as you showered your mercy on Abraham and the family of Abraham. You are the one worthy of praise and glory. O God, bless Muhammad and the family of Muhammad as you blessed Abraham and the family of Abraham. You are the one worthy of praise and glory."

The third cycle began with the imam saying the takbir aloud. This was followed by the silent recitation of a prayer for the deceased: "O God, forgive our people who are still alive and those who have died, those who are present here and those who are absent, those who are young and those who are elderly, those who are male and those who are female. O God, let the one from among us that you want to keep alive live according to Islam, and let the one from among us that you want to die die in a state of faith." Then came a personal prayer for the deceased, mentioning him by name, and asking for God's forgiveness and mercy on him.

The fourth and final cycle began with the imam saying the takbir aloud, followed by saying aloud the blessings that conclude the daily prayers, turning to the right and then the left while saying each time: "Peace be upon you and the mercy of God."

Having prayed this prayer a number of times, I needed to take the next step, which was to observe a funeral and burial. For this, I needed to go to another mosque in Southern California which had an Islamic mortuary.

The Islamic Society of Orange County: Funerals and a Burial

The Islamic Society of Orange County (ISOC) is the largest Islamic center in Southern California. Located in the city of Garden Grove in Orange County, about an hour's drive from Los Angeles, it was founded in 1976. In 2005, a mortuary was added, making it one of the few mosques in the area with an onsite mortuary. I met with Goulade Farrah, who is the funeral director. He said that the ISOC Mortuary averaged about twenty funerals per month. As a full-time funeral director, Farrah also works with the Jewish community, which has similar funeral rituals to Muslims, as well as with members of other faith communities—there is a large Vietnamese population in Garden Grove. Having been in many other funeral homes, I was struck first by the simplicity of his operation at the ISOC Mortuary. His office was not much bigger than a small closet, with only one small window in the door. His desk and chair were on one side of the space, and there were two chairs for people to sit on beside him. Farrah said that the average non-Muslim funeral he did in the area would cost around $18,000, while the basic funeral at the ISOC would average less than half that, at $8,500. The non-Muslim funerals would average about twenty-one days from the date of death to the actual burial, while the Muslim funerals would ideally happen within twenty-four hours of death.

Farrah then took me into the working area of the mortuary, which had one station to wash and shroud bodies. Behind this was the cold storage for corpses, with shelves on one side for women, and on the other side for men. Since the mortuary did not use any chemicals or do any embalming, it was considered a Green mortuary. In the mortuary, I met a staff member, Abu Ahmad. He was one of the people who would wash the bodies if it could not be done by family members of the deceased. The ISOC Mortuary had a list of volunteers they could call upon to do this, men who washed the bodies of males, and women who washed the bodies of females. Normally, it took three people to do the washing, since the corpse would often be rigid and slippery, requiring two people to hold it while the third person did the washing. There are similar volunteer societies across North America, with my mother belonging to one in Toronto at the mosque of the Islamic Society of North America.[7]

We then went across the hall to the other side of the mortuary. This consisted of the family lounge, as well as an area where people could view the body of the deceased once it had been washed and shrouded. The day that I was there, there were two funerals. One was a woman from Burma, the other a man from Jordan. What was striking to me was the gender breakdown of the two funerals. For the Burmese woman, a number of women were present to view the body. However, when it came time for the Jordanian man to be brought into the viewing room, there were no women present. This illustrates the differences in practices of different ethnic communities of Muslims.

Once each family had finished in the viewing room, the respective corpse was placed into a plain white panel van. This was one of the ways in which the ISOC Mortuary kept the costs down, with hearses being available at an extra charge. The van was driven by Farrah's son, who is another employee of the mortuary. The van drove around the property to the back entrance of the ISOC mosque, Masjid Al-Rahman. There, the two corpses were taken out and placed in a room that was screened off from the main prayer room in the mosque with a sliding door. They were lined up, with the head of one corpse next to the feet of the other corpse. The usual practice for funerals through the ISOC Mortuary is to pray the *dhuhr*, or noon prayer, and then pray the funeral prayer immediately afterward. The sliding door separated the corpses from the living during the noon prayer, and then the door was opened during the funeral prayer.

The imam explained that there were two funerals that day, and he gave the names of both of the deceased. Like the KFM, the ISOC mosque is gender segregated. In the case of Masjid Al-Rahman, there is one large prayer space on the main floor, with the men on one side of the room and the women on the other side of a glass wall that separates the two prayer spaces. The immediate male family members were invited to come to the front of the men's prayer area to be closest to the corpses of their deceased, and the imam led everyone in one funeral prayer for both deceased. In another situation, a family member might lead the funeral prayer. After the prayer the imam gave a short sermon about death in the Islamic tradition. This was not particular to either of the deceased, but a general reminder to the community that death will come to all of us, and a reminder to all of us to repent before we returned to God.

Once the funeral prayer was over, the body of the man from Jordan was taken and put in one of the white vans and driven by Abu Ahmad to the cemetery in Westminster, about two miles away from the mosque, for burial. Unfortunately, there was a delay in the burial of the woman from Burma. The electronic death certificate had not been entered into the California Electronic Death Registration System by the hospital where the woman had died. Without the proper registration of this death certificate, the woman could not be buried in the cemetery. Farrah had to call the hospital and ask the hospital staff to resend the certificate. This took two attempts, as the first time the fax transmission to his office from the hospital wasn't clear enough to be accepted. Another complication was that the health department was closed for their daily lunch break from noon to 1 p.m., so nothing could be done until the appropriate person returned to his office. This was particularly ironic as it was during the month of Ramadan, so the family members of the deceased, who were unable to eat lunch, had to wait until someone else's lunch hour was over before they could proceed with the burial. This is one of the issues that arises with trying to bury the body within twenty-four hours of death. Had it been a non-Muslim funeral taking place more than a week after the death, there would have been ample time to make sure the paperwork was properly filed and to correct any errors. Thankfully, the issue was resolved with a delay of only an hour. Farrah's son then put the woman's corpse into another van and drove it to the cemetery where she would be buried. There are five cemeteries that are used by the ISOC Mortuary.

I was able to go to the burial of the man from Jordan, who had been a member of the congregation at the King Fahad Mosque. The Westminster Memorial Park cemetery had a large section for Muslim burials. By 2013, the first 2,000 plots that had been purchased were already filled, and so space for another 3,500 plots was purchased. There were about 300 completed graves in that new section, with another 80 or so still unfinished, in two rows of 40. These were graves where people had been buried over the previous six months, with a mound of earth to mark their burial. Once the two rows were completely filled up, they would be finished like the other graves behind them, with a cement border between the graves, white gravel on top of them, and a simple headstone to mark each one.

When I arrived at the cemetery, Abu Ahmad was waiting to finalize the paperwork for the burial. There were approximately 150 men present, with no women in sight. I was told that this was the custom in Jordan, where women aren't present at the burial. There are also hadith, or sayings of the Prophet Muhammad, that discourage women from attending a burial.[8] Still, it was the first graveside service I had ever attended without any women present.

The workers at the cemetery had already dug out the grave and lowered a concrete vault into it. Since the deceased was to be buried without a casket, the cemetery required a concrete liner to comply with health regulations. Abu Ahmad opened the rear doors to the van and the immediate family lined up in two rows behind it to carry the bier to the grave. The bier was metal with a plastic backboard on the bottom where the shrouded corpse rested, covered by a cloth embroidered with Qur'anic verses. The man's family took turns carrying the bier to the gravesite about one hundred yards away, which had been fenced off with a temporary plastic fence.

Abu Ahmad and the cemetery workers lowered the body into the grave using the standard strap and automatic pulley system employed for this task. Once the straps were brought back up, a ladder was lowered into the grave. Abu Ahmad and two members of the deceased's family descended into it. They brought out the plastic backboard on which the corpse had rested. They also made sure that the body was positioned on its right side, oriented to the prayer direction. Finally, they put a few handfuls of earth into the grave, so that even though the corpse would be sealed into a concrete vault, there would be a symbolic amount of earth to which the body could return. With the body properly positioned in the grave, they came up and removed the ladder, and the cemetery workers used a bulldozer to lower the concrete cover down onto the vault to seal it.

Once the vault was sealed, the cemetery workers brought up a John Deere Dump Hauler that held the earth that had been excavated to create the grave. Abu Ahmad asked everyone present, beginning with the man's family, to take handfuls of dirt and fill in the grave. As people lined up to do this, he stood beside the grave and repeatedly recited the following words from the chapter of the Qur'an entitled *Taha*: "From the earth We (God) created you, and into it We will return you, and from it We will bring you forth a second time" (20:55). Once people had taken turns putting earth into the grave, using either their hands or shovels, the cemetery workers dumped in the remaining dirt. Abu Ahmad and a few members of the family then used shovels to create the rounded mound of earth on top of the grave.

With the burial completed, everyone gathered under the trees that marked the end of the Muslim section to listen to sermons that concluded the graveside service. Two imams gave short, five-minute exhortations about death and dying, and three members of the family also spoke in Arabic. The five speakers took less than twenty minutes altogether, and gave very little personal information about the deceased. Instead, the exhortations from the imams were similar to those heard in the mosque, reminding people of the inevitability of death and encouraging them to prepare by becoming more observant in their practice of Islam. The prayers by the three family members asked for the deceased's sins to be forgiven, for his good acts to be accepted by God, for him to be steadfast in answering the questioning angels in the grave, for his grave to be a window to paradise, and for the family to have patience and perseverance in the face of their loss. The family of the deceased lined up in a receiving line and shook hands with everyone who had attended the burial. Since it was Ramadan, there would be no immediate reception. It was about 3:15 p.m. when the funeral concluded, and the time to break the fast wouldn't be until approximately 8:05 p.m. Instead, we were told that the family would be hosting a reception at the mosque after the sunset prayer and the breaking of the fast. People returned to their cars; from start to finish the burial service had taken about fifty minutes.

While the sermons were going on, the cemetery workers had removed the temporary plastic fence around the grave. They helped Abu Ahmad put the metal bier and the coverlet embroidered with Qur'an verses back into the van and he drove back to the mortuary. I was able to wander around the Muslim cemetery to take a closer look at the graves. All the graves were identical in shape and size, with a black headstone that had three lines of text. The first line was either the *basmallah* (In the name of God, the Merciful, the Compassionate) or a line from the Qur'an commonly recited at funerals, "Indeed we belong to God, and unto God we are returning" (2:156). The second line named the person buried, while the third line gave the person's dates of birth and death. Some of the graves were decorated, but surprisingly few with any "Islamic" elements. Some had balloons and others ceramic angels, both decorations that could be found in any cemetery. Some graves had bird feeders installed over them; others had colored glass stones to contrast with the white gravel that covered each grave. A few had Islamic prayer beads or tiles inscribed with Qur'anic verses.

The Muslim section of the cemetery was marked by a large granite stone. On one side was the basmallah, and underneath that was a version of some lines from the funeral prayer, "O Allah forgive our living and our dead, those who are with us and those who are absent, our young and our old, our menfolk and our womenfolk. O Allah, to whoever you give life in Islam and whoever you take away from us, take him or her in a state of iman (faith)." Underneath that was the verse from Surah Taha (20:55) that was recited when people were filling the grave with earth. The opposite side of the marker had alternating text in Arabic and English. At the top was the line from 2:156 of the Qur'an followed by the English translation, and then the following hadith: "Peace be unto you, o people of the graves, may Allah forgive us and you. You are our predecessors and we are right after." These hadith and Qur'anic verses about death are well known; perhaps this is why there was no information to identify them as such.

The Muslim Mortuary and Cemetery Committee

A few days after the funeral, I was able to meet with Abdul Wahab, one of the directors of the Muslim Mortuary and Cemetery Committee (MMCC). The MMCC was established in 1991, and Abdul Wahab, who had been on the board of the ISOC, was asked to join in 1996. Prior to the establishment of the MMCC, the ISOC had been working with a cemetery in Riverside. However, issues arose because the workers in that cemetery's mortuary were not sensitive to the requirements of the Muslim community. So, for example, if a body was delivered to them, they sometimes left it naked on the trolley once it had been removed from the transportation bag. This violated Muslim understandings of modesty, which apply not only to the living, but also to the dead. The MMCC was formed to provide burials that complied with both Islamic ritual requirements and California law. Abdul Wahab and the MMCC created the forms and paperwork that allowed bodies to be buried within twenty-four hours of death if there was no need for a coroner to intervene.

Abdul Wahab explained to me that they had to wait at least three months for the earth in fresh graves to settle before they could be finished. Once the rows of graves were ready to be finished, they would add a cement border between the graves, so people could respect the dead and walk between them without having to step on any of the graves. This was also the reason for putting gravel over the graves. If the graves were covered with grass, the cemetery would go over them with mowers and tractors. The gravel prevented this from happening. The MMCC also made an effort to keep all the plots identical so that there would be no differentiation between rich and poor. Interestingly, in the Westminster cemetery, beside the plots managed by the MMCC, there were about twenty-five other assorted Muslim graves, some with more elaborate headstones or gravestones. So, those who wanted something other than what the MMCC offered had the option of working with another funeral director. Those who wanted to be buried beside loved ones could purchase adjoining or family plots. Otherwise, people would be buried in a grid in the order in which they died.

There are other rituals that take place after the funeral. Many families may gather to recite the Qur'an in its entirety, dividing up the chapters among them. Often there is an event to mark the fortieth-day anniversary of the death and another one to mark the one-year anniversary.

My conversation with Abdul Wahab also raised some issues specific to Muslim funerals in Southern California. One was the need to create a system whereby people could sign off on the appropriate paperwork to bury someone within twenty-four hours of death. Another was the need to bury indigent people. This had happened twice at the KFM in the past year, when they got calls from the coroner about people who had died with no next of kin and whose names indicated that they might have been Muslim. The KFM paid for these funerals through donations solicited from the congregation, another aspect of their communal obligation or fard kifaya. Another issue was to ensure that those who wanted to could receive an appropriate Islamic burial. For this purpose, the MMCC created and distributed cards that people could keep in their wallets, which declared them to be Muslim and asked that they be buried according to Islamic law and not be embalmed or autopsied. The cards also had information about the MMCC so that people could contact them to make arrangements (or ideally, prearrangements) for burial. The need to accommodate Islamic law to California law was demonstrated in the need for concrete vaults to line the graves since the bodies were buried in a shroud and not a casket.

Often, the issues for Muslims come from outside the Muslim community. There may be opposition to Muslim cemeteries due to Islamophobia. For example, in June 2016 the town of Dudley, Massachusetts, denied the local Islamic community the opportunity to build a cemetery on land that they had purchased. This was particularly ironic as the Islamic community in question, the Islamic Society of Greater Worcester, had founded one of the first Muslim cemeteries in the country almost a century earlier, in 1918.[9]

There may also be issues with Muslims who have family members who are Christian, and who may want the person buried with other family members in a non-Muslim part of the cemetery. Or issues may arise because the traditional Muslim funeral takes place within twenty-four hours of death, thus not allowing people to attend, as they might have done if it were a Christian funeral that would have taken place a week later. Christian family members might also want the body to be embalmed and have an open-casket funeral, which conflicts with Shariʿa for Muslims.

Muslim American Variations

Abdul Wahab mentioned that the MMCC was open to both Sunni and Shiʿa Twelver communities. Given the large number of Shiʿa Muslims in Southern California, it is not surprising that they have their own exclusive Shiʿa organization, the Muslim Burial Organization of Los Angeles (MBOLA), which buries people according to the Jaʿfari school of Shariʿa. The MBOLA manages two cemeteries of its own: Wadi-us-Salaam in LaVerne, whose plots sold out in 2010, and Wadi-e-Hussain in Pomona, which had 750 plots remaining. There are slight differences between the Shiʿa funeral prayer and the Sunni version described above. The main difference is that the prayer consists of five takbirat and not four, with the added cycle being another prayer of forgiveness for the deceased. After the fourth takbir, the following is recited before the pronouncement of the fifth takbir: "O Allah, indeed this is Your servant, son of Your servant and son of Your maidservant. He has become Your guest and You are the best of the hosts. O Allah, we do not know except good from him and You are more knowing than us. O Allah, if he had been a doer of good, increase his good deeds and if he had been a sinner and an evildoer, forgive his sins. And gather him on Judgment Day with the Prophet and the purified and chaste Imams."[10] Then the congregation raise their hands to the ears for the fifth takbir, ending the prayer.

If the funeral is for a female, the following prayer is recited after the fourth takbir:

O Allah, indeed this is Your maidservant, daughter of Your servant and daughter of Your maidservant. She has become Your guest and You are the best of the hosts. O Allah, we do not know except good from her and You are more knowing than us. O Allah, if she had been a doer of good, increase her good deeds and if she had been a sinner and an evildoer, forgive her sins. And gather her on Judgment Day with the Prophet and the purified and chaste Imams.

It is also notable that the Ja'fari school of Shari'a recommends the recitation of instructions to the corpse, reminding the deceased of the forthcoming visit by the angels who will ask him or her questions of faith. The Ja'fari school also recommends several prayers for the family and the community of the dead person. These prayers, which are also recited in Sunni traditions, include supplications asking God for forgiveness and to provide patience to the relatives of the dead. Family and friends gather to provide support and to ensure that the family is supplied with food for three days.

The Shi'a Isma'ili community has its own particular rituals. The body is washed and shrouded and if the services are not held in a funeral home, it is taken in a coffin into the Jamatkhana, or Isma'ili prayer space. There the community offers its own prayers, Qur'an recitation, and devotional hymns called *ginans* for the deceased before the coffin is taken to the cemetery for burial.[11]

The Nation of Islam (NOI) has a small presence in Southern California. NOI beliefs differ from those of other Muslims in that, according to the teachings of Elijah Muhammad, there is no life beyond the grave or spiritual resurrection after the death of the body. Instead, Elijah Muhammad taught about the "mental resurrection" that needs to take place while the person is still alive. It was the NOI that provided the United States with its most famous Muslim, the Greatest of All Time.

The Greatest of All Time

The first Muslim funeral most non-Muslim Americans have probably seen is the public funeral for Muhammad Ali. It was held during the first week of Ramadan on June 10, 2016, in his hometown of Louisville, Kentucky. Ali's funeral showed people's outpouring of love and support for him. This was a beloved American hero returning home. The funeral was by Ali's own design an interfaith event, featuring remarks by religious leaders, family members, celebrities, and politicians, concluding with a eulogy by former president Bill Clinton. The service began with a procession through the streets of his hometown that ended with his Muslim burial in the Cave Hill Cemetery. However, a day earlier, Ali had also had a traditional Muslim funeral service. At his passing, his body was washed and shrouded and prayed over in accordance with Islamic customs. Muslims across America and around the world were encouraged to pray the salah al-janaza for our deceased Muslim brother.

The Muslim funeral service prayer for Ali, held on June 9, 2016 at the Kentucky Exposition Center in Louisville, was extraordinary. The venue was next to Freedom Hall, where Ali had fought Tunney Hunsaker in his first professional fight on October 29, 1960. It was broadcast live across the country, and on the drive home I heard part of the Qur'an recitation from the funeral on CBS radio, the first time I ever saw or heard coverage of a Muslim funeral on the daily news.

The service was led by Imam Zaid Shakir, a noted American imam from California and the cofounder of Zaytuna College, the first accredited Muslim liberal arts college in the United States. Among the pallbearers who brought in the coffin was Shaykh Hamza Yusuf, another cofounder of Zaytuna College, and international recording star Yusuf Islam (the former Cat Stevens). Imam Zaid explained to the crowd what would happen during the salah al-janaza. The funeral prayer was performed, followed by a Qur'an recitation and a translation of the words recited by Shaykh Hamza. Then three people were invited to address the crowd in short sermons. They were Sherman Jackson, a professor at the University of Southern California and one of the most important Muslim scholars in the United States; Dalia Mogahed, the former director of the Gallup Center for Muslim Studies; and Khadijah Sharif-Drinkard, a lawyer who oversees business and legal affairs for the New York offices of Black Entertainment Television (BET).

Sherman Jackson's short sermon captured the intertwining of American and Muslim identities in the body of Muhammad Ali:

> As a cultural icon, Ali made being Muslim cool. Ali made being a Muslim dignified. Ali made being a Muslim relevant. And all of this he did in a way that no one could challenge his belongingness to or in this country. Ali put the question of whether a person can be a Muslim and an American to rest. Indeed, he KO'd [knocked out, eliminated] that question. With his passing, let us hope that that question will now be interred with his precious remains. . . . Ali helped this country move closer to its own ideals. He helped America do and see some things that America was not quite ready to do or see on its own. And because of Ali's heroic efforts,

America is a better place today for us all. And in this regard, Ali belongs
not just to the Muslims of this country, Ali belongs to all Americans. . . .
If you are an American, Ali is part of your history, part of what makes you
who you are, and as an American, Ali belongs to you, and you too should
be proud of this precious piece of your American heritage.

At another funeral service over fifty years earlier, on February 27,
1965 Ossie Davis gave the eulogy for Malcolm X. There, he famously
said, "Malcolm was our manhood, our living, black manhood! This
was his meaning to his people. And in honoring him we honor the best
in ourselves." Ali, as Professor Jackson pointed out, wasn't just for *his*
people, but for all people. If Malcolm was our manhood, then Ali was
our humanity, with a life lived for all the world to see. A life lived in
complexity and contradiction, triumph and tragedy. A life of change
and metamorphosis. A life which gave the lie to F. Scott Fitzgerald's line
about there being no second acts in American lives, by living out its successful second and third acts. A life which showed us, in the words of
the old cliché, that it's not about how many times you get knocked down,
but whether you get back up, and what you do when you get back up,
that truly matters. An iconic American life, lived by an iconic American
Muslim.

Conclusion

For Muslims around the world, the most important Muslim building
is the Ka'ba in Mecca. The second most important is the Prophet's
Mosque in Medina, which also contains the grave of the Prophet
Muhammad. For non-Muslims, perhaps the most famous Islamic
building is the Taj Mahal in India, which is also a mausoleum. Muslim
burial sites, then, are important to both Muslims and non-Muslims.
Perhaps the funeral of the most famous American Muslim, Muhammad Ali, helped to shed light on the practice of contemporary Muslim
funerals. But his funeral also evoked the presence of our Muslim
American ancestors, who have been buried in North American soil
since at least the 1600s.

In 1991, the African Burial Grounds were discovered in Lower
Manhattan. The African Burial Ground National Monument on

Duane Street was proclaimed a national monument in 2006 by President George W. Bush and dedicated in 2007. In July 2010 the remains of a ship were discovered nearby during the construction of the 9/11 memorial to the victims of the 9/11 terrorist attacks. That September, at the New York Academy of Sciences, researchers described the boat as a sixty- to seventy-foot Hudson River sloop from the first half of the seventeenth century (1727–1760, based on a coin found on the ship), which "may have traveled up and down the Hudson River and perhaps the Atlantic seaboard, ferrying goods like sugar, molasses, salt and rum between the warm Caribbean and the uniting colonies to the north."[12] That is a lovely pastoral image, until one remembers the Middle Passage, and that the "what" that was exchanged for the goods on that Hudson River sloop was not a "what" but a "who," slaves from West Africa. Some of those enslaved people were Muslim, and some of them were buried in the soil of Lower Manhattan. Muslims, it is important to remember, have for centuries been buried in America.

NOTES

1 My thanks to Shakeel Syed, the executive director of the Islamic Shura Council of Southern California, for helping to connect me with the relevant people responsible for Muslim burials in the greater Los Angeles area. Thanks also to the people interviewed for this chapter. Thanks to Edward Curtis and the authors who participated in the workshop that he organized for their feedback and comments on earlier versions of this chapter.

2 Also known as *zaman* or *al-ayyam* (the days).

3 I have consulted the Qur'an translations available on the quran.com website (especially those of Yusuf Ali, Marmaduke Pickthall, and Sahih International), but all translations are my own.

4 See Amir Hussain, "Death," in *The Oxford Encyclopedia of the Islamic World*, Vol. 2, ed. John L. Esposito (New York: Oxford University Press, 2009), 47–49.

5 See Rkia Elaroui Cornell, "Death and Burial in Islam," in *Voices of Islam*, Vol. 3, ed. Vincent J. Cornell (Westport: Praeger, 2007), 151–172.

6 On the differences between the schools, see Yasir Qadhi, "The Funeral Prayer in Absentia," available at muslimmatters.org.

7 For those interested in the details of the washing, this website provides an animated guide to the process: en.islamway.net.

8 For a discussion of these hadith and the permissibility of women visiting graves, see imamluqman.wordpress.com.

9   See Karen Smid, "Cemeteries," in *The Encyclopedia of Muslim-American History*, Vol. 1, ed. Edward Curtis IV (New York: Facts on File, 2010), 96–98.

10 I am grateful to Dr. Husein Khimjee for his help on this section, and for providing the texts of the prayers.

11 I am grateful to Dr. Hussein Rashid for his help on this section. There is also material on Isma'ili funerals available at this website: www.ismaili.net.

12 For more on the ship, see www.livescience.com.

PART IV

Islamic Ethics and Religious Culture

10

You Can't Be Human Alone

Philanthropy and Social Giving in Muslim Communities

DANIELLE WIDMANN ABRAHAM

Three young women sit on the wooden floor of an old house, with a dozen plastic bins around them. They chat as they place items in each of the bins. By the time they are done, each bin will hold a bottle of shampoo, a roll of toilet paper, a tube of toothpaste, a toothbrush, deodorant, a small brush, soap, and a package of sanitary napkins. Every woman who comes through the door of this transitional shelter for homeless women will get a bin, filled with these necessities of self-care. The young women are students at Boston University who are volunteering with an Islamic charity getting ready to open its first women's shelter in Dorchester, a mostly working-class community in south Boston. Like dozens of Muslim groups around the country, this organization initiated a project to help vulnerable people—in this particular case, women who are homeless. Boston winters are brutal for those who are unsheltered, and women often face even greater precarity than men do on the street. By putting together the bins, these three young women become part of the story of how and what Muslims give to help others. Islamic philanthropy in the United States becomes visible as a bin full of the items a woman uses in the bathroom to care for herself and to help her feel normal.

Islamic philanthropy takes many shapes and sizes in the United States. It can be the donation that enables a museum to host an exhibit of Islamic art, or a university to start an Islamic Studies program. It can be thousands of packages of ritually slaughtered meat given to Muslims by other Muslims so they can celebrate the end of Ramadan, the fasting month. It can take the shape of an after-school program that teaches working-class kids to code so they don't fall into the digital divide. It can be a fund-raiser held by Muslim university students to raise money for children living in refugee camps. It can be a shipment of blankets thousands of miles across the globe, to people whose homes were obliterated by waves of moving earth or water. In metropolitan Los Angeles, home to one of the most diverse Muslim populations in the world, Islamic philanthropy can be a forklift unloading a truckload of factory-new athletic socks—a practical and important item for those who are living on the streets, walking their days through the city. It can take the shape of a determined and quiet-spoken man in India who uses the donations of American Muslims to travel to a small village and pay off a moneylender who is keeping young kids as bonded laborers and it can also take the shape of a school that he then builds them, with the help of more funds from the very same group.

The gifts vary greatly, and so do the givers. Those who give based on their connection to Islamic tradition in the United States include people whose families came here four generations ago. They might remember grandparents passing out food on festival days, a time marked by joy and the desire to share it. Muslims who give are also those who just made their homes here in the past few months or even weeks. They might still be figuring out how to make their lives work in a bewildering new place, and they might give help to someone else who seems even newer and more excited or overwhelmed than they are. Muslim Americans are one of the most ethnically and culturally diverse demographic groups in the nation, and since giving is a way of making connections and establishing a sense of belonging, Muslim giving in the United States marks a wide and impressive range of actions by an exceptionally diverse group of people.

The diversity of ways that Muslims give is mirrored in Islamic tradition, which encompasses multiple modes of social giving. There is what some call an "alms-tax," *zakat*, which is a obligation upon all Muslims. It is giving that is required, *wajib*, to fulfill the commandments of scripture and it constitutes one of the five pillars of Islamic practice. In contemporary calculations, zakat is understood to be 2.5 percent of standing wealth that one has possessed for more than a year. The Qur'an delineates the categories of people who are to receive zakat, which includes widows, orphans, the needy, and the destitute, among others, so zakat must be given and it must be given to certain people. Because it is obligatory, some speak of it in terms of a "payment" rather than a gift.

In addition to obligatory giving, Islamic tradition also identifies *sadaqa*, extemporaneous giving. Sadaqa is not focused on particular groups of vulnerable people like zakat, but refers to voluntary giving. It thus reflects the reality that people live in varying contexts and as we move through these contexts, we encounter others and come face-to-face with their suffering. To give (or pay) zakat is to fulfill a duty to God and doing so grants the believer knowledge that their giving is righteous. Sadaqa, however, is different. It comes not from duty, but out of love, sympathy, hope, friendship, or compassion. When people give sadaqa, they make a choice about when and how to respond to another person. So these two types of giving complement each other: through zakat, Islam allows people to experience themselves as fulfillers of God's commands, and through sadaqa, Islam allows people to experience themselves in self-determined connections of compassion.[1]

These multiple modalities of giving in Islamic tradition emphasize how important it is to human experience and social life. Muslims are obligated to give and they are free to give; there are specific kinds of vulnerabilities people have to recognize, yet there is also the openness to respond to people whose situations move one's heart in the contingency of everyday life; there is a fixed amount one should give and an illimitable amount one could share; in giving there is choice and inclination, and in giving there is assigned responsibility. By placing these modalities of giving in parallel, the tradition of Islam puts people in proximity to two great forces of humanity, duty and love. Perhaps it even lets people see how duty and love might blur together, or, in some instances, why we might tease them apart.

It is clear that there is no way to practice Islam without giving, and different groups of Muslims have affirmed this in distinct ways. Muslims who follow Shi'a traditions of Islam recognize another mode of giving called *khums*. Like zakat, khums is obligatory, and like zakat, people speak of it as a payment. It is one-fifth of the surplus a person has earned in a year, over and above what one needs for household and family expenses. Shi'a Muslims maintain that authority over and responsibility for the broad community of believers lies with Imams, who provide guidance and inspiration. Although some Shi'as affirm a living Imam for their community, the majority of the world's Shi'as maintain the Imam is hidden, or in occultation, from our contemporary world.

In the absence of a living Imam, the highest human authority is a *marjaʿ al-taqlid*, which means "source of emulation," and refers to a person who can make definitive determinations about how to practice Islam. Khums must be given to the marjaʿ, who is required to spend half of it for the sake of people from the Prophet's family, *sayyid*s, who are poor, or orphaned, or stranded on a journey; the other half of it is spent as the marjaʿ wishes. Often, this second half supports schools and scholars.[2]

The multiple modalities of Muslim giving have been influenced by the contemporary social and political climate in the United States. Historian Kambiz GhaneaBassiri has noted changes in the cultural infrastructure among American Muslims in recent decades. The "dynamic development of Muslim institutions and communal relations" in the United States, GhaneaBassiri notes, has been motivated in part by the desire "to offset the stigmatizing effects" of popular discourse which marginalizes Muslims from public life.[3] Many institutions and social networks have been developed as vehicles of Islamic giving, both locally and nationally, and there has been an increase of projects and programs funded by Muslim giving in the post–9/11 period.

This growth has taken place in an atmosphere of heightened suspicion and mistrust of Muslims brought on by the war on terror, in which the United States and other countries targeted terrorists and terrorism, with a special focus on violent extremists with an Islamic background. After 9/11, several Muslim charities had their assets frozen and a few more faced further civil or criminal penalties or were shut down completely after being placed on a terrorism watch list.[4] New mechanisms for financial compliance and oversight have since been put in place, and they operate in conjunction with an ever-evolving and detailed legal framework of counterterrorism. In the contemporary United States, Muslim charities and philanthropic foundations must diligently comply with the intensifying financial and legal structures that ensure that they will not channel funds to terrorists. The Muslim charities and nonprofits that are operating today continue to function by virtue of their explicit commitment to regulatory compliance.

Giving to others and making obligatory payments from one's personal wealth are ways of participating in collective life. Social giving engages people by bringing together the material and the spiritual. It's about putting together bundles of new socks and underwear, and then putting that bundle in the hands of people who are homeless. At the same time, giving embodies deep values such as generosity, compassion, solidarity, and care. The combination of expressing values and acting with material things makes giving a compelling power in human life. We give in part because we see who we are through what we can give. Charity, philanthropy, and obligatory giving help us to establish the terms of our connections to others. When we give, we define ourselves by deciding with whom we will throw our lot. Social giving in Muslim communities involves expressing Islamic values in the distinct context of the United States. When we look at Muslim social giving, we can see the richly varied strands of Islamic tradition refracted through the multifaceted prism of American culture.

Social Giving in the American Shiʻa Diaspora

The Imam-e Zamana Mission (IZM) was founded in 1985 as a vehicle for the collection and distribution of zakat and khums. The organization is based in Hyderabad, India, but it is part of Muslim giving in the United States, since many Shiʻa Americans pay their khums to IZM. Giving to the organization, which then gives to others back in India, is part of how they practice Islam in America, as Indian Muslims living in a global diaspora. The organization traces its roots to influential Shiʻa clerics in twentieth-century Iran and Iraq who sought to reconfigure religious practices and institutions to make them beneficial in a modern society. From the 1960s onward, religious scholars and clerics participated in "intense discussion . . . concerning their role in society."[5] They saw Muslim societies as comparatively disadvantaged in light of the wealth and productivity of Western countries. Consequently, they called for Islamic scholars "to take a more active social role" in improving the quality of life and well-being of average people.[6] In tandem with Iranian intellectuals, religious scholars articulated a new understanding of Islam. They reinterpreted the relevance of Islamic tradition by emphasizing that "each Muslim has an obligation to strive for achieving the ideal Shiʻi society."[7] The active role of clerics and scholars in providing "social leadership" dovetailed with an increasing emphasis on education and the growth of nation-state bureaucracies throughout the twentieth century. The IZM was just one of dozens of organizations that emerged from global connections between laypeople and Shi'a clerics in the twentieth century, as religious leaders inaugurated educational institutions and charitable foundations that paralleled governmental efforts.

The contemporary development of religious organizations includes schools, universities, hospitals, and orphanages—all of which have been part of Muslim societies for centuries, through long-standing customs of elite patronage of education and social welfare. While these institutions are not new, their more recent iterations take a distinctly modern form in three respects. First, they have taken up the goal of international development, the broad project of improving the quality of life and socioeconomic standards in less industrialized societies. Second, such organizations have adopted modern, bureaucratic standards that value accountability and transparency. Finally, they are connected to diasporic networks of Shi'as who have migrated out of their nations of origin in pursuit of new global opportunities. All these trends are evident in the work of the Imam-e Zamana Mission.

Development emerged in the post–World War II world as a way of coordinating efforts to improve the quality of life of people in those societies that had not yet reaped the benefits of widespread industrialization and economic growth. One of the key claims of modern socioeconomic development is that poverty can be resolved through concerted effort. This marks a shift away from the premodern understanding of poverty, with its model of embodied care and responsibility for those in need. In the past, poverty was a reality to be endured; in our modern world, poverty is a problem to be solved and removed. While educational and social welfare institutions have long been a part of Muslim societies, such institutions now often reflect the new ambitions of development. "When I was growing up in Hyderabad," said Ali Ahmed, who lives in the Southwestern United States, "everyone in my family used to just give money to the orphanage and send them food during *Ramazaan* [Ramadan]. But things are different now." Today, the Imam-e Zamana Mission webpage demonstrates how the religious ideal of caring for the poor and vulnerable merges with the contemporary goal of redressing poverty. A banner at the top of the page quotes Ali, "If you want to pray to Allah for better means of subsistence, then first give something in charity." Below that lies one bold and simple claim: Education is a fundamental solution to poverty. Literacy has long been valued in Islamic culture as a way of enabling believers to engage the sacred text of Qur'an, and educational institutions were built on that foundation. IZM reframes this traditional value of education in the modern terms of development, as a solution that can be realized in society. This shift reflects the modern approach to poverty as a problem that can and must be solved.

Within the paradigm of development, poverty is also approached through the ideology of empowerment. If poverty is a problem to be solved, then part of the solution involves poor people playing an active role in transforming their own circumstances of poverty. When one of the leaders of Hyderabad's Shi'a community, Maulana Kamran Hyder, makes an appeal to fellow Muslims on behalf of IZM, he notes that the organization is "helping the poor to stand on their own feet." There are, then, two legacies that converge in projects like IZM: a religious tradition of giving to help the poor, and the development goal of helping the poor help themselves.

As an organization that bridges traditional social welfare and development, IZM operates in light of contemporary expectations of accountability and transparency. It is registered with the Indian state of Andhra Pradesh as a "public society," and licensed by the Indian government to collect contributions from abroad. As part of this official recognition, the government stipulates that IZM not engage in any kind of activity related to conversion, a highly charged activity in this Hindu-majority nation. But beyond this formal recognition, IZM itself engages in new types of reporting designed to satisfy the expectations of those who contribute to its projects. "They are doing this in a disciplined way and it gives people the sense that they were doing it for the community and not for themselves," said Ali Ahmed. "Previously, khums would be valid if the imam was there to collect it. Now, they have to specify that this money goes to those who are sayyids, this money goes to others, and when they release a report, they enumerate that." Expectations about organizational structure and communication have shifted in recent decades, such that religious projects like IZM are now evaluated by quasi-professional standards. IZM presents detailed figures about how many students are enrolled in its secondary schools and college, how many widows and disabled people it supports every month, and how many houses it builds for those who have no permanent dwelling. It also publishes the approximate costs for each of these activities, which enables those who give to track the outlay of expenses. Such practices of transparency and accountability are not limited to finances. IZM also digitally published its *ijaza*, its certificate of legitimacy that was granted in 1993 by Grand Ayatollah Ali al-Sistani, the preeminent Shi'a authority based in Najaf, Iraq, who is embraced by many Indians. Disclosing details of expenses and costs, providing a digital copy of its ijaza, and clarifying the composition of its Executive Committee helps those who are far away know and trust its efforts.

The vast majority of those who contribute to IZM are in the United States, Canada, and Europe. Although IZM was established by local elites in the Shi'a community of Hyderabad, it now functions as a source of social connection and religious devotion for those who have emigrated around the world. It is thus both a local and a global project. All Shi'as are obligated to give their khums to the marja' al-taqlid, the "source of emulation" or highest authority in Twelver Shi'a Islam (who in this case is Grand Ayatollah al-Sistani). The choice to give one's khums to IZM fulfills an important religious obligation, but it also enables those who now live far from their place of origin to feel that they are still connected to that original local world. IZM claims to provide "help to poor and needy people of our community." The "our" allows people living thousands of miles away to sense that they still belong to people like them in a place in which they no longer live, that they still are a part of the community that defines their roots. Khums must be given to the marja', and part of it must be distributed to poor sayyids. For Shi'as in the United States where there is no marja' and where there are few poor sayyids, khums functions as an inbuilt mechanism to connect to a homeland world that was once local and immediate and is now distant but dearly cherished.

African American Islam and Urban Social Change

The ILM Foundation is a community-based organization in Los Angeles that emerged from the congregation of Masjid Ibaadallah, or "the mosque of God's servants," and the commitment of its *imam*, the leader of the community, Saadiq Saafir to improve the lives of individuals in the neighborhood. Working with a coalition of other Muslim groups, the ILM Foundation has organized Humanitarian Day to meet the needs of homeless people living in Los Angeles. Since 2000, Humanitarian Day has been held every year during the fasting month of Ramadan, and has now spread from Los Angeles to other cities in the United States and three other countries. The ILM Foundation also hosts smaller-scale monthly Humanitarian Days with volunteers from the congregation. All these events grew out of the Muslim community of Los Angeles, whose members had, through various efforts, been serving food to the city's homeless for many years. In 2002, the ILM Foundation joined together with other Muslim organizations in the community to scale up their efforts during Ramadan. Today, Humanitarian Day is the "largest collective Muslim charitable event" in the United States, bringing together thousands of people to provide direct assistance to people living without shelter.

The ILM Foundation's efforts crystallized under the leadership of Imam Saafir. In recent years, he has received awards for his humanitarian work from the Islamic Society of North America and the Muslim Public Affairs Council, two important national Muslim American organizations. His journey to becoming a leader for social change in the community began with his own personal transformation. Imam Saadiq tells the story of how he came to Islam in 1970 after a man visited him every week for six months, selling *Muhammad Speaks*, the newspaper published by the Nation of Islam. One day, he finally accepted the man's invitation to go to the mosque. "I was really young, I was really running the streets," Imam Saafir says, "just trying to find something to get into. I went with [this brother] and heard the teachings. I wanted to go back and hear them again. The next week, I went back again, and I embraced Islam. I've been a Muslim ever since. That was the best move I ever made in my life."[8] Imam Saafir began meeting with other Muslims in a local home, and eventually he established Masjid Ibaadallah in South Central Los Angeles in 1986. The congregation is majority African American and working class.

As an imam, Saafir has focused on teaching Islam and supporting the personal development of the members of his congregation. "Islam is a social religion," he states, and in his role as a leader of the Muslim community, Imam Saafir has sought to communicate the values of Islam—knowledge, love, and mercy—to his students and congregants in order to help them thrive in society. For him, the truth of Islam is a message of empowerment.

Umar, who is part of the Masjid Ibaadallah community and who works with the ILM Foundation, described how meeting Imam Saafir changed him. "As a Muslim, I truly believe that you meet people on your path that you need to meet, that help you go forward. Imam Saadiq mentored me, he taught me, he helped me develop interests I didn't know I had. He taught me Islam, everything. He gave me an Islamic education and taught me to apply that education to my life." Imam Saafir came to Islam through a personal invitation from another African American man, and so too did Umar—this time, the invitation was from Imam Saafir himself. Umar's words reflect a sense that Imam Saafir was a singular and steady presence in his life, and a person who wanted to see him grow and learn.

Imam Saafir taught Umar about Islam as much by what he did as by what he said. "For Imam, Islam was a philosophy, a code, a protocol that you apply and that you live. It's about how to practice compassion. That's straight out of the Qur'an." Seeing Imam Saafir draw on religion to transform the local world deeply impressed him. "Imam Saadiq was real. He didn't just know about the *deen* [religion], he used it for peacebuilding and community building. He used it to train others. When I met him in Compton, he could articulate his experience, his learning, his emotional intelligence, and his cultural influence. For me and the people around me, they wanted to see who you are, if you showed up. I trusted him because of his actions and because he internalized the religion." Being drawn in to the Masjid Ibaadallah community through Imam Saafir's teaching changed the trajectory of Umar's life. "I was raised here in Compton and I traveled around. I engaged the community, the culture. The camaraderie on the streets is unique. Sometimes, it can get you into trouble, so that camaraderie is good but it can also be really bad. Most of us, you know, grew up. We don't have fathers. So he filled a void, he filled a void in my life. When you meet a group like that, that brotherhood, that's something you ain't never felt."

The mission of the ILM Foundation is to "teach life skills to replace social ills," and it reflects Saafir's vision of conjoining personal and community development in the name of Islam. ILM aims to "create an active network of multifaceted and talented caregivers that utilize their skills and resources to shelter those who don't have it, develop career or entrepreneurial goals, give care for those who require it, and provide additional educational (emotional intelligence) opportunity for those who want it."⁹ The name of the foundation, ILM, encapsulates this teleology with a play on the Arabic word for knowledge, 'ilm, and abbreviates the values of Intellect, Love, and Mercy that Imam Saafir and the Masjid Ibaadallah identify as foundational and empowering. The activism of the organization puts problem solving at the center: personal problem solving thus expands into efforts to solve social problems. In this model of giving, philanthropic outreach is combined with a human development approach in the hopes of promoting personal and collective empowerment. The hoped-for result is a resilient, creative, and collaborative social network that is galvanized by Muslim identity.

Humanitarian Day involves members of the Masjid Ibaadallah congregation along with people from other Muslim groups, religious organizations, and social service providers, all of whom work together to meet the needs of people who are homeless. This direct action, which involves Muslims as well as non-Muslims, comes out of the teachings of the Qur'an. "Our Creator instructs us to have the following attitude: *'And they give food in spite of love for it to the needy, the orphan, and the captive, Saying We feed you only from the love of God, we wish not from you reward or thanks.'* 78:6–7."¹⁰ ILM emphasizes how selfless giving to those in need expresses the love of God in an embodied, practical way.

This devotional and social action becomes situated in sacred time as Humanitarian Day, which is held every year during the month of fasting. Ramadan is a time to "revive, renew, and restore one's personal spirituality, families, and communities with a Divine Will for Good," according to the organization. "The Creator says, *'Ramadan is the month in which was sent down the Qur'an, as a guide to mankind, also clear (signs) for guidance and judgment (between right and wrong).'*"¹¹ The ILM Foundation links the sacred month of Ramadan, when Muslims fast from sunrise to sundown, to the act of feeding those who lack shelter, and thereby integrates care for others into the process of spiritual renewal. Thus the event of Humanitarian Day encourages people to act on "a social responsibility that *'enjoins what is right and forbids what is wrong,'*" and to embody qur'anic ethics in the local community.¹²

Humanitarian Day addresses the needs of those in Los Angeles who are homeless. The reality of ever-increasing numbers of people who are homeless within the city and county of Los Angeles is a crisis for community groups and public policy. The gap between wages and affordable housing has resulted in larger numbers of people living on the streets in what policy makers call "chronic homelessness." The Los Angeles Homeless Services Authority estimates that 75 percent of the roughly 47,000 people who are homeless go unsheltered every night.[13] This crisis reflects an acute racial disparity: although African Americans make up only 9 percent of the general population in Los Angeles, they are 40 percent of the homeless population.[14]

The ILM Foundation has taken a leadership role in coordinating Humanitarian Day which addresses some of the most important issues that affect the vulnerable: food, health, and hygiene. During Humanitarian Day, people are given a meal, foodstuffs to take home, and a bag filled with necessities: a toothbrush, toothpaste, clean socks, underwear, a comb, lotion, soap, and a washcloth. Medical checks for blood pressure and eye exams are performed by volunteers from the UMMA Community Clinic, a free clinic started by Muslim students from UCLA Medical School in 1992 in the wake of the Rodney King riots. Along with local Muslim organizations, groups such as the Los Angeles Police Department, the Church of Latter Day Saints, and Macy's department stores, among others, also support the event with donations in kind.

The ILM Foundation has ensured that Humanitarian Day is both collaborative and grassroots, working with organizations from across the city and registering volunteers from across the community. "Anyone can be involved," said Precious, who has volunteered during two Humanitarian Day events. "The policemen come in, the firemen stop by—it's really community oriented. And that puts power in the community. Being action-oriented, if you are with your fellow man, serving people, you're going to bond with them. Doesn't matter if you are Christian or Muslim. Last year, there were these two older African American women. They sat nearby, talking to people. They were having a great time. After a while, they asked me, 'If we help, can we get a T-shirt?' They couldn't stop laughing. That's what this does—it gives you entry to places, across walls that normally divide people."

For Precious, Humanitarian Day does indeed provide a kind of renewal, but she sees it as a renewal of the essence of being human. "Islam has zakat, sadaqa, philanthropy, but I don't think people separate these out much in real life. It's about the ethos of the practice, and that is definitely universal—as long as you don't put words on it. The words are from your community, but the action is from everyone. I think the experience of giving is instinctively part of the human experience. Religion amplifies it and gives it direction. For me, it is such an endorphin release. It's confirming our existence. We lose sight of that, you know. It gets blocked out because we are conditioned in this world and our mind is conditioned. So people get happy when they reconnect to that. I do. I feel at peace."

Humanitarian Day for Precious is about a way of experiencing herself in the course of helping others, a way of being released back into the essence of her human life. For Umar, who coordinates these daylong events, the personal experience of serving others is one half of the value of Humanitarian Day; the other half is taking on the responsibility of being in relationship with the people who are being served. "During Ramadan, you're fighting. You're fighting your hunger, your thirst. You totally tap into who you are. When you do this work, it's like that. You get a chance to see who you are and what you can do." That sense of being able to see something essential in oneself mirrors Precious's experience, yet for Umar a sense of connection to people who are being served is also crucial. "A lot of folks, they do some good will and bounce. We practice in the same location for our monthly Humanitarian Days that we do for our regular Humanitarian Days in Ramadan. One location. We stay in the same location to build a relationship with people. Because of that, Muslims have built a reputation to serve. We *built* that. And because of that, they have a different respect for Muslims. People there on Skid Row, they see you, they look for you. They'll say, 'You weren't here last week. You slackin' off?' They keep you accountable. *How* you do this work matters. The main objective is to connect with people. It's a sacred responsibility." This sense of responsibility and accountability in building relationships, which simultaneously builds people's respect for Muslims and Islam, complements the personal satisfaction that comes from being involved in meeting the needs of others.

In addition to personal satisfaction and interpersonal connection, Umar also describes Humanitarian Day as a way of socializing with others in a different way than they socialize every day. "We have people who come. We're not just someone they donate to, but they come do our work with us. You have wealthy people doing the work. You're giving them the opportunity to connect to who they are. It's not like they are just wealthy anymore. You got wealthy serving poor, poor serving wealthy. All of us feel wealthy together." Marking Humanitarian Day as an exceptional time—a day that is different from other days—and holding it during the sacred month of Ramadan doubly marks its contrast from everyday life, and this supports people in having a different experience of themselves and others, freed from the constraints of class differences which shape their everyday lives.

Umar describes students from the University of Southern California's Muslim Student Association who join as volunteers, and the way that the experience of volunteering becomes a kind of education that complements their university studies. "Students get a different type of education alongside their academic education. Some teachers teach only theories and these theories become so real to them that they forget about the application. Volunteering keeps students involved, and it gives them a chance to practice their religion. The fourth pillar of Islam is zakat, so they can see how to do zakat with us." Just as Umar himself was taught through the example of Imam Saafir, so too he now himself teaches Muslim youth how to practice Islam. He does this while maintaining a sense of accountability to those people who he knows rely on the support that the ILM Foundation provides. "It's a teaching ground, but I don't like to use a person's poverty as a petting zoo. It's the way that you teach about it so it doesn't compromise yourself or the person, your dignity and their dignity."

From the Islamic education program of a working class, African American mosque congregation came the ILM Foundation, and out of the ILM Foundation grew an extensive service network to meet the needs of increasingly large numbers of people who are homeless in greater Los Angeles. Social giving in this context is part of an effort of empowerment and community building, which is also a way of teaching people about Islam. Teaching people that they have the power to give and to sustain relationships of care and solidarity teaches them how to be Muslim in America.

U.S. Muslim Charity and Global Humanitarianism

A bag of rice, dry breakfast cereal, flour, two cans of baked beans, four cans of tuna fish, macaroni pasta, tomato sauce, sugar, salt, black tea, dates, and peanut butter. "If you say it's a Ramadan food parcel, you gotta have dates. That's a requirement. What wasn't there before is peanut butter. That's a big thing in America. People love peanut butter," said Ridwan, a staff member at Islamic Relief USA. "You gotta give people their comfort food at Ramadan." Every year during fasting month, hundreds of volunteers put these staples into cardboard boxes that are distributed to families across the United States. More than four hundred volunteers assemble five thousand boxes in Washington, D.C., Detroit, Dallas, and Los Angeles, giving people the basic supplies they can use to feed their families.

Feeding the poor during the fasting month is one of the oldest Islamic practices of giving, and yet this tradition takes on new significance with increasing food insecurity in America. Today there are more than 48 million people living in poverty in the United States, and yet this reality often goes unacknowledged.[15] "Hunger is a global epidemic, but when most people think of hunger, they don't think of the United States. It's true, in many ways, America is the land of plenty. But 1 in 7 of our neighbors will stare at empty plates while we prepare to enjoy our special Ramadan meals. As we strive to perfect our belief this Ramadan, let's remember the saying of our prophet (saw): 'He is not a believer who eats his fill while his neighbor beside him goes hungry.'"[16] Islamic Relief makes appeals to the Muslim community to recognize the reality of hunger that contrasts with American prosperity, and to take action to redress it. Like the ILM Foundation in Los Angeles, they see this as part of the spiritual practice of Ramadan.

Responding to hunger in the United States is a new effort of Islamic Relief, which has been primarily focused on international humanitarian aid and disaster relief. The U.S. office is affiliated with Islamic Relief Worldwide, an organization that grew out of efforts of Muslims living in the United Kingdom to help those suffering from famine in East Africa. Since the 1990s, Islamic Relief USA has worked in more than forty countries. It was only in 2013 that it developed a dedicated domestic program that focuses on helping people in the United States. That change came about in part because of the global commitment in Islamic Relief to fighting hunger, and the realization that people, especially children, are suffering from hunger in the United States. One of Islamic Relief's projects has been to work through the Department of Agriculture program that provides subsidized lunch in schools. Islamic Relief focuses on continuing that nutritional aid during the summer, when such programs usually take a hiatus. Yet integrating a concern for domestic issues of poverty and hunger in the United States also comes from scripture. "It says in the Qur'an, 'Have you seen those that rejected the faith? Those that rejected the orphan and urged not the feeding of the needy.' That's Surah al-Mawn, verses 1 through 3. That sura doesn't mention color, it doesn't mention sex, it doesn't mention religion, and it doesn't mention ethnicity. It says those who need it. And some of those who need it are our neighbors," said Anwar Khan, the Executive Director of Islamic Relief.

As a humanitarian organization, Islamic Relief is, by design, responsive to changing circumstances and needs. The organization works to adapt its structure and programs in a quest to be efficacious in confronting poverty and the effects of natural disasters. With an annual budget of approximately $60 million, its projects span the globe and it works in a variety of sectors to meet human needs. It still provides emergency response in disasters, but this initial commitment has branched out into more specific efforts, including early recovery, food security, water/sanitation/hygiene, health, and nutrition. There are also programs that work for the long term, such as education and economic development. Islamic Relief combines these humanitarian efforts with giving that is specifically Islamic, such as sponsoring orphans and distributing food boxes and halal meat during Ramadan. Both their humanitarian efforts and their Ramadan giving emerge from the ethical teachings of Islam. To be a Muslim means, in their view, to be humanitarian. Islam is a portal to the humanitarian work of taking care of those who are vulnerable and working to free the world from poverty.

Muslim culture in the United States has been shaped by immigration, which also affects patterns of giving to others. More than half the Muslim population is comprised of immigrants who have arrived since the 1990s. These recent immigrants often have strong family and cultural ties to their country of origin, as noted earlier in the discussion of Indian Shi'as. As Islamic Relief raises funds from Muslims in the United States, this demographic reality can be seen in the choices people make to donate to certain funds over others. Through its online portal for donations, Islamic Relief allows people to specifically designate the country they wish their donation to target. This results in many people designating their donation for their home country's fund. "Palestinians want to give to Palestinians, Syrians want to give to Syrians," said staff member David. "We're trying to convey that there's a problem in the world, the world needs your help. It's not just your country. It's our job to educate our donor base about the issues that they don't yet care about. Some countries get the support from everybody, like Palestine. If something escalates in Palestine, like it did in 2014, then the numbers come in. It's one of those easy sells—it's like Apple doing its iPhones. So what we're trying to sell is, like, Apple TV. It's not an easy sell."

Changing the culture of Muslim giving requires a conscious effort on the part of Islamic Relief staff. The organization now has a Media and Communications team to take on the work of helping their donors stay connected to their efforts while simultaneously changing their approach to giving. "We're trying to switch the people's thought-process from country-specific to sector-specific, say, for example, water. Then we could do water projects around the world," explains David. "It's hard to get somebody thinking from one way to another because they are so tied. You're taking that patriotism from their country and putting it in humanity. That's hard, obviously. Governments haven't done that, religious groups are still working on it. So here you have a non-profit like us trying to do that. It takes work." Being able to implement sector-specific projects in different parts of the world enables Islamic Relief to relocate its expertise in different contexts and further develop its organizational knowledge about effective program delivery.

Islamic Relief is trying to shift the orientation to giving in Muslim communities by developing a humanitarian consciousness in its donors: it wants people to respond to suffering whether it is affecting their own ethnic, national, religious, or cultural group or others beyond that identity group. By emphasizing the human experience of suffering, it encourages people to apprehend the universality of the struggle to overcome disaster and deprivation, and to make that the basis for action. When staff members reach out to different Muslim communities across the United States, they are speaking to people with a wide variety of religious commitments. Some kinds of giving are obligatory for Muslims, and others are voluntary. For Muslims who are committed to implementing the normative religious obligations of Islam, giving is not a matter of voluntary choice. "Those daily masjid goers, they are our strongest donor base, because for them, it's wajib [required]," said David. "It's the five pillars, it's their zakat. Fund-raising with them is about holding a bucket and making sure they see you." Giving, however, is a modality of action that cuts through the boundaries between people who maintain normative practices of worship and those who might have family roots in a Muslim culture but are not regularly involved in congregational worship. Both those who diligently maintain their daily prayers and those who rarely do, give. "You have people who won't go to masjid, but they'll show up for a janazah if someone dies, or they have a Muslim background. For them, we have to make sure that the message isn't confined—it can't be 'It's wajib.' They are here because they don't want to hear that it's wajib," David continues. "Somebody like that is going to give for the sake of 'Wow, I saw something on CNN about an earthquake in Ecuador and I really feel for those people because of the earthquake.' So if Save the Children is already there, they'll give to them. But if we go there first, they'll say, 'Hey, I'll give to Islamic Relief because they're Muslim and I'm Muslim too.' It's a messaging question." Being able to speak to people who reflect the great diversity of religious lives in the Muslim community—people who maintain the importance of normative Islamic religious practices and people who understand their Muslim identity more in terms of family or cultural background— requires the organization to blend distinct ways of talking about the value of giving. Through a language of giving that translates across different religious orientations, Islamic Relief affirms a variety of expressions of humanitarianism and Muslim identity.

Navigating the layers of diversity in Muslim communities in the United States and around the world places a significant emphasis on communication. Islamic Relief has, in recent years, hired a creative media team that takes on this challenge. Podcasts, social media posts, and print media play a critical role in fund-raising and organizational cohesion. Ridwan, who works with the media team, describes the effort and approach to visual media at Islamic Relief: "When I first came, some of the materials had, you know, the starving Somali kid or the refugee woman in tears. That gets an emotional reaction, but our job is working together to make a better world. We're not trying to show how bad it is. We know it's bad. We know that. And we will show how bad it is, but that's not the central part. The central part, at the end, is that we're trying to make something better, make something different. That's what I'm trying to show. When I take pictures, when I shoot, I am about this far away—four or five feet. Never more. You *know* I am taking your picture. I'm taking pictures, not hunting zebras in a safari from a huge distance. People tell me their stories. They gift me their image. So now it's my duty to try to tell you their story with their image." The goal of portraying the agency of people who receive humanitarian aid, their ability to make something different in a world that seems broken, guides the media team at Islamic Relief. Part of their humanitarian work thus involves humanitarian aesthetics and the impulse to create images that emphasize the possibility that people can work together to change suffering.

Being able to produce a humanitarian aesthetic across media platforms also works to establish organizational legitimacy. "Media has the potential to put us on the same level as Oxfam or the Red Cross—and us here means Muslims," says Ridwan, speaking from a photo shoot in the Islamic Relief headquarters. "The goal here was to have a 15-yr old kid look at our brochure and say, 'Damn, y'all *serious*.' That's the only reason this exists the way it does: so a 15-yr old kid can look at this and be like, 'Wow, *we* are *real*. We can be real.' We have one audience: Muslims. It says Islamic in our name and it's important that it's Islamic. Kids who are growing up can say, 'They do good work. And this stuff is badass. Look at how good their design work is, look at how good their photography is. I'd totally work there, I'd totally donate there. And they're Muslim, and they're not like the uncles at the masjid who are yelling at me for playing with my camera.' You can make a difference as a photographer, as a designer. The potential to do good for Muslims in America is there. Some kid will be like, 'Man, they get *down*.'" The images of recipients of aid show their potential to effect change, but those very images can also effect changes in the Muslim Americans who see them. Images within this humanitarian aesthetic also give their Muslim viewers an opportunity to see their own selves in a more humanitarian way. As Ridwan puts it, such media can allow them to put aside the normative judgments of other Muslims in favor of affirming their own creative potential. Islamic Relief thus produces a humanitarian aesthetic that can reshape the self-understanding of American Muslims, emphasizing that they, just like the recipients of aid, have the creative potential to make a difference in the world.

The work of representing the global Muslim population and their humanity in the face of poverty and suffering happens within the context of the contemporary United States, where the war on terror has reshaped the domestic security regime. Every program and project within the organization has to pass clear protocols that are put in place to address concerns that Muslim charities may be funding extremist terror. All people responsible for implementing program grants must pass through the Anti-Terrorism Screening of the U.S. government. This scrutiny happens at the level of program staff, project directors, and the Board of Islamic Relief. After September 11, 2001, Islamic Relief was placed under the oversight of the Attorney General of Los Angeles. For five years, it was required to submit all its financial and communication records for counterterrorism screening. It is committed to complying with U.S. government regulations, and has even shifted its headquarters to the suburbs of Washington, D.C., in order to establish collaborative relationships with regulatory bodies and other faith-based nonprofits. "The safety and security of the organization are our first priority," says one board member. "If we don't get it right, no matter how good you are, no matter how much money you have, you can be shut down." Maintaining compliance is not just a matter of organizational sustainability: it's a responsibility to the American Muslim community. Domestic program staff member Naeem put it this way: "Our community needs us to be global. We can't be this little pocket charity off to the side. They'll see something on the news and the next thing, they'll call us and ask 'Are you there? And if not, why not? Get there!' That's how they see us. We have to act in a huge way, a big way. One time, this brother came up to me and said, 'We can't have *any* bad news coming out of Islamic Relief. No. Not you guys. Keep your house in order, whatever you got to do.' That is what it means to be here. Muslims want to feel that they are part of something big and we're that big thing for them." The organization does humanitarian work, but it also plays a crucial cultural role by fostering the imagination of Muslims as being part of a global, constructive project of making the world a better place. It's about connecting American Muslims—those born here, and those born far away—with a project that is bigger than their suburban life, their urban environment, their own family, and even their own religious community. It helps people act on the biggest shared world of our globe. Through their humanitarian work, they help Muslims see themselves as part of what can bring into being that better global reality.

Conclusion: The Sustaining of Muslim America

The various modes of social giving bring to light the forces that are shaping the arc of Muslim experience in the United States. Poverty and hunger, both in the United States and around the globe, motivate Muslim giving. Whether that giving becomes direct aid—socks, schools, and sanitary pads—or whether that giving takes the form of education, Muslim Americans make consistent and concerted efforts to redress human deprivation. We see what sociologist Robert Hefner calls "organizational vigor" come out of American Muslim communities as they creatively seek out more effective ways to provide care to those who are vulnerable.[17]

Social giving is part of what sustains Muslims in America. It organizes the way in which people join with other Muslims, in shared efforts to live out what they see as the truth of Islam in empowerment and compassion, and also how they join with others who are not Muslim, collaborating with other organizations and local government bodies. Obligatory giving shapes the connections between Muslims. American Shi'as can keep alive their attachment to the local world of Hyderabad, India, even as they are making their life in the United States. Paying khums to an organization that is endorsed by Grand Ayatollah al-Sistani confirms their multiple identities, as Shi'as, as Hyderabadis, and even as Americans. They have a way of sharing the benefit of the opportunities they have found in immigrating to the United States with those who want to develop their own cities and villages in countries across the globe.

For Muslims involved with the ILM Foundation, giving charity expresses their active solidarity with other Angelenos. It is a way of sustaining their city in the face of public crisis, and making space to dignify those who have fallen through the cracks of American social policy, especially African Americans. Islamic Relief encompasses obligatory Islamic giving within a broad affirmation of humanitarian possibilities.

Islam, in its view, makes it paradoxically possible for Muslims to apprehend the transcendent value of every human life and of the totality of humanity.

Giving—from duty or love, or both—pulls people into the social world of collective life and lets them access expansive hopes and visions and new ways of knowing themselves. Social giving reminds people that we need others to know who we are: no one can be human alone. When people give, they are feeding others, taking care of their material needs, and simultaneously also feeding their imaginations of themselves, their neighbors, their communities, their countries, and their world. It is this imagination of belonging and community that makes us human. Muslim practices of giving, in its many forms, allow people to see themselves in light of Islamic tradition, as part of American society, and within the broadest community of humanity. Islamic philanthropy, charity, zakat, and khums are a crucial part of what makes Muslims Muslim. And now, these Muslim practices of giving also stand as part of the humanitarian potential of American society writ broadly.

NOTES

1 For more information, see the entries for "zakat" and "sadaqa" in *Oxford Islamic Studies* online, www.oxfordislamicstudies.com.

2 The mechanisms through which ayatollahs develop institutional patronage are discussed by Annabelle Böttcher, "Sunni and Shi'i Networking in the Middle East," in Barbara Allen Roberson, ed., *Shaping the Current Islamic Reformation* (London: Routledge, 2003), 40–61; multiple case studies of "charitable-educational complexes" sponsored by various marj'as are presented in Elvire Corboz, *Guardians of Shi'ism: Sacred Authority and Transnational Family Networks* (Edinburgh: Edinburgh University Press, 2015).

3 Kambiz GhaneaBassiri, *A History of Islam in America* (New York: Cambridge University Press, 2010), 375.

4 Shortly after the 9/11 attack, President Bush signed Executive Order 13224 to prevent the financial support of terrorists and terrorism. Under this order, the Department of the Treasury was authorized to designate an organization as a terrorist organization and then seize its assets and shut it down, regardless of whether there was a subsequent criminal indictment. It also enabled the Treasury Department to seize the assets of people or organizations that provide material aid to terrorists or terrorism. These new counterterrorism regulations allowed federal authorities to freeze a group's assets while it was under pending investigation, before any formal designation or indictment. Nine U.S.-based Muslim charities have been closed as the result of a federal terrorism designation or inves-

tigation; six were designated and had their assets seized and organizational status revoked; one more was not designated but had its assets frozen; two others closed while under investigation. Of these nine, three involved criminal indictments for aiding terrorists, and only one case resulted in a conviction. Other organizations and leaders faced criminal charges of tax fraud and violating sanctions in Iraq during the 1990s, but were not prosecuted for terrorism-related activities. For more information, see American Civil Liberties Union, *Blocking Faith, Freezing Charities: Chilling Muslim Charitable Giving in the "War on Terrorism Financing"* (New York: ACLU, 2009). For a global overview of Islamic charities in the contemporary world, see Jon B. Alterman and Karin Von Hippel, eds., *Understanding Islamic Charities* (Washington, D.C.: Center for Strategic and International Studies, 2007).

5 Moojan Momen, *An Introduction to Shi'i Islam: The History and Doctrines of Twelver Shi'ism* (New Haven: Yale University Press, 1987), 256.

6 Ibid., 257.

7 Ibid., 259.

8 www.youtube.com, accessed May 9, 2016.

9 www.humanitarianday.com, accessed May 9, 2016.

10 humday.blogspot.com, accessed July 20, 2016.

11 www.humanitarianday.com, accessed July 20, 2016.

12 Ibid.

13 documents.lahsa.org, accessed July 20, 2016.

14 Ibid.

15 U.S. Census Bureau, "Income and Poverty in the United States: 2014" (Washington, D.C.: U.S. Government Printing Office, 2014), www.census.gov.

16 www.launchgood.com, accessed June 10, 2016.

17 Robert Hefner, "Religion and Modernity Worldwide," in Peter Clarke, ed., *The Oxford Handbook of the Sociology of Religion* (New York: Oxford University Press, 2009), 153.

11

Food Practices

The Ethics of Eating

MAGFIRAH DAHLAN

Part 1: What Is Halal?

What does it mean for Muslims to eat *halal*? If the average American knows anything about what Muslims eat—or do not eat—it's that Muslims don't drink alcohol and don't eat pork. As I asked this question to Muslims in the United States, they said something similar. But their answers go beyond what is strictly prohibited, or *haram*, into an area that is less clearly chartered and therefore requires more careful navigation. Sure, a McRib is haram, but what about a Big Mac? Is a bacon-free deluxe Chicken Sandwich from Chick-fil-A okay? How about the General Tso's chicken from one of those ubiquitous Chinese restaurants? Or the all-beef hot dogs served at cookouts? Does it make a difference if the hot dogs are Hebrew National kosher? Although Islamic dietary laws may seem to be monolithic to outsiders, the answers to the question of what it means to eat halal vary from one Muslim to another.

As I interviewed a number of Muslims for this study, I could sometimes guess how they would answer the question of what halal means based on the location they chose for the interview. But I was sometimes surprised. If a Muslim orders a vegetarian burger from Burger King, or a fish sandwich from McDonald's, I can have a relatively high degree of confidence that she only eats *zabiha*. Zabiha is a term that Muslims in America use to indicate the meat of halal, or permissible animals that have been slaughtered according to the strictest Islamic requirements. The requirements include, at the very least, the presence of a Muslim who pronounced the name of God at the time of the animal slaughter. This person should also ensure that the animal dies from the bleeding of the cut of the throat and not from any other causes or injuries.[1] Although the location of the interview and what someone orders can give me some clue as to what eating halal means for a Muslim, I cannot know for sure until I ask the person this question specifically. Some people prefer meatless meals even if they consider certain meat to be permissible. One participant I interviewed, for example, ordered Taco Bell's seven-layer burrito. When I asked her about her choice, she told me that she does not limit herself to zabiha meat. She just loves the burrito because it is delicious.

I also discovered that asking the question, "What is your interpretation of halal?" can lead to some defensive responses. All the participants in this study had agreed to answer this question and were willing to give more comprehensive, well-thought-out answers. But I also often have to ask this question in an informal setting as a member of a Muslim community and not only as a researcher. And the answers I have received, regardless of whether the person has a stricter or less strict interpretation of halal, seldom take the simple form of: "This is what eating halal means for me." More often than not, the answer is followed by a somewhat lengthy explanation not only of why they choose to interpret eating halal a certain way, but also of the anxiety that comes with the varying interpretations of the concept in Muslim communities.

This anxiety can be understood in terms of the importance of our food choices to our identity. With regard to religious dietary choices, this identity is not simply an individual matter. Arguably more importantly, it is also a matter of communal identity. As a Muslim, one's interpretation of halal situates oneself in the community. It determines not only what one can eat but also how one can eat with others. Every person I have asked about his or her interpretation of halal has asked me my own interpretation of halal. In terms of research, there has never been an option for me, in carrying out this study, to be an objective outsider whose interpretation does not matter to the participants. More importantly to me, however, in terms of being a member of a Muslim community, the issue of my interpretation of halal affects my interactions with other Muslims. If, for example, a Muslim finds that my interpretation of halal is not strict enough, she may not be comfortable consuming certain food as a guest at my dinner party. Similarly, if a Muslim thinks that my interpretation of halal is stricter than hers, she may feel the need to let me know how she will accommodate for my stricter interpretation when she invites me to dinner.

The different interpretations of eating halal result from the gray area in the purview of religious dietary laws. American Muslims generally agree on what is haram, or clearly prohibited. However, when it comes to halal animal species, such as chicken and beef, Muslims disagree with regard to applying the religious dietary laws to contemporary conditions of life in a modern multicultural society. More specifically, Muslims in non–Muslim majority countries such as the United States have different interpretations of the permissibility of consuming the meat of animals that are slaughtered by non-Muslims. As previously mentioned, some Muslims believe that Muslims should eat the meat only of animals slaughtered by Muslims, or at least in the presence of a Muslim who pronounces God's name at the time of slaughter. Iskandar, a Muslim who was born and raised in Indonesia, and came to the United States in the late 1990s as a graduate student, interprets halal in this way. I interviewed him at his home in Richmond, Virginia. To him, the pronouncement of God's name during the slaughter of an animal defines the permissibility of its meat. He shares his home with his wife, who was also born in Indonesia but had grown up in the United States, and their two American-born children.

When I asked Iskandar why he understands halal the way he does, he cited the Qur'anic verse that many Muslims are familiar with. The verse speaks to the importance of the method of slaughter, "Eat not of (meats) On which Allah's name Hath not been pronounced: That would be impiety" (6:121). Iskandar was not the only participant I interviewed who made specific reference to this textual basis for an interpretation of halal. Another participant, Ahmad, also discussed this verse when explaining his similar interpretation of halal. Ahmad is a medical school professor who was born in Pakistan and studied in Egypt in his early twenties before he came to live in the United States. I interviewed Ahmad at an Islamic community center in Roanoke, Virginia, where he had been serving as a community leader for more than a decade. In addition to citing the same qur'anic verse, Ahmad also made reference to the *hadith*, the sayings of Prophet Muhammad and part of the larger prophetic traditions, or the *Sunna*.

Those with a different interpretation of halal, however, also have a textual basis for their view. A different verse of the Qur'an speaks to this,

"This day are (all) things Good and pure made lawful Unto you. The food of the People of the Book is lawful unto you. And yours is lawful Unto them" (5:5). Many Muslims consider people who profess an Abrahamic religion (i.e., Judaism and Christianity) to be People of the Book. Although Muslims with this view of halal agree that the method of slaughter is important, to them it is an ideal but not necessarily a practical requirement, given the context of a non–Muslim majority society. Amina is a Muslim convert who was born and raised in the United States. She was one of the founders of an Islamic elementary school in Richmond, Virginia, and had been serving as the school's principal for many years at the time of the interview. She described her view of halal as including the meat of halal animal species that have not been slaughtered following the requirements of zabiha. She used the example of meat from the grocery store and hamburgers from McDonald's as being halal because they came from animals slaughtered by the People of the Book.

Practicality plays a key role in one's interpretation of halal. Many Muslims who view the food of the People of the Book as halal follow a stricter definition of halal when zabiha meat is abundant, such as when they travel to larger cities where zabiha stores and restaurants are ubiquitous, or when they are in a Muslim-majority country where all halal meat is zabiha. Amir, a graduate student from Morocco at the time of the interview, explains to me that he follows the opinions of Muslim scholars whom he respects, including those who allow Muslims living in a predominantly non-Muslim country, especially in small towns where zabiha meat is not easily accessible, to eat the meat of the People of the Book. Amir explains that when he goes to Morocco to visit his family, he eats only zabiha meat because he understands the scholars' opinion to mean that the availability of zabiha meat cancels out the permissibility of non-zabiha meat.

Among those Muslims who do not observe the stricter zabiha requirement, I found different ways of delineating the permissibility of the food of the People of the Book, since they don't know exactly how and by whom the animals have been slaughtered. Most of them view the United States as a "pretty much Judeo-Christian" society, as Amir describes it. Therefore, all non-haram meats are considered halal. A smaller number of Muslims who subscribe to this view would eat kosher non-zabiha but not non-kosher non-zabiha meat because kosher meat comes from animals slaughtered following a specific set of dietary laws from an Abrahamic religion (i.e., Judaism). For these Muslims, kosher serves as an intermediate category; it is less ideal than zabiha but better than non-kosher.

Another way Muslims distinguish the permissibility of non-zabiha food is to exclude the food of those they consider to be outside the category of the People of the Book. Amina, for example, explains to me that while she considers meat from regular grocery stores and McDonald's to be halal, she views Chinese restaurants to be off-limits because she assumes that the owners of those restaurants are Buddhists and do not belong to the category of the People of the Book. These variations between Muslims who view non-zabiha meat as acceptable are not as pronounced as the main difference between Muslims who eat only zabiha halal and those who eat non-zabiha halal meat.

As I mentioned briefly earlier, Muslims in the United States are well aware of the different interpretations of halal with regard to the method of slaughter, which can be a source of anxiety. Many of those I interviewed acknowledged the varying interpretations and they would say what halal meant to them or their family, rather than what halal is in absolute terms. Arif was another graduate student in Blacksburg, Virginia, at the time of the interview. He had been living in the United States for six years, having come from Indonesia with his wife and two children. His view of halal includes the food of the People of the Book based on the aforementioned qur'anic verse; however, he quickly added, "not everyone agrees." He explains that this disagreement could stem from a more fundamental disagreement on who should be considered the People of the Book. Some Muslims, who hold the stricter view of halal, believe that the term the People of the Book only refers to the Jews and Christians who coexisted with the earliest community of Muslims during the the Prophet's lifetime. Therefore, the qur'anic verse on the permissibility of their food no longer applies to Muslims today. Other Muslims, including Arif, believe that the designation of the People of the Book applies to contemporary Christians and Jews with regard to the method of slaughter of permissible animals, although the permissibility of their food does not override the prohibition of pork.

In general, Muslims' interpretations of halal are not only diverse but also fluid. Most of the people I interviewed have changed or modified their view depending on their circumstances. One circumstance that I had not anticipated being of importance is that of an expectant mother. I did not have a specific question on this and yet three women voluntarily brought up their experience of craving certain foods while they were expecting. All three women—who were interviewed in different cities and did not know of one another—had a stricter interpretation of halal and would only eat zabiha meat under normal circumstances. During their pregnancies, however, each of them had a craving for non-zabiha food—a chicken sandwich from Chick-fil-A or a cheeseburger from Wendy's. All of them decided to eat those foods—one of them told me a story about her cousin who decided not to give into her pregnancy craving—although they maintained their stricter view after the end of their pregnancies.

The choices that Muslims make with regard to their food practices are also somewhat dependent on the practicality of following the stricter interpretation of halal. Many Muslims who live in small towns or rural areas where zabiha meat is not conveniently available follow a more flexible interpretation. The same people consume only zabiha meat when they move or travel to places where it is more abundant. Within this gray area, when Muslims consider their interpretation to be correct, they believe other interpretations are not necessarily incorrect. As one interviewee told me, although she does not eat non-zabiha halal meat, she does not judge those who do so.

Although not very common, sometimes members of a single family hold a variety of interpretations. For example, Ahmad, a Muslim who grew up in Pakistan and came to the United States two decades ago as a college student, eats non-zabiha halal meat. In contrast, Sarah, his American-born and -raised wife of Pakistani descent only eats zabiha halal. As part of their agreement when they got married, they only eat zabiha halal at home and when they go out together. However, when he travels by himself for work, which he does quite often, she agrees that he is free to eat non-zabiha halal. Additionally, as Sarah explained to me, they have also agreed to raise their son to eat only zabiha halal. She said, "He cannot take our son to Chick-fil-A, or bring home a Chick-fil-A sandwich to eat in front of our son." Although she would rather he only ate zabiha halal, she believes that it is not something that she can or should force on him.

Having non-Muslim family members can also influence a Muslim's decision on how to negotiate the gray areas. This is the case for Khadijah, a teacher from Durham, North Carolina, who was born and raised in a Muslim family. Her husband grew up in a devout Christian family and converted to Islam in his thirties. Khadijah told me that although she, her husband, and their sons only eat zabiha halal meat, they make an exception when they are guests of her husband's non-Muslim parents. She explains that while eating zabiha halal is important to her, it is more important not to draw what she considers to be an unnecessary distinction between her and her husband's parents when it comes to foods that are not clearly forbidden. Outside the boundaries of family, I have also heard about this type of negotiation among Muslims who prepare and eat only zabiha halal at home but accept non-zabiha halal as guests in other people's homes. Some of them attribute this to the importance of honoring one's hosts in prophetic traditions.

Some Muslims view having a different interpretation of halal from their parents in particular as an important part of developing a more conscious Muslim identity. This was the case with Naila, who was a twenty-one-year-old student in Blacksburg, Virginia, at the time of the interview. Born and raised in the United States, Naila described her experience of growing up with her parents, who eat only zabiha halal food. They had come to the United States from Bangladesh in the 1970s and would take Naila and her siblings for regular visits to Bangladesh every few years as the children were growing up. When Naila left her parents' house for college, she began to think more consciously about the importance of zabiha for herself. She attributed the slow and deliberate shift in her interpretation of halal to her active participation in campus life, including serving as the president of her campus Muslim Student Association (MSA), and classes that she had taken, such as an ethics class. Over the course of her four-year undergraduate experience, she developed a different interpretation from that of her parents. While she still considers zabiha to be the ideal, she has slowly accepted the permissibility of non-zabiha halal, starting with kosher to, later on, other non-zabiha halal such as organic chicken purchased from regular grocery stores.

Because of the variation in the interpretations of halal meat, Muslims employ different strategies when dining with others who do not share the same interpretation or when dining with non-Muslims. Some of those who eat only zabiha halal ask, while others consider it to be impolite to do so and assume it is zabiha unless it is clearly specified otherwise. As I mentioned previously, some Muslims make distinctions between what they eat at home and what they eat as guests of others. They explain this in terms of the importance of following the example of the Prophet, who was known to respect his host when he was a guest. Conversely, being a good host and respecting their guests is also part of the Prophet's Sunna, so some Muslims who have a more flexible interpretation of halal serve zabiha halal meals to their guests or bring zabiha halal meals to potluck Muslim gatherings. As the principal of her Islamic school, for example, Amina ensures that all the food served in the school is zabiha halal to accommodate those with the strictest interpretation.

The ability of Muslims to dine together with others who may not share their personal understanding of halal is highly dependent on the level of trust within a particular Muslim community. Sarah, who only eats zabiha halal, told me of her experience with a Muslim community she grew up with. She overheard a member of the community telling others that a non-zabiha halal meal was zabiha halal. That caused her to avoid sharing communal meals and other activities with that community. Another way to negotiate the gray area is for Muslims who observe zabiha halal strictly to eat either vegetarian or seafood dishes. All vegetarian dishes are halal as there are no restrictions on the type or method of preparation. For many Muslims, especially Sunni Muslims, seafood is also a safer option as the slaughter requirements for land animals do not apply to sea animals. For Shi'a Muslims in general, fish without fins or scales (such as catfish and eels), crustaceans (such as crawfish, crab, and lobster), and mollusks (such as squid, octopus, and oyster) are prohibited animal species. Some Shi'a Muslims consider shrimp to be *makruh*, an intermediate category between halal and haram (forbidden), or food that is not forbidden but best avoided.

Part 2: Islamic Food Traditions and Food Ethics

In the remainder of this chapter, I will discuss the different ethical concerns that the interviewees shared with me. They include their concerns over both the way the animals are treated prior to their slaughter and the conditions of the mechanical zabiha slaughter method. More specifically, many of the people I interviewed brought up their concerns over animals being raised in a packed feedlot, the use of hormones and unnatural diets, and the long-distance transportation of live animals.

When I asked the Muslims I interviewed about halal food, some of them explained to me that they had thought about Islamic dietary laws beyond the matter of how the animals were slaughtered. Many of them voiced their concern about the way the animals were treated. Safiya was a graduate student in Blacksburg, Virginia, at the time of the interview. She was born in Jordan but had grown up in a different part of the United States before living in the small town in Virginia. When I asked her about what halal meant to her, she reflected on how the classes she had taken as part of her education had led them to think of halal in a different way. In one of her classes she had learned about the effects of the hormones used in large-scale cow and chicken farms. Her concern extended beyond the health effects for the people who consumed the meat of these animals. She considered the use of hormones an inhumane way of treating the animals. In large-scale farms, she said, "the animals are treated like [they are in] a factory. They are not animals, they are just products." Safiya used the term "true halal" to describe meat that comes from animals not only slaughtered following zabiha standards, but also raised in accordance with Islamic standards in which the animals are raised naturally and not subjected to hormones that are not necessary for their well-being. For her, if she cannot have such true halal meat, it is more important to make sure that the animals have been raised humanely than to make sure that they are slaughtered according to the zabiha method. She prefers to buy meat from her local farmer's market than the zabiha store because, as she puts it, "these [farms] are small scale, so they are treating the animals better as opposed to [a] big factory that's just pumping out mass products."

This belief is shared by Aishah, a writer who was born and raised in the United States and whose family came from Syria. She explains how she views halal as an ethical standard and that halal isn't just about the way the animals die but also, and perhaps more importantly, about how they live. Throughout the interview, she explains that her understanding of the importance of the humane treatment of animals derives from the prophetic traditions. She told me, "A Muslim is supposed to be invested in the good quality of life, not just the human beings, but with animals too. There are plenty of stories in Islamic history of the Prophet telling us of the people that were either granted heaven despite a long time of sins for their kindness to an animal, or sent to hell for punishment because of their cruelty to an animal." Like Safiya, Aishah also prefers to buy her meat from the farmer's market, from a farmer "who I know loves her cows and treats them with the best care and does not just slaughter them for profit."

Aishah finds zabiha meat from animals slaughtered using a modern mechanical slaughter method to be particularly problematic. She told me of her friend who made a documentary about halal slaughterhouses in New York. This documentary revealed to her that the distinction between zabiha and non-zabiha meat is minimal. As she put it, "I was really disappointed when he would tell me that some [halal slaughterhouses] were practically indistinguishable from a Tyson plant. Except for the fact that people had to say Bismillah [in the name of God] before they did it and that's not the point of it. [. . .] The point of [pronouncing the name of God] is supposed to be that you are engaged with it [the animals slaughtered], understanding what you are doing, you care about what the animal experiences." Muslims who find large-scale industrial farming and mechanical slaughter to be problematic see a direct contradiction between these practices and the basic teachings of Islam. To them, Islam's requirement that Muslims show kindness and compassion to animals means they have a responsibility to ensure that, for example, the animals have been fed their natural diet, are allowed to grow at a healthy rate, are not subjected to unnecessary antibiotics and growth hormones, and are given the opportunity to behave naturally.[2]

Another participant, Elizabeth, who converted to Islam in her early twenties, shares a similar concern about the unethical treatment of animals in large-scale industrial farming and slaughterhouses. She describes the problem of large-scale industrial farming and slaughterhouses as a lack of respect for the spirituality of animals as part of divine creation. In such a system, she says, "There isn't respect for animals, for what they eat, and their place in the world, their purpose in the world. It is just really mechanized. [. . .] In Islam, you respect animals, you respect their lives and their rights to clean food, good food, what they would naturally eat on their own. [. . .] You have to respect that; that is part of Allah's creation." Other participants also pointed to the condition of animal confinement and transportation as a sign of society's disrespectful attitude toward the animals we consume. For Muslims such as Elizabeth, animals raised in smaller-scale, local, organic farms and slaughtered using the traditional method fulfill religious requirements in a way that industrial farms and mechanical slaughterhouses do not. In addition to the term "true halal" that Safiya used in my interview with her, Muslims have used other terms such as "eco-halal," "organic halal," and "green zabiha" to make the distinction between what they consider to be the ideal and simply zabiha, which is less than ideal.

However, very few of the participants that I interviewed considered vegetarianism or veganism as a solution to the ethical problems of eating meat from animals raised and slaughtered in this system. Aishah, who was one of these few, shared with me her experience of being a vegetarian for several years when she was a teenager. She decided to return to meat eating partly because she found that limiting herself to consuming no meat at all was inconsistent with her understanding of Islamic teachings and traditions. However, she thinks that the amount of meat consumed by most contemporary Muslims in advanced industrial societies to be in contradiction with prophetic tradition. She believes that following the example of the Prophet would require Muslims to consume only a fraction of the amount most people consume.

Although most people I interviewed do not consider vegetarianism to be Islamic, the topic of Islamic vegetarianism has been of increasing interest to Islamic studies scholars. These scholars' arguments for an alternative reading of Islamic dietary laws, one that specifically prohibits meat eating, have developed mainly as a response to the modern condition of industrial farming. One argument for Islamic vegetarianism focuses on the religion's virtue of compassion. According to this argument, the permissibility of meat eating as delineated by the religious slaughter requirements in Islam is not absolute. Rather, when the dietary laws and slaughter requirements are considered in context, Muslims will understand that the intent and purpose of the laws may be that meat eating should be prohibited. More specifically, according to this argument, the dietary laws were revealed to Muslims in the context of seventh-century Arabia, where meat eating was essential to one's survival. Given that Muslims in America live in a radically different context, specifically one in which their survival no longer depends on meat eating, it is now incumbent upon Muslims to refrain from meat eating to embody the most compassionate attitude toward animals.[3]

Another recent argument for Islamic vegetarianism is based on a feminist ethical approach. Like the argument based on compassion, the feminist argument challenges the absoluteness of the permissibility of meat eating and takes historical context into consideration. According to this argument, given the exploitative human-animal relationship in which contemporary American Muslims live, a similar reinterpretation of the religious permissibility of meat eating is necessary. By appealing to Islamic teachings on both equality and justice, this argument promotes Islamic vegetarianism as a way for Muslims to practice the virtues.[4] As I have previously mentioned, although these arguments are gaining traction in academic circles, most Muslims I have encountered currently do not consider Islamic vegetarianism to be consistent with their understanding of Islamic dietary laws.

Conclusion

When we think of what it means for Muslims to practice Islam, it is understandable that the images that come to mind are often of rituals and places of worship. But Muslims also practice their religion in the mundane act of eating their daily meals. For many Muslims who live in non-Muslim-majority countries such as the United States, this act of choosing what to eat acquires greater significance. To them, food is an important part of their religious identity. Their understanding of what it means to be Muslim, especially as a minority group surrounded by nonpermissible food, is translated literally into their bodies through the food choices that they make daily. In this chapter, we have seen how many Muslims refer to scripture for guidance on the permissible and the forbidden to inform their food choices. More importantly, however, a diversity of interpretations is evident in the different ways Muslims embody their religious dietary laws. A Muslim's understanding of how to best practice these dietary laws affect his or her interactions with others, Muslims and non-Muslims alike. Furthermore, at least for some

Muslims, this understanding is specifically informed by a critical view of the ethics of the modern food system. As such, the focus of their interpretations moves beyond permissibility to wholesomeness and the religion's fundamental virtues such as equality and justice.

NOTES

1 Mian N. Riaz and Muhammad M. Chaudry, *Halal Food Production* (Boca Raton, Fl.: CRC Press, 2004).

2 Nadia Arumugan, "The Eco-Halal Revolution," www.culinate.com (November 4, 2009).

3 Richard Foltz, *Animals in Islamic Tradition and Muslim Cultures* (Oxford, U.K.: Oneworld, 2006).

4 Kecia Ali, "Muslims and Meat-Eating: Vegetarianism, Gender, and Identity," *Journal of Religious Ethics* 43, 2 (2015): 268–288.

12

The Qur'an

Studying, Embodying, and Living with the Word of God

MUNA ALI

As you open the door to this large rectangular building, you are greeted by a melodic, rhythmic humming in different pitches. Walk in and enter a large carpeted room bare except for framed Arabic calligraphy hanging on the walls and a few chairs stacked in a corner. This space is occupied by seven groups of four to ten youngsters sitting on the floor facing low and narrow unfinished-wood tables on which their open books are placed. Ranging in age between five and eighteen and divided by age and sex, the groups scatter around the room, illuminated by natural light filtering through the large windows. The groups are instructed by young men in their twenties and thirties wearing skullcaps and long white robes or South Asian tunics. The youngest groups trace their index fingers on the pages of a photocopied booklet of Arabic letters, rhythmically reciting "*Alif,*" "*Baa,*" "*Taa,*" and so on. The slightly older cohorts read and then recite in unison a selected chapter from the Qur'an. In the oldest groups, students read different chapters while one of them recites from memory to the teacher. All around the room, the reciters' bodies sway back and forth to the rhythm of their voices.

Taking in these sights and sounds, one might feel transported to a *madrasa,* or school, in a village in a Muslim-majority country were it not for the visual and auditory interruptions of the ethnic diversity, English signage around the space, and the unaccented American English instructions that punctuate the children's recitation. This is the Qur'an Academy of an Islamic center in an affluent suburb in Arizona. The academy was established and led by two young American-born imams of immigrant parentage who memorized the Qur'an years earlier in their mosques. In the past two years, these imams have led the community in prayers during Ramadan, reciting each night over one-thirtieth of the Qur'an. As the imam's recitation proceeds through the night, one frequently hears sniffles or quiet sobbing from some congregants who, though they may not understand Arabic, are nevertheless moved to tears by the divine speech penetrating their hearts. Beyond words and their meanings, this ability to "hear with the heart" is what anthropologist Charles Hirschkind called "sensorium." It is a whole body experience where "a complex synthesis of disciplined moral reflexes" enables the cultivation of a level of piety to which one aspires.[1]

There is extensive scholarship by Muslims and non-Muslims on the Qur'an's origins, authenticity, and interpretations but less has been written about how ordinary Muslims engage the Qur'an. This chapter aims to contribute to this area by exploring how American Muslims engage the Qur'an and how their religious minority status in America impacts this engagement. American Muslims are unique both in America and in the *ummah,* or Muslim world community, in their diversity.[2] The majority are immigrants, but there are also nonimmigrant groups with an African American plurality. The Qur'an knits this ethnic, sectarian, interpretive, and socioeconomic diversity into a religious community striving to connect with and draw on the Qur'an as it tries to manage its diversity and create a cohesive political community. This chapter will explore how Muslims recite the Qur'an as individuals and community; how, in mastering its recitation and interpretation, they authenticate their religious authority and piety; and how they appeal to it to resolve their differences and from it summon their evidence for needed community "reform."

The first section briefly introduces the reader to the history of qur'anic revelation through the experience of a Muslim American determined "to connect" with the Qur'an. It will then explore what this quest reveals about Muslim America and it will present the journeys of diverse Muslim Americans learning to recite and understand the Qur'an and the impact of these experiences. The next section examines how the Qur'an punctuates the social life of Muslim Americans. In births, child socialization, weddings, graduations, illness, and death, and during all community events, the Qur'an is recited to bless, inspire, comfort, and console. The social and the political blur when issues of belonging to the community and to the nation are at stake. The third section explores how Muslim Americans are highlighting the presence of the Qur'an in the nation's past and present to assert their belonging. It will also show how the Qur'an inspires their work for social justice within and outside their community and creates scholarship responding to the important issues of the day. The last section considers how the Qur'an is experienced aesthetically as a melodic recitation and how it engages Muslims' creative imagination and inspires cultural production as poets incorporate it into verse and visual artists inscribe the sacred words on walls, canvases, mirrors, and candles to bless and beautify the walls of their institutions and homes.

The Story of the Qur'an through American Eyes

Revelation

When reciting the Qur'an, Muslims encounter verses about its purpose, when it was revealed, and its inimitability. Muslims, however, generally learn the story of revelation by learning about the Prophet Muhammad's life. Meraj Mohiuddin, a young Arizona physician, learned this story and qur'anic recitation from his parents as a child. As an adult, he "struggled to connect with the Qur'an" because, as a non–Arabic speaking Muslim, the English translation veiled the "Qur'an's meaning and majesty" and limited his experience of it.[3] Excelling in medical school made him painfully aware of his deficiency in comprehending the Qur'an. He felt "lopsided and restless."[4] Because learning Arabic demanded more time, he decided that grasping the life of the Prophet was the key to understanding the Qur'an. He likened the Prophet to a "container" which must be grasped for the holy liquid (Qur'an) it held to be drunk.[5] Mohiuddin was dissatisfied with the available biographies of the Prophet for citing too little of the Qur'an and containing too many "men all named 'Abd Allah" as companions of the Prophet[6] whose role in the story was not clear. Drawing on his medical school study skills, he recorded verses and catalogued the Prophet's experiences, contemporaries and their lineages, and all the major events of his life. His various iterations of the notes and graphs grew over ten years into a unique book: *Revelation: The Story of Muhammad*, released in early 2016.[7]

Mohiuddin begins the story, as it always begins, in the pre-Islamic Arabian city of Mecca where several tribes lived around the sacred shrine of the Ka'ba built long ago for the worship of the One God by their ancestors Abraham and his son Ishmael. Deviating far from Abraham's monotheistic tradition, these tribes filled the Ka'ba with idols they worshiped. The tribe of Quraysh, headed by the family of Bani Hashim, managed the pilgrimage to the Ka'ba. It is to this family that Muhammad, who came to restore monotheism, was born in 570 C.E. While acknowledging the nobility of Meccan Arabs, Muslims generally call this pre-Islamic period a time of *Jahiliyya* (ignorance), when idols were worshiped and social injustices prevailed. Muhammad was an orphan in a patriarchal society where one's well-being was determined by whose son one was; Muhammad's noble character, however, earned him the epithet "the truthful and trustworthy." A mark of distinction on his back was identified as the "seal of the prophet" by a Christian monk after noticing a cloud shading young Muhammad as he worked in a trading camp.[8] Though his family was the guardian of the idols in the Ka'ba, Muhammad did not partake in idol worship. On a spiritual quest and troubled by the social ills and injustices of his time, he regularly sought seclusion in the mountains outside Mecca.[9]

But to connect with the Qur'an and know its history "inside out," Mohiuddin was not content with merely reciting history and quoting verses. Instead, he used the Qur'an to frame the book and symbolized it by the letter "Q," representing the twenty-three-year timeline of revelation. It begins on "Qur'anic year" one (QY1), when one night during seclusion outside Mecca, the Archangel Gabriel came to Muhammed and commanded him to "Recite," to which Muhammad responded, "I cannot recite."[10] After a third command and the same reply, Gabriel recited: "Recite in the Name of thy Lord Who created, created man from a blood clot. Recite! The Lord is most noble, Who taught by the Pen, taught man that which he knew not."[11] Muhammad was shaken by the extraordinary experience and questioned its authenticity but was reassured by his wife and her Christian cousin that he was the prophet foretold by previous scriptures and that persecution by his own people awaited him.[12] Though Muhammad was initially followed by mostly poor and marginalized Meccans, the Quraysh saw in Muhammad and his message a threat to the social order and alternated between enticing and harassing him while persecuting his followers to dissuade him, but to no avail.

Over the next twenty-three years, the Prophet would receive the word of God through Gabriel in various contexts. At times, the physical toll of the revelation on him would be apparent to those around him.[13] Muhammad would, in turn, recite these words to his followers, who memorized them, and to scribes, who transcribed them on various media and who recited them back to the Prophet and among themselves. *Iqra'* (recite), the first word revealed, and all revelation that followed became collectively known as the Qur'an (recitation). Mohiuddin's book stops in 632 C.E. (QY23) with the death of the Prophet and the end of revelation, but the recitation continues over fourteen hundred years later by generations of Muslims who, like Mohiuddin, want to grasp its message.

Mohiuddin's book details the story and historical context of the Qur'anic revelation, but his book also reveals another story and historical context: Mohiuddin's post–9/11 Muslim America where questions about faith, its relevance, and the authenticity of its sources are debated by Muslims and non-Muslims and where non-Muslim questions about the character of the Prophet and the content of the Qur'an are routine. To focus on the Qur'an, whose authenticity is unquestioned by Muslims, and cognizant of debates about the authenticity of some prophetic traditions, Mohiuddin quotes 89 out of the 114 chapters of the Qur'an because "wherever and whenever the Qur'an can tell the story of its own revelation, it should tell the story."[14] Much of the story is presented as answers to over four hundred questions which confront Muslim Americans, particularly the young, at this historical juncture when they are viewed by many in post–9/11 America as its newest "problem people." Mohiuddin says he could not ignore questions like "Why did young Muhammad feel so disillusioned with Mecca? Why did he condone caravan raiding? Why did he marry so many women? Why did he command his companions to take captives? Why didn't he stop the execution of the Jewish tribe of *Qurayzah*? Why did he forgive his fiercest opponents? Why was he worried if he knew he would succeed?" But the most difficult questions, Mohiuddin says, were "Why does this bother me?" and "Why can't I come to terms with this?"[15]

Many young Muslims find in Malcolm X, the African American Muslim leader of the 1960s, a model for how to be authentically Muslim and American, and Mohiuddin quotes Malcolm in the epigraph. And aware of intracommunity tensions and the critical role played by Sherman Jackson, an African American Muslim scholar, in shedding light on the roots of this tension, Mohiuddin delayed releasing the book to secure a foreword by Jackson. Confirming the indispensability of grasping the historical context and Muhammad's life to understanding the Qur'an and Islam, Jackson connects this history and the message of the Qur'an to Muslim America. He reminds readers that as Muhammad embraced and changed his society for the better, so should they. Additionally, as the survival of the early Muslims depended on the support of their non-Muslim clansmen, in the American context the African American community has served this critical role but is unrecognized and unappreciated by Muslims.[16] In reclaiming the story of revelation for his generation, foregrounding Malcolm X, addressing controversial issues, and securing the endorsement of prominent Muslim American scholars, Mohiuddin reclaims and authenticates the two sides of this hyphenated identity.

Compilation

The Qur'an consists of 114 *suwar* (sing. *Surah* [enclosure], translated as "chapter"), which vary in length from 3 to 286 *ayat* (sing. *Ayah* [sign], translated as verse) totaling over 6,200 verses divided into thirty parts.[17] While there is consensus on the order (revealed, not chronological) of the chapters, Sunnis and Shi'a differ on when and who initiated the compilation. The Shi'a believe that Ali, the Prophet's cousin and son-in-law and their first Imam, compiled the Qur'an into a book within six months of the Prophet's death. Sunnis believe it was the first Caliph Abu Bakr, the Prophet's father-in-law and best friend, who charged the Prophet's scribe and prominent memorizers with this task, producing a *mushaf* (pronounced mus-haf), a codex of the Qur'an, a year after the Prophet's death. A copy of it was entrusted to the Prophet's wife Hafsa.

The second phase of compilation occurred when the third Caliph, Uthman, charged the Prophet's scribe and memorizers to produce new copies, using Hafsa's copy and following Meccans' recitations, to put an end to differences in copied versions of the Qur'an. Uthman then recalled all other copies from the provinces and sent new copies and qualified reciters to teach people. This "Uthmani mushaf" is the sacred book that all Muslim sects recite today.[18] However, because the Qur'an is foremost a recitation, most Muslims first encounter the Qur'an as an aural experience. The Qur'an conveys doctrinal messages about God and the nature and purpose of mankind and creation. It exhorts the reader to ponder the ayat, or signs, of the Qur'an and those of creation, which all point to God. The Qur'an contains historical narratives of theophany that serve as models for the believers' edification and ethicolegal instructions. Because it touches on every aspect of Muslim life, Muslims consider it the primary source of the *Shari'a* (Islamic law or way of life) and the foundation of all knowledge from jurisprudence, theology, and philosophy to the humanities and the social, physical, and biological sciences. Seyyed Hossein Nasr, a Muslim American philosopher and Islamic studies scholar, asserts that all these sciences, for which the West is indebted to Muslims, are actually "commentaries on it [the Qur'an]."[19]

Preservation through Embodiment

Aisha, the Prophet's wife, is reported to have said that Muhammad's "character was the Qur'an." But while Muslims believe the Prophet is the vessel and embodiment of revelation, the Qur'an unequivocally asserts its unearthly origins and its eternal inimitability and preservation.[20] Commonly called al-Qur'an (the Recitation), Muslims also refer to it as *al-furqan* (the Criterion), *al-kitab* (the Book), *al-Huda* (the Guidance), and *al-dhikr* (the Remembrance). Lecturing on the "Miracle of the Qur'an" in Tennessee, Yasir Qadhi, a second-generation Pakistani American Islamic studies professor and a popular preacher, reminds his audience that pre-Islamic Arabs were masters of eloquence who "valued the power of the spoken word." Because prophets' miracles are always context relevant, Muhammad's ultimate miracle was "a speech like no other speech . . . the most eloquent of all books."[21] Qadhi then elaborates the Qur'an's divine origins, citing its themes, including scientific concepts unknown to seventh-century Arabia, such as the orbiting of heavenly bodies and stages of human development. The miracle is also evident today, he says, in the sectarian and ideological diversity of Muslims who nevertheless all read the same Qur'an and are "mesmerize[d] and transfix[ed]," even if they do not understand Arabic.[22]

Explaining the impact of the Qur'an on its listeners, Ingrid Mattson, a Canadian American Muslim scholar, notes that the sound of the recited Arabic words communicates meaning analogous to the meaning music conveys, which transcends lyrics. Mattson adds that beyond the "melodic techniques" reciters employ, qur'anic "verses are imbued with rhyme, assonance, and rhythm" by which the Qur'an at once draws on and distinguishes itself from pre-Islamic poetry.[23] In popular workshops like the *Undeniable Linguistic Miracles of Qur'an* and academic works like *The Quran as Literary Masterpiece*, Muslim Americans continue the age-old tradition of contemplating the literary structure, forms of argumentation, imagery, and concepts in the Qur'an as evidence of its divine origin and its inimitability (*i'jaz al-qur'an*).[24]

This literary structure facilitates its memorization and preservation in the hearts of Muslims, even non–Arabic speaking ones like Yaser, the imam and attorney who established the Qur'an Academy described earlier. Learning his first verses in the family car at age three, nine-year-old Yaser, who by then had memorized four-thirtieths of the Qur'an, received a *mushaf* with the dedication "to *hafiz* Yaser, in sha'a Allah" from his teacher. Never considering it before, the inscription inspired him to become a Qur'an *hafiz* (a preserver through memorization). This required great effort by him and his parents, both physicians, including driving twice a week to the nearest city with a Qur'an teacher. Yaser was also attending public school and playing sports. The family sacrifices enabled Yaser to become a hafiz at age fourteen "without understanding one word of Arabic," which itself affirmed to him "the miracle of the Qur'an."[25] He memorized the Qur'an by adhering to the strict rules of *tajweed* [26]governing articulation and intonation. After college, Yaser traveled to Jordan to learn Arabic and to obtain an *ijazah* (memorization certification) indicating that his recitation was authenticated by a master hafiz whose own recitation was authenticated by another master, each becoming a link in the sacred chain of those who recite the Qur'an as perfectly as the Prophet recited it to Archangel Gabriel.[27]

Memorizing the Qur'an, Yaser says, has had an "incredible" impact on his life, from the parent he aspires to be to how he spends his time. He reviews his memorization daily, has weekly private Arabic and Qur'an classes with a teacher, and fulfills his communal "obligation and privilege" of leading congregational prayers on Fridays and during the long nightly Ramadan prayers (*taraweeh*). He also represents the community in interfaith events and in meetings with local officials.[28]

The 1990s were a critical juncture in Muslim American history when a quest for religious knowledge took many students overseas.[29] But it was also a time when institutions like Darul Uloom in New York and

Dar-us-Salaam in Maryland were created to educate future imams and hafiz, combining the state curriculum and qur'anic studies for young students. Khalid Herrington, an African American in his thirties, converted to Islam in his teens after being convinced of the Qur'an's divine origin by "the first seven verses."[30] For years, he studied with a local imam and after college joined a full-time hafiz program in a Midwestern city, later becoming an imam of an Islamic center.

While men's memorization often earns them the public role of leading communal prayers, the aspiration to become a hafiz is not limited to men and Qur'an schools enroll both sexes. Maryam Amir, a second-generation Iranian American, learned Qur'anic recitation as a child and in her teens wore hijab only to impress "older and cooler" hijab-wearing visiting cousins. Otherwise, she "hated [her] identity and questioned Islam being true" and focused on being popular in school.[31] When she was fourteen, she grudgingly went to Mecca with her parents. There, the sight of the Ka'ba profoundly affected her as she experienced the "unexplainable, fully tangible presence of the Creator of the Universe." She began to "bawl" and was overcome with regret for wasted time.[32] Trying to sustain this nascent spirituality when she returned home, Maryam read five pages of Qur'an daily. Not having read it in years, this was "painfully slow," so she read two pages in English translation daily. Understanding the meaning of what she read provided Maryam a "connection to God that [she] couldn't have even fathomed." This "transformed [her] core" from being a "self-absorbed" girl made "insecure" by "negative media-messaging about the female body," to becoming a "passionate, independent advocate for social justice."[33] A desire for an "intimacy with the Creator's revelation" and the ability to recite from memory inspired her to memorize it.[34] After a seven-year journey, she became a *hafiza* (female hafiz). Except for eleven months in Egypt learning Arabic and memorizing, Maryam's memorization occurred in the hubbub of her American life juggling college, work, family, and community work. She now teaches *tafsir* (exegesis) and writes for the *Virtual Mosque* blog, inspiring Muslims to connect with the Qur'an. This connection, she says, entails sincerity and consciousness of "the heavy responsibility and glorified honor of living as Allah's servant and carrying His words in [one's] heart" and acting upon it.[35]

The Islamic Society of North America holds an annual National *Qira'at* (recitation) Competition in which state finalists, grouped by age, compete. The preparation for these competitions is demanding. Twelve-year-old Zayna, a third-generation Syrian American, hoped to win her Islamic school's competition and qualify for the state competition. Learning tajweed in first grade, Zayna has read three-quarters of the Qur'an and memorized two of its thirty parts. To prepare for the approaching competition, she spent nearly twenty hours a week reciting with four teachers. Missing third place by "only 0.01% point," she nevertheless feels she "won the biggest prize with Allah" and is preparing for next year.[36]

Some might view rote memorization of the Qur'an as pointless or worse, as mindless indoctrination. However, rote memorization of sacred texts is a common methodology in religious traditions to cultivate personal piety and inculcate communal values and norms.[37] As noted by both Mattson and Moore, the power and meaning of the Qur'an is not limited to its lexico-semantic aspects but is also conveyed in the sound of recitation and contributes to Muslims' moral and spiritual character development.[38] Additionally, memorization is not the end but the beginning of learning and of a process of embodiment in which the Qur'an, as an oral text, comes alive "through the mental and physiological capabilities of the students' bodies."[39] As Boyle says, what is imprinted on their memories springs forth through their lips to be shared, taught, contemplated, and inspired by.[40] Emulating the Prophet's embodiment of the Qur'an is the pedagogical objective for Muslim religious education. It involves the refinement of the body, behavior, and character and disciplining the self by cultivating qur'anic virtues. This embodiment is evident in the transformative experiences that Yaser and Maryam narrate and which inspire them to learn Arabic to deepen their understanding of the Qur'an.

Recognizing a growing interest in learning Arabic, new programs offering training have sprung up across the country. The *Bayyinah Dream*, founded by Nouman Ali Khan in Texas, is the most popular program. Khan's story is a quintessentially American story of redemption and success. Born in Germany to Pakistani parents, Khan moved to the United States as a teenager and became an atheist in high school. Then, through friends, he returned to Islam in college. Finding translations of the Qur'an cumbersome and the available Arabic classes unsatisfactory, he educated himself, then designed a "Divine

Speech" course in which sharing "one of the linguistic gems" of the Qur'an captivates the audience. Khan argues that the literary beauty of the Qur'an cannot be fully translated, but it must be attempted so non-Arabic speakers can "taste the sweetness" of the Qur'an.[41] For this purpose, he created the Bayyinah Institute and equipped it with state-of-the-art "technology and innovative educational tools," which attract thousands of students onsite and online. Graduates speak of the life-altering impact of connecting with the Qur'an through this program[42] and some magnify Khan's impact by meticulously cataloguing his online Qur'an lectures.[43]

Bayyinah students are primarily young men and women of all backgrounds who can afford the time and fees. But Muslims of all ages strive to learn Arabic to understand the Qur'an. Seventy-five-year-old Frieda, an African American, has been trying to learn Arabic since she converted in 1972 through local and international, college-level summer Arabic intensive programs and Bayyinah's online courses. Though critical of its cost, pace, and methodology, Frieda loves that Bayyinah draws entirely on Qur'anic Arabic. During Ramadan when many Muslims strive to recite the entire Qur'an, Frieda was gratified to spend it looking up the meaning of every word in the longest chapter of the Qur'an.[44]

Grasping the meaning of the words is important but understanding and implementing the message requires that it be made relevant to one's life. Most mosques have study circles where a teacher expounds on traditional tafsir and exhorts participants to heed the message. But innovative projects like the Arizona-based Good Tree Institute (GTI) eschew this traditional method to "provide an experiential educational study of the Qur'an."[45] Here, the teacher provides the literal meaning of the words, then facilitates a collective contextual interpretation[46] of the verses and a group-generated "take away message." Created by young women of immigrant background to teach their children the Qur'an without "cultural or political baggage,"[47] GTI over time added adult programs. The aim is to facilitate critical thinking and spiritual development for a deeper "relationship with God that cultivates individual and communal transformation."[48] Nadia Katrangi, the resident scholar, is a medical doctor certified in Qur'an memorization and tafsir. In GTI's "Seeds of Wisdom: Spiritual Health and Fitness" weekend workshop, Katrangi guides forty men and women, diverse in age and ethnicity, in an "experiential" exploration of the last ten chapters of the Qur'an, which, Katrangi says, summarize its message. In examining chapter 99 (The Earthquake), which describes the awesomeness of the day of judgement when the earth releases its burdens and is inspired to "tell its news," the group's hourlong reflection leads them from the horror of the scene and the accountability for every seemingly insignificant act, to the conclusion that all of creation is alive and humans are accountable for how they treat it. After each chapter, they engage in a learning activity and participants are offered a tiny key to take home with a message like "make space [for God] in your heart" or "renavigate your intention."[49]

The Qur'an in the Muslim Life Cycle

Whether they recite it or it is recited on their behalf, the Qur'an accompanies Muslims from birth to death. Muslim children may encounter the Qur'an in the womb as echoes of their mothers' recitations. To ease the birthing process, Abbas, a Shi'a Iraqi American, says family members read the chapter of Mary from the Qur'an for the mother-to-be. Once the child is born, the parents recite the *shahada* (declaration of faith) and *adhan* (call to prayers), which include qur'anic formulae, in the baby's ears and they may place a small Qur'an in the crib for protection. Salwa Ali, a second-generation Pakistani American, says that some families look in the Qur'an for "beautiful names" or "role model" namesakes for their children.[50] As the children begin to speak, they learn phrases like "*bimillah ar-rahman ar-raheem*" (in the name of God, the most compassionate, the merciful) before eating and "*al-hamdulillah*" (praise be to God) after eating, "*masha' Allah*" (as God has decreed) when admiring something, and "*in Sha' Allah*" (God willing) when they plan to do something. These qur'anic formulae pepper Muslim speech in everyday social interactions. As toddlers, many children begin to recite the Qur'an with their parents and join others in Qur'an school at the local mosque.

The *madrasa*, or school, where Muslim children learn to recite and memorize the Qur'an, is an old and critical institution for the socialization process of becoming Muslim. In the United States, Muslim communities, small and large, organize Islamic weekend or full-time schools where, alongside other curricula, children learn to recite the Qur'an.

Children's ability to recite is an occasion for certificates, gifts, and cel-ebrations. South Asian American Muslims mark a child's first official reading with a "*Bismillah*" (in the name of God) party which begins with the child repeating *Al-Fatiha*, the first chapter in the Qur'an, after the teacher. When the child completes reciting *juz Amma* (the last thirtieth of the Qur'an with the shortest chapters, which is learned first) there is an *Ameen* party. Speeches, prayers for the child and parents, food, gifts, and flower garlands mark the festivities. These celebrations hold partic-ular meaning in America as articulated by Nadia. A second-generation immigrant of Indian parentage, Nadia fondly remembers her *bismillah* and *Ameen* parties and continued the tradition with her children be-cause "in a religion that isn't really known for fun traditions—from a child's perspective—particularly compared to the dominant culture—with Christmas, Easter, Bar/Bat Mitzvah, Hanukkah—this [celebration] provided a fun way to introduce religious practice to a child's life and hopefully get them excited about learning to read the Qur'an."[51] Chil-dren also learn that the Qur'anic text must be handled with reverence and *adab*, or etiquette. It should not be placed on the floor, nothing can be placed on top of it, and if open, it should not be turned upside down. Many Muslims also believe ablution must be performed before touching the Qur'an or a clean barrier, such as the digital screen or gloves, must be used. Damaged pages of the Qur'an are burned, shredded, or buried so they are not sullied in waste baskets.[52]

The Qur'an is read in graduation parties and at all community events. Nuptial engagements are sealed by reciting *al-Fatiha*; and during mar-riage officiation, Qur'anic verses remind the couple that, like "garments," they are a source of comfort and security to one another. Among the wedding gifts, there often is a copy of the Qur'an and recitations and copies of the Qur'an bless new homes or cars. The Qur'an is central to all worship rituals (prayers, fasting, and pilgrimage) but reciting or lis-tening to it is itself an act of worship.[53] For example, Ahmad, a twenty-four-year-old second-generation immigrant of Bangladeshi background, starts and ends his day with the Qur'an "to receive guidance and inspi-ration." He reads "surah *Yasin* in the morning for forgiveness, surah *al-Waqi'ah* after maghrib [or sunset] because it increases one's sustenance [and], Surah *al-Mulk* after *isha* [or at night], because it protects one from the punishment of the grave."[54]

A Cure and Mercy

For many Muslim Americans in hardship, recitation or *dhikr*, the remembrance of God, consoles their hearts and contemplating sacred historical narratives in the Qur'an about pre-Islamic prophets whose faith turns trials into triumph is instructive. The narrative, however, is not a historical record but, like all good storytelling, is significant for its ethical and spiritual lessons. Through relatable events and characters, these narratives teach Muslims that they have within themselves the "qualities of Moses and those of Pharaoh, the beauty of Joseph and the conniving of his brothers" and that in the struggle between good and evil, with faith in God, patience and perseverance, good eventually triumphs over evil.[55] These stories, which comforted early Muslims in their struggles, give solace today to Muslim Americans encountering Islamophobia, racism, and challenges within their diverse communities.

At the height of presidential candidate Donald Trump's anti-Muslim rhetoric in early 2016, in a Friday sermon in a Phoenix mosque, the imam reminded his audience that "Allah is teaching [us] that if we have the right focus, Allah will create a way out for us. Because Allah says 'whoever fears Allah, He will make a way out for him and will provide for him from where he does not expect.' And whoever relies upon Allah, then Allah is sufficient for him."[56] The imam then demonstrated the meaning of this verse by connecting the struggles of Muslim Americans with historical narratives in the Qur'an. He told his audience that "Allah is not telling us bedtime stories." These stories were narrated "so we can see how this connects to our lives." He then retold the qur'anic story of Moses and his people coming face-to-face with Pharaoh's army. At that moment, the imam told his audience, surrounded by a vastly militarily superior army, the Israelites said, "'We are overtaken' because they focused on being trapped like we are today." In contrast, Moses "focused on something else" and said, "'No! Indeed my Lord is with me'[57] and Allah open[ed] a path for him in the sea." The imam reminded the congregants that Moses did not have a plan but he "had *tawakkul* [reliance on God] and we too must trust in the unseen." He then reminded them that reliance should not be mistaken for inaction but that they should at once trust God and work diligently without despair.[58] In analyzing this Qur'anic narrative and making it relevant to the current context, the imam hoped his audience would be simultaneously consoled and called to action.

The Qur'an says, "And We send down of the Qur'an that which is a cure and a mercy for the believers."[59] Consequently, for those who believe in its guidance, the Qur'anic "words affect the very flesh and viscera."[60] They cure physical and mental ailments, including ignorance, hypocrisy, and enmity; and as a mercy, they enable the acquisition of virtues and "adorn one with wisdom and knowledge."[61] Fatima, a Somali American, diligently tried to manage her son's epilepsy with medication, but without success. Then it came to her in a dream that if the entire Qur'an was read over him, he would be cured. So, on a Saturday, the imam and thirty reciters sat in a circle around her son and, since they all could benefit, the rest of her children joined him. For an hour, the children sat in the center mesmerized as the melodic recitation reverberated around their house. The healing session ended with supplication for healing and commenced with a special home-cooked lunch. Fatima says her son has never had an epileptic seizure since. As she sees it, healing can be done with the Qur'an and/or with medication; after all, healing is from God and He can heal with a pill or His words. But there is no cure for death and the Qur'an says "every soul shall taste death."[62] If able, those dying recite the Qur'an and strive to exit the world while saying the *shahada* (declaration of faith). At their deathbed, gravesite, and long afterward, loved ones recite the Qur'an for their benefit and to console themselves. In the afterlife, the Qur'an stands witness and "speaks" about its relationship with the dead.[63]

Qur'an, Identity, and Belonging

Identity formation is not a solitary internal project but a process of becoming in and through social interaction within a cultural and historical context. The preceding passages shed light on the role of the Qur'an in socialization processes that shape one's Muslim identity. But Muslim Americans are also shaped by and engage multiple historical and contemporary narratives—"Islam and West," national identity, and the "war on terror." In these narratives, the Qur'an is used as an example of Muslim Otherness and belonging. For example, Keith Ellison, the first Muslim elected to the U.S. Congress in 2006, made headlines for planning to take the oath on the Qur'an during his swearing-in ceremony. Keenly aware of rising anti-Muslim rhetoric and the inherent symbolism of his choice, Ellison swore on Thomas Jefferson's Qur'an to demonstrate the Qur'an's early presence in American history and the Founding Fathers' belief "that knowledge and wisdom could be gleaned from any number of sources, including the Qur'an."[64]

Periodic reports about alleged desecration of the Qur'an by U.S. military personnel and headlines like the 2010 planned burning of the Qur'an by a Florida pastor demonstrate how Muslim reverence of the Qur'an can be used to taunt them. But these episodes also create a space, however narrow, for public conversation situating the Qur'an in the nation's history. To correct misconceptions about, and hopefully prevent desecration of the Qur'an, the Council on American-Islamic Relations (CAIR) began two campaigns—"Explore the Qur'an" and later "Share the Qur'an"—during which they distributed free copies of Muhammad Asad's English translation. Because Asad was a European Jewish convert to Islam, CAIR considers his translation more effective in explaining Islam to the West.[65] Besides explaining Islam, Muslim Americans are also asserting their belonging to the nation by revisiting U.S. history to unearth Islam's deeper roots in America. They highlight the Qur'an copies of early Muslims like Jansen Van Salee (1607–1676), the first settler of Brooklyn, and enslaved Africans like Ayyub (Job) ibn Sulaiman Diallo (1707–1773), who transcribed the Qur'an in Arabic, and Omer Ibn Said's Arabic manuscript containing Sura *Al-Mulk* (Sovereignty).[66] They also point to the Supreme Court's carved marble frieze of the greatest lawgivers, including the image of the Prophet Muhammad holding an open Qur'an.[67] The selection of a Qur'anic verse to be among the "greatest expressions for justice in history" in Harvard Law's "Words of Justice" exhibit was widely publicized by Muslims as evidence of the just nature of the Qur'an to counter allegations that it inspires violence.[68] Qur'anic recitations during interfaith dialogue and in prayers for the nation during moments of tragedy are also considered symbolic events of belonging.[69] Muslims are not the only ones who highlight the historical presence of the Qur'an in response to Othering discourses. Brown University library director and historian Ted Widmer, for example, confirms the presence of Qur'an copies in American libraries as early as 1683 and details how enslaved African Muslims preserved the Qur'an by reciting from memory or, in a few instances, like Bilali in Georgia's Sea Islands, smuggling copies.[70]

The history and sociocultural context Muslims share with other Americans produces particular "habits of mind or thought," which inform their engagement with the Qur'an.[71] Therefore, the book *The Study Quran: A New Translation and Commentary* (2015) aims to both help Americans of all traditions gain deeper insights into the Qur'an and to make it relevant to Muslim American lives. When Seyyed Hossein Nasr was approached by his publisher to be the chief editor of the Study Qur'an project, Nasr's humility as a "student of Qur'an[,] not a scholar of it" prevented him. But after considering the gravity of having to answer to God for declining such an important task, Nasr agreed.[72] Cognizant of the effects of these habits of mind, Nasr insisted that only Muslim scholars participate and that all politically tainted fundamentalist and modernist interpretations/commentary be excluded. *The Study Quran* is unique in being a compound commentary of Sufi, Sunni, and Shi'a interpretations and linguistic, philosophical, mystical, and historical commentaries. Being a Shi'i Muslim, Nasr deliberately chose four Sunni American general editors (three converts and one Muslim-born, three men and one woman) in order to transcend sectarian divisions fueled by geopolitical interests and to highlight how Muslims understand the Qur'an and its diverse classical commentaries.[73] The two-thousand-page book also contains fifteen essays written by prominent Muslims of diverse backgrounds. The essays address critical issues salient in public discourse including women in Islam, human rights, war and peace, Islamic law, and conversion to other religions. To approximate, however inadequately, the literary beauty of the Qur'an and reflect the habits of the minds of the editors as much as of the readers, the editors draw from past and present luminaries of English-language literature.[74] Presales of *The Study Quran* so exceeded the publisher's expectations that another thirteen thousand had to be printed. The book has won high praise from leading Muslim and non-Muslim scholars of Islam in the West, but there were also critics who accused the editors of misinterpretation and of confusing readers by including too many interpretations.[75]

Constructing the American Ummah

Being the most diverse religious community in both the United States and the global Muslim world presents Muslim Americans with challenges and opportunities for collaboration and for the construction of a cohesive political identity. The major fault line among Muslim Americans is framed in terms of "immigrant" and "converts/indigenous." While these terms are contested, they have currency in intracommunity discussions, and the matter of religious authority is central.[76] Immigrants are often blamed for a number of things, including importing or internalizing America's antiblack racism; expecting converts to become culturally Arab or South Asian or African in order to be "true" Muslims; and monopolizing religious authority as if, the argument goes, the understanding and interpretion of religious texts is a birthright of Muslims of "olive skin"[77] rather than the result of authoritative knowledge. Debates on intracommunity tensions have intensified in the context of the Black Lives Matter social justice movement and the rise of Islamophobia, resulting in calls for solidarity work. As an intervention, diverse young Muslim Americans created the Muslim Anti-Racism Collaborative (MuslimARC) for the purpose of "racial justice education for Muslims by Muslims." MuslimARC grounds its work in the qur'anic verse featured on its homepage, "And of His signs is the creation of the heavens and the earth and the diversity of your languages and your colors. Indeed in that are signs for those of knowledge."[78]

Though there is ethnic variation, tensions also exist across gender lines. Debates on religion and gender occur in all traditions. However, gender in Islam is a globally debated issue in which orientalist,[79] feminist,[80] and fundamentalist (secular and religious) tropes are invoked. In these debates, the Qur'an is cited by supporters of patriarchy who draw on literal interpretations of sacred texts and by patriarchy's critics who highlight the Qur'an's egalitarian message. In her book, *Qur'an and Woman: Rereading the Sacred Text from a Woman's Perspective* (1999), Amina Wadud, an African American Muslim scholar and a prominent figure in the Islamic feminist movement, explores whether the prevalent gender inequality among Muslims is religiously based or a cultural and human shortcoming. To do so, she decided to access the Qur'an "unfettered by centuries of historical androcentric reading and Arabo-

Islamic cultural predilections." The research confirmed to her that the Muslim "female person was intended to be primordially, cosmologically, eschatologically, spiritually, and morally a full human being, equal to all who accepted Allah as Lord, Muhammad as a prophet, and Islam as *din* [religion]." Consequently, she argued, Muslim women can ground themselves in the egalitarian spirit of the Qur'an to challenge inequality.[81] Other works by female Muslim scholars have followed, including Nimat Hafez Barazangi's *Women's Identity and the Quran: A New Reading* (2004); Laleh Bakhtiar's *The Sublime Qur'an* (2007), the first translation by an American woman; Asma Barlas's *"Believing Women" in Islam: Unreading Patriarchal Interpretations of the Qur'an* (2012); and Aysha Hidayatullah's *Feminist Edges of the Qur'an* (2014).[82] Though the "woman in Islam" topic dominates public and Muslim discourses, discussions about Muslim masculinities are emerging in the community. An example of this is the 2015 community-organized "Muslim Masculinity in an Age of Feminism" conference. While acknowledging that models of masculinity change over time, Naeem, a conference speaker, argued that Islam presents foundational characteristics of love and mercy found in the Qur'anic description of the Prophet as "a mercy to all mankind."[83]

Both inside and outside the community, Muslim social justice advocates draw on the Qur'an to motivate themselves and others and to persevere in the difficult work for justice. Rami Nashashibi, a prominent Muslim activist from Chicago, cites a qur'anic verse and points out that while the verse cites important foundational articles of faith, these are invisible inner states of belief. However, the verse raises services for the poor and the disenfranchised, which are "clearly measurable instances of righteous actions," to the highest level of worship.[84]

Qur'an-Inspired Art

The Qur'an, as recitation and written text, has always been central to Muslim religious art. The poetic rhythm and musicality of the qur'anic recitation is an aural aesthetic experience capable of bringing listeners to tears in "ecstatic reactions," and is a significant aspect of religious practice.[85] This intrinsic musicality is amplified by reciters' beautiful voices and the use of melodic scales, elevating recitation to an art form and drawing large followings online and in mosques. But Muslim Americans are also incorporating the Qur'an into poetic expressions. For example, starting as the Qur'an does with "*bismillah ar-rahman ar-raheem*," spoken word poet Amir Sulaiman connects injustices against African and Native Americans with ones committed in the "war on terror." He then quotes the verse "Allah will not change the condition of the people until they change what's within themselves" to argue that overcoming these injustices necessitates transformative inner work.

It is, however, in the visual realm that the Qur'an is most ubiquitous as art. Because many Muslims believe there is a prohibition on figurative religious art, the word of God inscribed in diverse media has always been a central feature of Islamic art. Today's Muslim Americans are contributing to this tradition with verses handwritten in elaborate Arabic calligraphy and engraved in mosque walls; painted on canvas; printed on wall clocks, iPhone covers, calendars, and cups; or etched into jewelry. There are graduation sashes with the verse "my Lord increase me in knowledge," and rings and pendants intended to "announce one's faith to others and remind the wearer of the creator's greatness and beauty."[86] And "[e]verywhere, the protective, blessed, and talismanic presence of the Word of God is experienced."[87]

Muslim America's master Arabic calligrapher, Mohamed Zakariya, a white covert from California, is also world renowned. He created the 2001 U.S. Eid postage stamp and the plaque of Qur'anic verse President Obama presented to the King of Saudi Arabia. Because calligraphy's impact transcends the word's meaning, Zakariya describes it as "music for the eyes," which like all great arts "gives truth more clarity" and for Muslims serves to "support and strengthen the spiritual edifice of faith."[88] Lubna Shaikh, a young Californian woman, articulates this role of art. She is inspired by the Qur'anic verse "Without doubt in the remembrance of Allah do hearts find rest" and features it on her website. She sees her work as "a means to this remembrance" and carves, paints, prints, and embroiders Arabic calligraphy into everything from glass to wax.[89] Young Muslim American artists also merge traditional calligraphy with urban graffiti art, creating calligraffiti in a synthesis that renders the sacred word in a new cultural garb. Haseena Mirza, a designer of Islamic art decals, expresses the sentiments of many Muslim Americans whose art is "a little traditional and a little contemporary modern—like how we live our lives."[90] In doing so, they contribute to tradition by making it relevant to a new context. These artists also note that their works aim to educate the public to change its harsh image of Islam.

Conclusion

The Qur'an is the type of text which Bruce Fudge, a scholar of Arabic, notes is "granted unimpeachable authority, unquestioned authenticity and most importantly a cultural and intellectual centrality"[91] for Muslims everywhere. This centrality is evident in the significant role of the Qur'an in the socialization process of becoming Muslim. From the recitation of its formulae in the newborn's ears and reading it while dying, to the embodying impact of memorizing it and the transformative effects of understanding and implementing its teachings, to seeking healing and comfort within it, to adorning oneself and spaces with its written and recited word, the Qur'an accompanies Muslims throughout their day and life cycle. Qur'an scholar and former president of the American Academy of Religion Jane McAuliffe sums up Muslims' relationship with the Qur'an as threefold: carnal, conceptual, and communal. She explains that for most Muslims, the Qur'an is "heard, viewed, touched, and sometimes ingested, long before it is ever read," and it is generally "'embodied' within Muslim life and material culture."[92]

In the Islamic tradition, the Qur'an is a timeless universal message and Muslim Americans draw on that narrative to "own" the Qur'an in their cultural context. They preserve and embody it through memorization and seek spiritual nourishment and inspiration from it for their creative endeavors and civic engagements. Continuing the Islamic tradition in the sociocultural context of America, they create institutions and innovative programs to lift the linguistic veil preventing them from directly accessing the revelation in its original language. Some of these programs, like Bayyinah, extend their reach internationally, helping Muslims elsewhere to "taste the sweetness" of the Qur'an. Muslim American scholarship on the Qur'an is educating the public, redefining gender in Islam, and producing new translations that attempt to at once revive traditional commentaries in their diversity, to transcend ideological and sectarian trappings, and to make the Qur'an relevant in the contemporary context. To affect change in their community, activists draw on the Qur'an's authority and authenticity and highlight its message of justice and unity to confront internal divisions. Muslims are also seeking inspiration and solace in the Qur'an's historical narratives of trials and triumph as they struggle against anti-Muslim bigotry. Additionally, they are finding the Qur'an's presence in America's past and present as evidence of their roots and belonging. In inscribing the sacred word in works of art, they at once engage in an act of worship, creative individual self-expression, and a form of cultural activism and civic engagement to challenge stereotypes and marginalization.

NOTES

1 Charles Hirschkind, "The Ethics of Listening: Cassette-Sermon Audition in Contemporary Egypt," *American Ethnologist* 28, no. 3 (2001): 623–649.

2 Mohamed Younis, "Muslim Americans Exemplify Diversity, Potential," *Gallup Center for Muslim Studies*, March 2, 2009, www.gallup.com.

3 Meraj Mohiuddin, *Revelation: The Story of Mohammad* (Phoenix: Whiteboard Press, 2015), 21.

4 Ibid.

5 Miraj Mohiuddin, personal interview, March 23, 2016.

6 Mohiuddin, *Revelation*, 21.

7 Mohiuddin, *Revelation*.

8 Ibid.

9 Ibid.

10 Ibid.

11 Qur'an 96:1–5.

12 Mohiuddin, *Revelation*.

13 Ibid.

14 Mohiuddin, interview.

15 Mohiuddin, *Revelation*, 24.

16 Sherman Jackson, "Foreword," in Mohiuddin, *Revelation*, 19–20.

17 Ingrid Mattson, *The Story of the Qur'an: Its History and Place in Muslim Life* (Malden, Mass.: Blackwell Publishing, 2008).

18 Ibid.

19 Seyyed Hossein Nasr, "General Introduction," in *The Study Quran: A New Translation and Commentary*, ed. Seyyed Hossein Nasr, Caner K. Dagli, Maria Massi Dakake, Joseph E. B. Lumbard, and Mohammed Rustom (New York: HarperOne, 2015), xxviii.

20 Mattson, *The Story*.

21 Yasir Qadhi, "The Miracle of the Quran," YouTube video, 48:08, August 2013, www.youtube.com.

22 Ibid.

23 Mattson, *The Story*, 32–33. In verses 17:89, 10:37–38, 2:23, and 11:13 the Qur'an challenges its deniers to produce a verse like it.

24 FreeQuranEducation, "Undeniable Linguistic Miracles of Quran, Nouman Ali Khan," YouTube video, 1:58:42, October 25, 2014, www.youtube.com; Muhammad Omer Iqbal, "The Quran as a Literary Masterpiece within Its Historical and Religious Milieus," M.A. thesis, University of Washington, 2013.

25 Yaser Ali, personal interview, May 11, 2016.

26 One could read the Qur'an without knowing how to properly recite it according to the rules of tajweed, but mastering these rules is strongly encouraged as it is essential to the aesthetic, and thus the spiritual, experience of the Qur'an. To learn tajweed, a teacher who demonstrates proper articulation and the complex intonations is needed. Those who cannot find a local teacher often rely on YouTube videos or online teachers.

27 Mattson, *The Story*.

28 Ali, interview.

29 Zareena Grewal, *Islam Is a Foreign Country: American Muslims and the Global Crisis of Authority* (New York: NYU Press, 2013).

30 Al Hikmat, YouTube video, 38:34, July 26, 2012, www.youtube.com.

31 Maryam Amirebrahimi, "10 Tips to Becoming One of Allah's Special People," May 4, 2012, www.virtualmosque.com.

32 Ibid.

33 Maryam Amirebrahimi, email communication, May 17, 2016.

34 Ibid.

35 Amirebrahimi, "10 Tips."

36 Zayna Kabbani, email communication, May 2, 2016.

37 Helen Boyle, *Qur'anic Schools: Agents of Preservation and Change* (New York: RoutledgeFalmer, 2004).

38 Mattson, *The Story*; and Leslie Moore, "Body, Text, and Talk in Maroua Fulbe Qur'anic Schooling," *Text & Talk—An Interdisciplinary Journal of Language, Discourse Communication Studies* 28, no. 5 (2008): 643–665.

39 Boyle, *Qur'anic Schools*, 98.

40 Ibid.

41 FreeQuranEducation, "The Life of Nouman Ali Khan—VIP Show," March 16, 2014, www.youtube.com.

42 Bayyinah, "about," bayyinah.com.

43 itunes.apple.com.

44 Frieda Mawwakil, phone interview, May 2, 2016.

45 The Good Tree Institute, "About Us," www.goodtreeinstitute.com.

46 Believing in the Qur'an's authenticity as the Word of God is an article of faith foundational to being a Muslim. While this authenticity has been agreed upon by Muslims through the ages, the interpretation of what the Word of God means has always been contested. There is a rich classic and contemporary scholarly tradi-

tion that shows how Muslims try to understand the Qur'an and make it relevant to their lives in their time.

47 Muna Ali, "Generation Next: Young Muslim Americans Narrating Self while Debating Faith, Community, and Country," Ph.D. dissertation, Arizona State University, 2013.

48 Good Tree.

49 Field notes, February 20, 2016.

50 Salwa Ali, email communication, March 24, 2016.

51 Nadia Rivero, email communication, May 15, 2016.

52 Mattson, *The Story*.

53 Ibid.

54 Ahmad Abdulqadir, email communication, May 3, 2016.

55 Nasr, "General Introduction," xxvii.

56 Qur'an 65:2–3.

57 Qur'an 26:62–63.

58 Islamic Center of North East Valley, Friday sermon by imam Moutaz, March 25, 2016.

59 Qur'an 17:73.

60 Mattson, *The Story*, 165.

61 Seyyed Hossein Nasr et al., *The Study Quran*, 719.

62 Qur'an 3:185.

63 Mattson, *The Story*.

64 Frederic Frommer, "Congressman Uses Thomas Jefferson's Quran at Swearing In," *Associated Press*, January 4, 2007, old.seattletimes.com.

65 Korva Coleman, "Muslims Want More People to Read the Quran," August 31, 2009, www.npr.org.

66 Muhammed Al-Ahari, "The Qur'an as Part of American History," March 2, 2016, chicagomonitor.com.

67 Abdul Malik Mujahid, "Prophet Muhammad Honored by the U.S. Supreme Court as One of the Greatest Lawgivers of the World in 1935," n.d., www.soundvision.com.

68 Council on American Islamic Relations, "Harvard Recognizes Quranic Verse as One of the Greatest Expressions of Justice," March 11, 2015, www.cair.com.

69 Mike Ghouse, "A Muslim Leap of Faith: Offering Interfaith Prayers for Newtown," *HuffPost Religion*, December 12, 2012, www.huffingtonpost.com.

70 Ted Widmer, "People of the Book: The True History of the Koran in America," *Boston Globe*, September 12, 2010, archive.boston.com.

71 Seyyed Hossein Nasr, keynote address at "New Approaches to Qur'an and Exegesis," October 23–24, 2010, islamicstudiescenter.gmu.edu.

72 Politics and Prose Bookstore, "Sayyed Hossein Nasr, 'The Study Quran,'" YouTube Video, 1:02:50, January 21, 2016, www.youtube.com.

73 Ibid.

74 Ibid.

75 For praise, see the publisher's website at www.harpercollins.com. For an example of critics, see Dr. Shadee Elmasry, November 25, 2015, www.facebook.com

76 Ali, *Generation Next*.

77 Sherman Jackson, "Muslims, Islam(s) and Race in America," in *Islamophobia and the Challenges of Pluralism in the 21st Century* (Washington, D.C.: Center for Muslim-Christian Understanding, Georgetown University, Occasional Papers, 2008), 80–87.

78 The Muslim Anti-Racism Collaborative, Qur'an 30:22, www.muslimarc.org.

79 *Orientalism* is the title of a 1979 book by the late Edward Said, a professor of English history and comparative literature at Columbia University. In this book, he introduced the concept of orientalism to describe the ways European travelers, artists, historians, and scientists depicted people from the "Orient," namely, from Arabia, Africa, and Asia, during Europe's imperial conquest of these regions. Said argued that the knowledge produced by these Europeans created images of people from the "Orient" that were not based on these peoples' complex realities which change with time. Instead, they contracted them as exotic others frozen in history who are in every way the opposite of Europeans. This knowledge, which is produced by powerful Europeans about the less powerful people they colonized, continues to shape the way people from that part of the world are viewed in the West today.

80 Feminism is a theoretical project and a sociopolitical movement with different strands (first-wave feminism, second-wave feminism, third-wave feminism, Jewish feminism, Christian feminism, and Islamic feminism). Despite some differences, these strands of feminism share a focus on examining and revealing how social institutions and cultural practices privilege male ways of knowing the world and serve male interests while marginalizing female ways of knowing and disadvantaging women in the social, political, and economic spheres. Whether they draw on secular or religious traditions, the objectives of feminist scholars and activists are to identify these male-female social and cultural dynamics and to bring about change that improves the status of women and creates a more just society for both men and women.

81 Amina Wadud, *Qur'an and Woman: Rereading the Sacred Text from a Woman's Perspective* (New York: Oxford University Press, 1999), ix–x.

82 Nimat Hafez Barazangi, *Women's Identity and the Quran: A New Reading* (Gainesville: University Press of Florida, 2004); Laleh Bakhtiar, *The Sublime Quran* (Chicago: Kazi Publications, 2007); Asma Barlas, *"Believing Women" in Islam: Unreading Patriarchal Interpretations of the Qur'an* (Austin: University of Texas Press, 2012); and Aysha Hidayatullah, *Feminist Edges of the Qur'an* (New York: Oxford University Press, 2014).

83 Asma T. Uddin, "Muslim, Man Up?" *Newsweek Middle East*, May 18, 2016, newsweekme.com.

84 Rami Nashashibi, "Moving beyond Ritual This Ramadan: The Importance of Righteous Actions," *Huffington Post*, August 17, 2010, www.huffingtonpost.com.

85 Navid Kermani, "The Aesthetic Reception of the Qur'an as Reflected in Early Muslim History," in *Literary Structures of Religious Meaning in the Qur'an*, ed. Issa Boullata (Richmond: Curzon, 2000), 255–76.

86 "Jewels of Faith," *Azizah Magazine* 5, no. 2 (2009): 26.

87 Mattson, *The Story*, 144.

88 Mohamed Zakariya, "Music for the Eyes: An Introduction to Islamic and Ottoman Calligraphy," n.d., mohamedzakariya.com.

89 "Muslim Women in the Arts: An Interview with Lubna Shaikh, Arabic Calligrapher," www.muslimness.com, March 13, 2011.

90 Rose Rashad, "Contemporary Tradition," *Azizah Magazine* 6, no. 4 (2011): 77.

91 Bruce Fudge, *Qurʾānic Hermeneutics: Al-Tabrisī and the Craft of Commentary* (London: Routledge, 2011), 2.

92 Jane McAuliffe, "Reading the Qur'an with Fidelity and Freedom," *Journal of the American Academy of Religion*. 37, no. 3 (2005): 621.

Edward E. Curtis IV is Millennium Chair of the Liberal Arts and Professor of Religious Studies at the IU School of Liberal Arts in Indianapolis. A recipient of Mellon, NEH, Fulbright, and Carnegie fellowships, Curtis is author of *Muslims in America: A Short History* and editor of *The Encyclopedia of Muslim-American History*.

ABOUT THE CONTRIBUTORS

Muna Ali (Ph.D., Arizona State) is an expert in Muslim American studies and a full-time instructor of physical therapy at the Mayo Clinic in Scottsdale, Arizona. She is the author of several refereed articles and is currently working on her first book about Muslim American youth.

Rose Aslan (Ph.D., North Carolina), a scholar of Muslim sacred spaces and material culture, is assistant professor at California Lutheran University. She is a coauthor of "Red, White, and Blue: American Muslims on Hajj and the Politics of Privilege."

Rosemary R. Corbett (Ph.D., Columbia) is faculty fellow at the Bard Prison Initiative. She is the author of numerous articles on Islam in the United States. Her first book is *Making Moderate Islam: Sufism, Service, and the "Ground Zero Mosque" Controversy.*

Maria F. Curtis (Ph.D., Texas) is associate professor of anthropology and cross-cultural studies at the University of Houston-Clear Lake. She has penned numerous articles and book chapters on topics related to Islam and food, mothering, music, and women's leadership.

Magfirah Dahlan (Ph.D., Virginia Tech) is an instructor at Craven Community College. Her dissertation examined progressive Muslim attitudes and practices related to the production and consumption of food.

Juliane Hammer (Ph.D., Humboldt) is associate professor of religious studies and Kenan Rifai Scholar at the University of North Carolina, Chapel Hill. She is the author of *American Muslim Women, Religious Authority, and Activism: More Than a Prayer* and coeditor of *The Cambridge Companion to American Islam*, among other books.

Marcia Hermansen (Ph.D., Chicago) is professor of theology and director of the Islamic World Studies program at Loyola University, Chicago. The author or editor of five books about Islam, she has also authored dozens of articles about Sufism in the United States.

Amir Hussain (Ph.D., Toronto) is professor of theological studies at Loyola Marymount University and former editor of the *Journal of the American Academy of Religion*. His many books and articles include *Muslims and the Making of America*.

Michael Muhammad Knight (Ph.D., North Carolina) is the author of over ten books including *The Taqwacores, The Five Percenters: Islam, Hip Hop and the Gods of New York*, and *Magic in Islam*. He is also a scholar of textual representations of the Prophet Muhammad.

Hussein Rashid (Ph.D., Harvard) is an adjunct faculty member at Hofstra University as well as a blogger, writer, and consultant. An advocate of religious literacy, he publishes in both specialized journals and general audience forums on Islam and Muslims in the United States.

Jackleen Salem (Ph.D., Wisconsin-Milwaukee) has published numerous book chapters and articles on Arab American immigrants in the United States. She is currently revising her history of one Chicago Muslim community into a book.

Danielle Widmann Abraham (Th.D., Harvard) is assistant professor and holder of the Livingston Wright Chair in Middle East Studies at Ursinus College. She has also served as cochair of the Contemporary Islam Group at the American Academy of Religion.

INDEX

abaya (long dress), 26–27, 154

Abdullah, Husain, 31

Abdullah, Tahir Umar, 85, 88–89, 91, 132

Abraham (Ibrahim): and birth rituals, 150; and *dhikr* rituals, 50; and funerals/death rites, 192; and the Hajj, 60, 72; and interpretation of the Qur'an, 248

Abrahamic cultures, 142, 152

Abraham's Tent, 90

Abu Bakr (Caliph), 108, 110–11, 115, 250

accommodations, religious, 20–21

accountability, 216

adab (etiquette), 130, 257

Adam and Eve, 60, 126, 177

Adawiyya, Rabia al-, 178

adhan (call to prayer): and birth rituals, 142, 146–47, 149, 162, 163; and the Muslim life cycle, 256; and prayer practices, 22–23, 27

African American Muslims: and Ashura commemorations, 114–15; and birth rituals, 149–50, 152; and charity/social giving, 216–22; and *dhikr* rituals, 38; and early American Muslims, 4; and Milad/Mawlid celebrations, 134; and philanthropy and social giving, 216–22, 229; and prayer practices, 25; and Qur'an studies, 253, 255; and Ramadan, 86–87; and weddings/marriage, 166–70, 182. *See also* Nation of Islam (NOI)

African Burial Grounds National Monument, 204–5

African Muslims, 134. *See also* African American Muslims

Aga Khan, 5, 24, 30

Ahl al-Bayt (people of the house), 111, 115

Ahl-e hadith (people of the hadith), 127, 137n15

Ahmad, Abu, 194, 195–98

Ahmad, Hajj, 16–18, 21–24, 28, 33n11

Ahmad, Jalal Al-e, 68

Ahmad, Tahera, 132–33

Ahmadi community, 150

Ahmed, Ali, 214

ahwal (ecstatic state), 55

air travel: "Flying Imams Incident," 31; preparing for Hajj, 66

Aisha (Prophet's wife), 108, 240–42, 251

alcohol prohibition, 1–2, 232

alhamdullilah, 28

Ali, Muhammad, 202–4

Ali, Muna, 245–66

Ali, Salwa, 256

Ali-Asghar, 110

Ali ibn Abi Talib, 62, 93, 108, 110–11

Allahu akbar (God is the greatest) 23, 28

All Dulles Area Muslim Society (AD-AMS), 101

Aly, Eman Hassaballa, 90, 100

Ameen parties, 257

Amen, Suehaila, 62, 77–78

American Muslim Civic Leadership Institute, 75

American Shi'a diaspora, 213–16

American Society for Muslim Advancement, 55–56

American Sufi Muslim Association (ASMA), 50, 54–55